WORKING FUTURES?

Disabled people, policy and social inclusion

Edited by Alan Roulstone and Colin Barnes

First published in Great Britain in November 2005 by

The Policy Press
University of Bristol
Fourth Floor
Beacon House
Queen's Road
Bristol BS8 1QU
UK

Tel +44 (0)117 331 4054
Fax +44 (0)117 331 4093
e-mail tpp-info@bristol.ac.uk
www.policypress.org.uk

© Alan Roulstone and Colin Barnes 2005

British Library Cataloguing in Publication Data
A catalogue record for this book is available from the British Library.

Library of Congress Cataloging-in-Publication Data
A catalog record for this book has been requested.

ISBN 1 86134 626 3 paperback

A hardcover version of this book is also available

Cover design by Qube Design Associates, Bristol.
Printed and bound in Great Britain by MPG Books, Bodmin.

Contents

List of figures, tables and boxes

Figures

Tables

Box

Preface

This collection of writings emanates from a national invited seminar that took place in Sunderland in the autumn of 2003. The contributors included academics, disability activists, senior civil servants and representatives of voluntary sector opinion formers. The event was an exciting fusion of ideas and was one of the first of its kind to look in depth at the question of disabled people and employment in the 21st century. The seminar brought together disabled people and activists with established and new policy writers and analysts. It was felt important to provide a forum for an exchange of views to take place at a time that disability and employment had become a major focus for government attention. Indeed, we had no difficulty attracting a colleague from the Prime Minister's Strategy Unit to the event.

While diverse views and specialist papers were presented, there was some sharing of concern that disability employment policy, despite the mountain of paper and initiatives it produced, was not making significant inroads in enhancing the employment openings for disabled people. It was also felt that the terrain of discussion should widen beyond simply that of access to paid work and the need to look more creatively at the economic and social contributions made by disabled people outside of paid work, hence the title of the seminar and book, *Working futures?* Here, 'work' can be taken to mean much more than paid employment, while 'working' relates to new policy ideas that function to include rather than exclude or coerce disabled people. However, it was felt that paid work remained a key building block of a just society and that disabled people required better, more focused and evidenced policy. Current policy was like the 'curate's egg', good in parts. However, questions were asked as to why disabled people were not more fully included in the policy process and the book begins to broach this issue.

The ideas represented in this collection are entirely those of their authors and do not necessarily represent the views of funding agencies or indeed their employers. The introductory and concluding chapters are both a distillation of the wider commentary provided in the book and some more daring thoughts about enabling futures which, although challenging, attempt to move debate forward. A key point made is that much disability employment policy fails to engage with the nature of work. This would be unthinkable in, say, policy writings about disabled people's education. Future credibility is likely to more fully attach to policy analyses that take more cognisance of the nature of work and social inclusion (does one provide the other?) and which include the voices of disabled people.

Alan Roulstone
Colin Barnes
August 2005

Acknowledgements

Gratitude needs to be extended both to the Joseph Rowntree Foundation and Lorraine Gradwell of Breakthrough UK, without whom the Working Futures seminar would not have taken place. Thanks also go to staff at The Policy Press who provided guidance and a sense of reality in turning these ideas into a book. Thanks to Laura Greaves, Rowena Mayhew, Dawn Rushen and Emily Watt for their support and also to the very rigorous but helpful commentary of the anonymous reviewers of the book – only you know who you are. We hope you enjoy the book.

List of abbreviations

ACAS	Advisory, Conciliation and Arbitration Service
ACDET	Advisory Committee on Disability Employment and Training
AtW	Access to Work
BCODP	British Council of Disabled People
BDA	British Deaf Association
BSL	British Sign Language
CBI	Confederation of British Industry
CCETSW	Central Council for Education & Training in Social Work
CEC	Commission of the European Communities
DCIL	Derbyshire Coalition for Inclusive Living
DDA	Disability Discrimination Act (1995)
DEA	Disability Employment Adviser
DEAC	Disability and Employment Advisory Committee
DfEE	Department for Education and Employment
DH	Department of Health
DLA	Disability Living Allowance
DPTC	Disabled Person's Tax Credit
DRC	Disability Rights Commission
DSS	Department of Social Security
DWA	Disability Working Allowance
DWP	Department for Work and Pensions
EC	European Commission
ES	Employment Service
GDP	Gross Domestic Product
GSCC	General Social Care Council
HR	human resources
ICB	Incapacity Benefit
IES	Institute for Employment Studies
ILM	Intermediate Labour Market
ILO	International Labour Organization
IPPR	Institute for Public Policy Research
LA	local authority
LFS	Labour Force Survey
MIND	National Association for Mental Health
NDDP	New Deal for Disabled People

OECD   Organisation for Economic Co-operation and Development
ONS   Office for National Statistics
OPCS   Office of Population, Censuses and Surveys
PMSU   Prime Minister's Strategy Unit
RNIB   Royal National Institute of the Blind
RNID   Royal National Institute for Deaf People
SEU   Social Exclusion Unit
TUC   Trades Union Congress
UN   United Nations
UPIAS   Union of the Physically Impaired Against Segregation
VCS   voluntary and community sector
WFTC   Working Families Tax Credit
WTC   Working Tax Credit

Notes on contributors

Dr Pauline Banks is a Senior Research Fellow in the West of Scotland Research Centre for Theraputic Practice (Health QWest), based at Bell College in Hamilton. Prior to taking up the post she was Deputy Director of the Strathclyde Centre for Disability Research at the University of Glasgow. Her research interests include disability, the impact of chronic illness on individuals and families, health and ageing, education and employment. Among her recent publications are articles in *Disability and Rehabilitation, Journal of Sexual Relationship Therapy, British Journal of Guidance and Counselling* and *Policy & Politics*.

Colin Barnes is Professor of Disability Studies in the Department of Sociology and Social Policy, University of Leeds. He is also founder and Director of the Centre for Disability Studies at Leeds. Colin is very well known for his contribution to disability studies and has presented on disability issues in many countries worldwide. He has published many books on disability including *Disabled people in Britain and discrimination* (1991), *Disabled people and social policy* (1998 with Mike Oliver), *Exploring disability: A sociological introduction* (1999, with Tom Shakespeare and Geof Mercer) and latterly has co-edited a series of books with Geof Mercer on applying the social model of disability. Colin is Executive Editor of *Disability and Society,* founded the UK Disability Archive and the Disability Press and an independent disability studies publishing outlet based at the University of Leeds.

Peter Coleridge is a world expert on disability and development and has done much to bring the social model of disability to Africa, Asia and the Middle East. Peter has been at the forefront of successfully applying self-help principles to disability development which works closely with disabled people in partnership. Peter is author of numerous publications including *Disability, liberation and development* (Oxfam Publishing, 1993). He has worked closely with Oxfam, the United Nations and the International Labour Organisation in fulfilling these goals.

Anne Corden is a Research Fellow in the Social Policy Research Unit at the University of York. Her interests have focused on social security, family policy, employment and disability, and she has conducted long programmes of work on take-up and delivery of benefits and tax credits, and transitions to and from paid work. Anne specialises in qualitative research methods and has also conducted comparative and evaluative research. Anne also worked within the Disability Services Research Partnership carrying out work for the Employment Service.

Ardha Danieli is Lecturer in Qualitative Research Methods and Organisational Analysis in the Industrial Relations and Organisational Behaviour Group (IROB), Warwick Business School, University of Warwick. Her interests include inequality in the labour market, particularly in relation to disabled people and women. She is currently conducting a participatory research project with disabled people funded by the European Social Fund examining barriers to implementing the business case for the employment of disabled people.

David Gibbs is Research Manager at the Derbyshire Coalition for Inclusive Living. This centre has been at the forefront of translating the social understanding of disability into practice by challenging established research and policy and by undertaking research within a social model of disability. Since 1992, the DCIL has aimed to create a direct and vigorous exchange between a group of disabled people and the research community. David's research includes locally commissioned projects, national development with other disability organisations and academic collaborations to research disabled people's own perceptions and evaluations of service outcomes. Insights from the research community have informed DCIL's strategic planning, monitoring and its approach to a civil society.

Dan Goodley is Reader in Applied Disability Studies in the School of Education, University of Sheffield. He has published and researched widely on disability issues and has contributed to the development of post-structuralist ideas and researching the position of people with learning difficulties in contemporary society. Dan is currently undertaking research ('Jobs, Not Charity') into the employment position of disabled people funded by the European Social Fund and the role of professionals in the post-natal support of disabled babies (ESRC). Dan is on the editorial board of *Disability and Society*.

Lorraine Gradwell is Chief Executive of Breakthrough UK Ltd, a cutting-edge social model organisation that is run by a majority of disabled people and provides employment and training opportunities, support and advice to disabled people. Lorraine has had a long involvement with the disabled people's movement and is Deputy Chair of the Manchester Coalition of Disabled People. She has much experience of working with the wider voluntary and statutory sectors and is a member of a number of influential committees including the Disability and Employment Advisory Committee (DEAC) and the UK Small Business Federation.

Bob Grove joined the Sainsbury Centre for Mental Health in March 2003 to lead the Employment Programme, which advises government and local authorities on policy implementation. He is currently seconded part-time to the Department of Health, working with the Department for Work and Pensions on setting up condition management programmes as part of the Incapacity Benefit Pilot Reforms. He has written widely on disability and employment issues. Recent books include *A framework for supported employment* (Joseph Rowntree Foundation, 2001), *Working towards recovery* (IAHSP, 2002) and *Hidden skills, hidden talents* (IAHSP, 2003).

Jennifer Harris is a Senior Research Fellow at the Social Policy Research Unit, University of York. Jennifer's research interests are the social model of disability and services for deaf and disabled people in the UK. Her publications include *The cultural meaning of deafness* (Avebury Press, 1995) and *Deafness and the hearing* (Venture Press, 1997). Jennifer is on the editorial board of *Disability and Society* in which she has made contributions on housing issues for disabled people, and deaf people's access to services. Her current work includes a project for the Department of Health, entitled 'Health Outcomes for Disabled Service Users', which aims to introduce a focus on outcomes in professional practice with disabled people in contact with social services.

Jeannine Hughes is a qualified and experienced social worker. She has taught and researched at the Universities of Durham and Sunderland and has completed much research in the field of domestic violence. Jeannine has much experience of the changing professional frameworks in social work and their impact and challenge for inclusive practice in social care.

Jennifer Hurstfield is Principal Research Fellow at the Institute for Employment Studies. She has previously held posts as Research Manager at IRS Research, senior lecturer in sociology at the City of London Polytechnic and lecturer in sociology at the University of

Leicester. She is a specialist in labour market disadvantage and has conducted research on disability, gender, and race discrimination. At the Institute for Employment Studies with Nigel Meager, she led the third phase of research for the Disability Rights Commission on the implementation of the Disability Discrimination Act (DDA), and has completed research on the implications of the extension of the DDA to qualifications bodies and trade organisations.

Neil Lunt is Senior Lecturer in Social Policy at Massey University (Auckland), New Zealand. He teaches in the fields of policy analysis and research methods. Research interests include welfare reform, globalisation, disability employment policy, and the role of 'evidence' in policy and practice. He previously worked at the Social Policy Research Unit, University of York and co-authored (with Patricia Thornton) a cross-national study of disability employment policy.

Nigel Meager is a labour economist and Director of the Institute for Employment Studies, having previously held posts at the Wissenschaftszentrum Berlin für Sozialforschung and the Universities of Bath and Glasgow. His personal research interests include labour-market disadvantage and the evaluation of active labour market measures. He has a long track record of research on issues related to disabled people in the labour market. He has recently completed studies of the impact of the DDA and the Disabled Person's Tax Credit, and is involved in a major evaluation of the New Deal for Disabled People and has published widely on related topics.

Geof Mercer is Reader in the Department of Sociology and Social Policy and is a member of the Disability Research Unit at Leeds. He has published extensively on the subject of disability and along with Colin Barnes has been at the forefront of the championing of the social model of disability and in confronting traditional dependency creating welfare, professional and service structures. Geof is co-editor with Colin Barnes of the series of writings on applying the social model including *Disability policy and practice: Applying the social model* (Disability Press, 2004) and *Implementing the social model: Theory and research* (Disability Press, 2004). Geof has recently been engaged in a research project on job retention.

Hannah Morgan is Lecturer in Applied Social Science at the University of Lancaster. Hannah lectures and researches in the fields of disability and ageing and has research interests in disability studies,

EU social policy, citizenship and migration. She has published in a range of publications with recent work focusing on service users' involvement in health and social care and disabled people and citizenship in the European context. Hannah has a key role in organising the UK Disability Studies Association Conferences.

Ghashem Norouzi is a postgraduate student at the University of Sheffield. His research explores the employment barriers faced by people with learning difficulties in contemporary society. He has worked for many years as a rehabilitation director and lecturer in Iran.

Mark Pearson is Head of the Social Policy Division, OECD, responsible for policy advice to governments on how best to integrate income transfers with social and employment services in order to help individuals to fulfil their potential and to support a dynamic economy. Previously, he has worked on employment related social policy at the OECD, working on reform of the tax and benefits systems, links between social protection, inequality and economic growth. He previously worked at the Fiscal Affairs Division of the OECD and at the Institute for Fiscal Studies in London.

Christopher Prinz is a policy analyst in the OECD's Directorate of Employment, Labour and Social Affairs, with an interest in employment-oriented social policy (pension reform, family policy, disability policy, older workers). He recently authored the OECD report, *Transforming disability into ability: Policies to promote work and income security for disabled people* (OECD, 2003), edited *European disability pensions policies* (Ashgate, 2003) and is co-editor of *Transforming disability welfare policies: Towards work and equal opportunities* (Ashgate, 2004). He is currently leader of the OECD team reviewing sickness and disability policies in selected OECD countries.

Sheila Riddell is Director of the Centre for Research in Inclusive Education and Diversity at the Moray House School of Education, University of Edinburgh. She previously worked as the Director of the Strathclyde Centre for Disability Research, University of Glasgow. Her research interests are equality and social inclusion, with particular reference to gender, social class and disability in the fields of employment, education, training and social care. Sheila has published widely in the fields of education, disability, learning difficulties and social capital.

Alan Roulstone is currently Reader in Disability Policy at the University of Sunderland and was previously Deputy Director of the Strathclyde Centre for Disability Research, University of Glasgow. He has published widely in the field of disabled people and employment and has completed research funded by the European Commission, Disability Rights Commission, Joseph Rowntree Foundation, Social Care Institute for Excellence and the Economic and Social Research Council. He is on the editorial board of *Disability and Society*. Alan's most recent writings embed a social model of disability and disabled people's perspectives into UK policy analyses.

Bob Sapey is Senior Lecturer in Applied Social Science at the University of Lancaster. He is interested in disability research and its application in the field of social work. Specific areas of disability research have included the social implications of wheelchair use, employment, housing and technology. He has published widely in disability studies and was co-author with Michael Oliver of the second and third editions of the key text, *Social work with disabled people* (Palgrave, 1999, 2006: forthcoming).

Jenny Secker is Professor of Mental Health with Anglia Polytechnic University and the South Essex Partnership NHS Trust. Her research interests centre on the development of employment services that are effective in enabling people with mental health needs to find and keep a job. In her previous post at King's College London she worked with Bob Grove on an ESRC-funded study of employment support. She is currently working with Bob Grove and colleagues from Durham and City Universities on a national evaluation of supported employment and is assisting the South Essex Partnership NHS Trust in the development of an evidence-based vocational service.

Philippa Simkiss is Assistant Director (Employment) at the Royal National Institute of the Blind (RNIB) and has a senior policy and development role with the organisation. Alongside contributing to debates on the employability of people with visual impairments, Philippa has a long track record of parliamentary and voluntary sector change agency and is an advocate of a range of employment options for people with visual impairment including intermediate labour market. Philippa has contributed to publications in the field of employment and visual impairment.

Bruce Stafford is Director of the Centre for Research in Social Policy at Loughborough University. His research interests focus on policy evaluation and social security issues. Currently, he is leading an international consortium evaluating the New Deal for Disabled People. He has also recently undertaken research on the implementation of the 1995 Disability Discrimination Act. He has published widely in the field of policy studies.

Kate Stanley is Head of Social Policy at the Institute for Public Policy Research (IPPR). Her research interests include welfare reform, children and young people, family policy, homelessness, asylum, disability issues and employment policy. Her recent publications include *Fit for purpose: The reform of Incapacity Benefit* (IPPR, 2004), *Sanctions and sweeteners: Rights and responsibilities in the benefits system* (IPPR, 2004, with Liane Lohde and Stuart White) and *The missing million: Supporting disabled people into work* (IPPR, 2003, with Sue Regan).

Patricia Thornton was until recently Senior Research Fellow in the Social Policy Research Unit, University of York. Patricia is a social policy analyst and evaluator specialising in employment and income policies for disabled people and people with health problems. From 2000 to 2005, she led the research partnership evaluating established employment programmes for disabled people on behalf of the Department for Work and Pensions. She recently worked on evaluations of the New Deal for Disabled People and the Job Retention and Rehabilitation Pilot. Patricia has recently embarked on a career with Voluntary Services Overseas (VSO) working with disabled people in Papua New Guinea.

Jon Warren currently lectures in the Department of Sociology and Social Policy at the University of Durham. He previously lectured in disability studies and youth and community studies at the University of Sunderland. Jon has research interests in theories of social inequality and social inclusion and is currently completing a PhD in the sociology of employment based on primary research of UK call centres. Jon has contributed to research funded by the Disability Rights Commission, ESRC and the Social Care Institute for Excellence.

Carol Woodhams is a Senior Lecturer in Human Resource Management. She has taught and researched at Manchester Metropolitan University Business School since 1993 after a career in hospitality management. She has published widely in issues of equality.

Her doctoral thesis examines equality theory and disabled employment. Publications include articles in *Human Resources Management Journal, International Journal of Research Methodology* and *Journal of Social Policy*. She has led and contributed to disabled employment research funded by the Nuffield Foundation, the European Social Fund and the Economic Social Research Council. She is a Chartered Fellow of the Chartered Institute of Personnel and Development.

Working futures: disabled people, employment policy and social inclusion

Introduction

Few areas of social policy have received more attention than disability and employment policy during the lifetime of the New Labour governments (DSS, 1998; DWP, 2001, 2002a; PMSU, 2004, 2005). The urgency and weight of issues are illustrated in the myriad policy and programme changes that have taken place since 1997 (Burchardt, in Millar, 2003, pp 145-66). However, an essential paradox remains: how is it that, despite much policy effort in the UK to enhance the employment activity of disabled people, these efforts have not been reflected in significantly enhanced employment outcomes (Burchardt, 2000; ONS, 2002; Labour Force Survey, 2003; Stanley and Regan, 2003)?

A number of possible explanations can be posited for the continued difficulty in increasing disabled people's employment. First, policy solutions are essentially sound, but not fully or widely implemented. A related position might be that the coverage of a given policy, benefit or programme is uneven and a lottery of provision has prevailed. Alternatively, one could view the policy framework at a macro-level as essentially sound, but observe factors that severely militated against the effective application of a policy, for example labour market conditions (Beatty et al, 2000; Faggio and Nickell, in Dickens et al, 2003), structural benefit traps (O'Bryan et al, 2000) and perceptions and suspicion of state interventions (Drake, 1999; Roulstone, 2000). Perhaps more fundamentally, the view might be taken that disability and employment policy is premised on an inappropriate model of disability; that policy details and employment programmes may have failed or been severely weakened due to a misunderstanding of the 'disability problem' (Oliver, 1990; Barnes, 1991; Abberley, 1992; Saraga, 1998; Oliver and Barnes, 1998; Roulstone, in Barnes and Mercer, 2004, pp 18-34). Indeed, the historical predominance of a medical model in UK disability policy more widely is hard to dispute. All of these explanations may of course hold clues as the disability and employment paradox.

Attempted discursive solutions to this paradox have been framed in diverse ways that include: social inclusion (Cabinet Office, 2004; PMSU, 2004, 2005); formal legal equality (DRC, 2001); civil rights (Barnes, 1991; Gooding, 1994); the business case (Zadek and Scott-Parker, 2001) and human rights discourses (Daw, 2000). Of note, a critical appraisal of the value of these competing discourses has yet to be undertaken in the field of disability and employment policy. The 'confusion' as to the nature of the 'disability employment problem' is manifest in recent discussions of disabled people as 'customers' rather than claimants. Here, it is conceivable where labour-market conditions are poor that disabled people may be 'customers' who may not want to 'buy' that which is 'not available' (DWP, 2002b). An honest and critical analysis of a disabling society, prevailing levels of human capital among disabled people, labour market characteristics and the interplay of state and the market are *all* prerequisites of a radical disability employment policy.

Although not offering a single framework or solution to the complex issues at stake, *Working futures?* pulls together in a new way the many valuable contributions that are being made to our understanding of the efficacy, limitations and challenges for disability and employment policy. This book aims both to engage with detailed policy evaluations, but also aims to catalyse more theoretical debate about the nature of disability, employment and policy. To draw on the formative ideas of Kurt Lewin, there is nothing "more practical than a theory" (Lewin, 1935, pp 36-48). Here, the explicit attempt to locate disability and employment policy into an ideological and political context is made. This reflects the view that policy is not inherently linear or progressive, and that power is not marginal to social policy decisions (Pierson, 1991; Oliver, 1992; Williams, 1998; George and Wilding, 1994; Ellison and Pierson, 1998; Oliver and Barnes, 1998). For example, within disability employment policy, paid work is largely presented a priori as a homogeneous and self-evident social phenomenon. Yet, the research evidence suggests that paid employment is the area of social life most susceptible to and reinforcing of major social inequalities and divisions (Joyce, 1987; Gallie, 1988; Pahl, 1988; Russell, 1998; Brown and Scase, 1991). Indeed, the employment contract might well be viewed as the power relation par excellence to which few other social relations compare. There is authoritative evidence that poor employee training and skills investment characterises the part-time and peripheral labour market segment (Felstead et al, 2000).

Arguably, the shift towards social inclusion discourses has taken critical analysis ever further away from the core issues of social inequality, class divisions and engrained poverty (Jordan, 1997; Northway, 1997; Levitas, 1998; Byrne, 1999; Percy-Smith, 2000). Distinctions between types of work, entry-level work versus professional work, manual versus non-manual work, seem to feature less in the mainstream social sciences than prior to the New Deals being mooted (Lee and Loveridge, 1987; Brown and Scase, 1991; White, 1994; Gregg and Wadsworth, 1998).

Social constructions of meaningful work and citizenship are rarely debated within disability and employment policy writings (Burden and Hamm, in Percy-Smith, 2000, pp 184-200). The idea that disabled people may contribute economically and socially outside of paid work has not yet impacted much policy analysis, arguably due to the ablist cultural hegemony that attaches to disability in linking disability with inability (Barnes, 1991).

Rather than argue, however, that social inclusion discourses have no inherent value, it could be argued that some approaches have begun to comprehend the multi-factoral influences that lead to social and economic marginalisation (Commission for the European Communities, 1993; SEU, 1997; DSS, 1999; Burchardt et al, 1999; Percy-Smith, 2000). A key message in *Working futures?* is that both policy frameworks and programme detail are unlikely to enhance disabled people's social inclusion if they fail to engage disabled people themselves in the policy solutions. Arguably, disability employment policy (compared, say, to independent living) has been almost hermetically closed to disabled people's influence (Roulstone, in Barnes and Mercer, 2004, pp 18-34). The paradox of social inclusion policy for disabled people of working-age being premised on almost complete exclusion from policy involvement itself has only recently been addressed (PMSU, 2004, 2005).

There is still a long road to travel in raising awareness of the above paradoxes and the need for example to ask more searching questions as to why most disability employment services have been provided by predominantly non-disabled people and premised on often disablist assumptions about the disability problem. We only need to look for parallels in the women's and black rights movement to begin to question whether it is acceptable for most policy and programme research, design and review to have been the province of largely non-disabled people and whether the equivalent would be acceptable in terms of ethnicity or gender policy (Rex, 1984; Lonsdale, 1986; Williams, 1998; Modood et al, 1997).

Alongside an appraisal of disability and employment policy to date, an enabling evaluation of the nature of paid work is also required. The increasing assumption that work and welfare are synonymous (DWP, 2002a) and that work provides social inclusion while supportable in principle, needs to be researched more fully. We know, for example, that workers in the UK work the longest hours in Europe (ILO, 2000; ONS, 2001; Roulstone, 2002). We also know from these same data sources that a lot of sickness absence is due to stress. There is also growing evidence of an intensification of working practices in the UK (Green, 2001). The imperative in the near future then is for a broader appraisal of factors that impact the nature and availability of paid work (Parkinson, 1998; Chanan, in Percy-Smith, 2000, p 201; Roulstone et al, 2003). The relationship between the rigidities and intensification of industrialised production and attempts to adjust and make more flexible working life are also central to our understanding of disabled people's access to the labour market.

The last 10 years have witnessed many positive developments in disability employment policy (Burchardt in Millar, 2003, p 145-66) and great promise inheres in current plans to revise policy further (PMSU, 2005). However, for every positive development there have been policies that have set back the trust between disabled people and the 'employment system'. The New Deal for Disabled People was paralleled by the Benefits Integrity Project (Drake, 1999). Job Retention pilots have been floated amidst a renaissance of media concern about a sickness culture. Recent ministerial commentary has arguably added to the divisive potential of policy change when he referred to the importance of distinguishing between the 'back problems' and 'severe disability' in the population of Incapacity Benefit claimants (DWP and IPPR, 2005). Disabled people, their bodies and very identity continue to be argued over in a way that makes many fear an increase in surveillance and harsher return to work policies. The role of enhanced trust, alongside involving disabled people in reshaping their life chances, seems the sine qua non of enabling disability employment policy worthy of the 21st century.

This collection of writings, then, acknowledges that alongside detailed policy appraisal is an urgent need to bring together new epistemological frameworks and possibilities to the study of disabled people's employment and valued living options. The following questions are addressed:

- What are the factors that continue to limit disabled people's access to paid employment, and what currently works in enhancing employment options for disabled people?
- How can increased policy and programme efforts be squared with the limited employment opportunities available to disabled people?
- Is there currently symmetry of activation activity aimed at both disabled people and employers?
- What can we learn from the wider European policy agenda about policy enhancement?
- Should we be questioning the 'Work First' agenda more fully, its potential for disabled people, or simply improving it?
- What alternative enabling futures should we validate in policy and cultural terms?
- What are the values that our economic and social system attaches to work and workableness and what are the implications for disabled people?

Reading this book

The following chapters provide detailed accounts of disability and employment policy. They offer a wide range of policy analysis that looks at access, enhancement, equality and retention policy. Chapters also attempt to link employment-based policy to the wider policy context and to the benefits system. The changing nature of paid work and future policy options are also explored where they seem to have a bearing on disability policy and disabled people. The book makes clear the continued weight of barriers faced by many disabled people at the beginning of the 21st century, while also looking at the effectiveness of policy responses to the particular challenges faced by people with mental health problems, sensory impairments and learning difficulties. The authors include researchers, policy commentators and senior civil servants with established expertise in the field of disability and employment policy and practice. New policy writers and themes are also introduced to afford more broad ranging and critical evaluations of disability and employment policy. The book also showcases new writings from disabled people, disability activists and those working at street-level to enhance disabled people's employment position. This is the first time this range of authors has worked together to respond to these key policy issues.

The book is in three main parts. Part One – 'Work, welfare and social inclusion: challenges, concepts and questions' – provides two introductory chapters designed to provide a critical reflection on the challenges of employing more disabled people. It is argued that part of this problem is conceptual and discursive confusion as to the nature of the 'disability and employment' problem. Part One also provides an introductory framework with which to make sense of the detailed policy chapters that follow in Parts Two and Three of the book. These chapters also draw on the stark data that convey the significance of barriers to the contemporary labour market and the urgent need to reform disability and employment policy.

Roulstone and Barnes (Chapter One) provide an overview of the policy area as a primer with which to read the rest of the book. Their chapter discusses the weight of barriers to gaining and keeping employment, the strengths and weaknesses of past policy and the tensions at the heart of recent ideological and policy shifts towards a work-first agenda. Stanley (Chapter Two) explores in some depth the broad policy challenges that face governments in reducing welfare spending, while dovetailing this with a social inclusion agenda. Stanley points to the importance of linking policies on disability, poverty and childcare to effect positive changes to the wider position of disabled people. The key characteristic of disability and employment policy is its labyrinthine and often uncoordinated nature according to Stanley.

Part Two – 'The current policy environment' – presents a detailed appraisal of current or recent disability employment policy writing, each chapter looking in some depth at key policy initiatives, programmes and practice. Stafford (Chapter Three) presents evidence on the effectiveness and limits of the flagship policy New Deal for Disabled People (NDDP). Stafford notes that, while our picture of the effectiveness is growing, most policy attention has been on process effectiveness rather than hard outcomes. The chapter addresses the challenges to smoothing a pathway to paid employment and ways in which the NDDP scheme could be enhanced to fulfil the significant potential New Labour have placed in it. Riddell and Banks (Chapter Four) look at another pre-employment programme, 'Work Preparation'. They argue that despite being sound in principle, the scheme offers very little in the way of progressive employment support in being based on a 'train and place' model. The latter is largely rejected by disabled people's organisations and with the advent of US-style supported employment, which adopts a 'place and train model', one more likely to foster sustained employment. The authors also point to the need to evaluate the programme more fully if it is to become better value for money. Meager and Hurstfield (Chapter Five) present recent research findings on the efficacy and limitations of the Disability Discrimination Act (DDA) 1995. Their findings suggest that despite the significant potential that inheres in the act, the DDA and the wider objectives it was meant to fulfil are substantially weakened by the use and interpretation of the law itself.

Danieli and Woodhams (Chapter Six) provide a complementary chapter in looking at the merits of the proposed Disability Bill (now the Disability Discrimination Act, 2005). They base their chapter on their evaluation of the likely effectiveness of proactive legislation that aims to encourage employers to workforce plan for disability through substantial employment monitoring and action planning. While supportive of a social model of disability, the authors note the difficulties of adopting the model for employment monitoring purposes. Mercer (Chapter Seven) looks at the now highly topical subject of Job Retention and Rehabilitation Pilots. This focus then is on why disabled people leave the labour market early and the likely effectiveness of the above pilots in enhancing disabled people's retention opportunities to stay in paid work. Corden (Chapter Eight) widens out the focus of discussion by looking at the complex nature of the disability benefits system. Corden addresses possible reforms to the benefits system that would help make paid work and benefits mutually compatible and non-stigmatising. She argues that there has been progress in aiding the pathway between benefits and paid work, and that there is still much to do to enhance disabled people's employment position and to make work pay. Pearson and Prinz (Chapter Nine) highlight the extent of disabled people's unemployment in OECD countries. Labour-market barriers, failure to activate disabled people into employment and perverse benefit incentives all serve to militate against disabled people's employment in the 'developed' world. The authors provide policy direction for enhanced future employment activation.

Thornton (Chapter Ten) highlights the tensions that sit at the heart of recent disability advisor developments. Noting the EC's impetus towards mainstreaming disability services, Thornton notes the recent preference of the UK Department for Work and Pensions for specialist disability advisers. The dangers of this approach are spelt out as they may militate against the development of disability expertise among mainstream programmes and further ghettoise work with disabled people.

Lunt (Chapter Eleven) provides a picture of the complex interplay of federal, national, and global interactions between capital, labour, the state and policy making. Adopting a multi-layered policy perspective, Lunt rejects a mono-causal approach based on global drivers of policy and employment change. He notes the relationship between these macro-level forces and the complexities of state, federal and cultural factors (for example, first-nation struggles) that impact disability and employment policy in commonwealth countries. Coleridge (Chapter Twelve) provides an appraisal of the role of paid work in the lives of some of the poorest disabled people. Drawing on his extensive work with disabled people in Africa and beyond, he posits that notions of employment and work are very different in these contexts. Many Africans simply 'make out' in informal but essential economic contexts. Coleridge points to the challenge of translating World Bank, International Labour Organization (ILO) and World Health Organization (WHO) policy measures in society where little if any policy infrastructure obtains. Coleridge points to what might be called 'appropriate disability policy', one which takes account of the economic, cultural and familial structures onto which policy objectives are placed. This chapter cautions against a 'one size fits all' approach to policy solutions. Coleridge reminds readers of the wider global links between disability, poverty and worklessness in the 'first', 'second' and 'third' worlds.

Although there are many barriers remaining in the current policy context, part two highlights throughout those policies that offer the most enabling outcomes for disabled people and also offer specific policy recommendations for the future.

Part Three – 'Towards inclusive policy futures' – addresses the limitations of policy laid out in Part Two by looking at how new discourses, structures, policies and programmes can be introduced and how innovative social model ideas can be adopted to radically change disability and employment policy. Gibbs (Chapter Thirteen) offers a viewpoint of the deficits of current disability and employment policy, both at a conceptual (theoretical) and practical level. Gibbs argues that the disabled people's movement in the UK has a number of key contributions to make, both in redefining key ideas around the 'disability and employment' problem, but also a number of tangible ideas that if heard will improve the shape and delivery of these policies in the future. Secker and Grove (Chapter Fourteen) provide a critical history of the impact of segregation on the employment expectations attached to people with mental health problems. Drawing on recent research they note the need to go beyond a 'train and place' approach to employment access, to a 'place and train' approach, which is developmental and crucially does not assume that mental health problems have entirely dissipated before employment begins. The authors offer some policy prescriptions for more enabling futures for people with enduring mental health problems. Goodley and Norouzi (Chapter Fifteen) provide a radical critique of current policy geared to the needs of people with the label of learning difficulty. They note how the essentialist view of 'mental retardation' has continued to dominate mainstream views of what is essentially a powerful social construct. The authors note that despite the promising language and reach of the 'Valuing People' White Paper, and of positive developments in the field of US-style supported employment, there are still profound cognitive and policy barriers to the further economic and social inclusion of people with learning difficulties.

Harris and Thornton (Chapter Sixteen) are also critical of current provision for Deaf and hard of hearing job seekers and workers. Beyond some very basic (and imperfect) data on employment rates for this group, we know little in detail about their labour market and employment experiences. The chapter makes both theoretical and practical suggestions for employment policy and practice that would be more inclusive of issues of access to communication and cultural identity of deaf people in the labour market. Simkiss (Chapter Seventeen) also deals with issues of sensory impairment and the unmet needs of disabled workers. Here, Simkiss looks at the continued barriers facing workers and jobseekers with visual impairments. The author notes the proposed shifts to wholesale commitments to mainstream employment, asserting that there will always remain some requirement for some intermediate labour market activity for blind and partially sighted adults, especially those currently some distance from the world of work. Simkiss sees diverse routes to social inclusion, and a virtue attaching to a range of employment choices, rather than full-time mainstream employment being accepted as the norm.

The theme of the challenges to social inclusion is central to Morgan (Chapter Eighteen). Here the promise of formal legal equality and rights to citizenship in a European context are explored. Morgan argues that until recently the ability to work was at the centre of the EC's definition of citizenship. Increasingly this notion has shifted both towards more substantive human rights and through EC activities towards a greater valuation of EU citizens. While there are still challenges and the paradigm shift is incomplete, there are some promising developments within European policy that may signal the greater social and employment integration of disabled people.

Gradwell (Chapter Nineteen) provides a very cogent appraisal of the promise and limitations of much current voluntary and community sector (VCS) activity in the field of disability and employment provision. Although acknowledging where good employment enhancement work is taking place, Gradwell notes the often unevaluated nature of much VCS activity and the need to employ more disabled people in that sector as a role model to other employers. This greater employment of disabled people would also be symbolic of their commitment to disabled people's employment more widely. Gradwell contrasts 'disability organisations' and 'organisations of disabled people' seeing these organisations as based on very different appraisals of disability.

Sapey and Hughes (Chapter Twenty) point up the overly homogenised policy perception of employment by looking at the policy implications of professional change. Professional level work rarely receives explicit attention in policy terms, itself a noteworthy phenomenon that requires further research. Sapey and Hughes, both former practitioners, explore the changing nature of professional accreditation and the often awkward fit between these codes, requirements and stipulations and the opening up of professional work to more disabled people. The chapter begs questions about the future of policy and policy impact in these employments.

Warren (Chapter Twenty One), provides a chapter, deliberately designed to look back at the origins of welfare and work policy. By doing this, Warren highlights the continuities and breaks with tradition in policy thinking and the changing conception of the disability employment problem. Warren argues that work continues to be premised on narrowly defined notions of wage labour and with the longer run drift to neoliberal policy underpinnings risks losing much of the corporatist tradition that emphasised collective futures and solutions. The growth of conditional welfare risks an exacerbation of the very social exclusion policy makers and politicians are seeking to diminish

While highly supportive of greater employment opportunities for disabled people, Barnes and Roulstone (Chapter Twenty Two) are concerned that the 21st century has not witnessed more creative policy solutions, ones that question whether paid work is the only legitimate source of social citizenship and inclusion. Should disabled people's economic roles as employers of personal assistance, their positive activism for more enabling environments and their often unpaid input to the community and social governance not be accepted as alternative sources of social value? The chapter makes a plea that, alongside employment enhancement measures, policy makers and the visionaries of the 21st century be allowed to think beyond the orthodoxies inherited from the Poor Law of 1601.

References

Abberley, P. (1992) 'Counting us out: a discussion of the OPCS disability surveys', *Disability, Handicap and Society*, vol 2, no 1, pp 139-55.

Barnes, C. (1991) *Disabled people in Britain and discrimination*, London: Hurst and Co.

Barnes, C. and Mercer, G. (2004) *Disability policy and practice: Applying the social model*, Leeds: Disability Press

Beatty, C., Fothergill, S. and Macmillan, R. (2000) 'A theory of employment, unemployment and sickness', *Regional Studies*, vol 34, pp 617-30.

Brown, P. and Scase, R. (eds) (1991) *Poor work: Disadvantage and the division of labour*, Buckingham: Open University Press.

Burchardt, T. (2000) *Enduring economic exclusion: Disabled people, income and work*, York: York Publishing.

Burchardt, T., Le Grand, J. and Piachaud, D. (1999) 'Social exclusion in Britain 1991-1995', *Social Policy and Administration*, vol 33, no 3, pp 227-44.

Byrne, D. (1999) *Social exclusion*, Buckingham: Open University Press.

Cabinet Office (2004) *Mental health and social exclusion*, London: Cabinet Office.

Commission of the European Communities (1993) *Social exclusion, poverty and other social problems in the European Community. Background Report*, Luxembourg: CEC.

Daw, R. (2000) *The impact of the Human Rights Act on disabled people*, London: Disability Rights Commission.

DSS (Department for Social Security) (1998) *A new contract for welfare: Support for disabled people*, Cm 4103, London: DSS.

DWP (Department for Work and Pensions) (2001) *Strategy for increasing the employment rates for disabled people*, DWP Research Paper, London: DWP.

DWP (2002a) *Pathways to Work: Helping people into employment*, Green Paper, London: DWP.

DWP (2002b) *New Deal News*, issue 4, Autumn, London: DWP.

DWP and IPPR (2005) The Future of Incapacity Benefit Seminar and published proceedings, Senate House, University of London, 7 February.

Dickens, R., Gregg, P. and Wadsworth, J. (eds) (2003) *The labour market under New Labour*, London: Palgrave.

DRC (Disability Rights Commission) (2001) *Strategic plan 2001-2004*, Stratford-Upon-Avon: DRC

Drake, R. (1999) *Understanding disability policies*, Basingstoke: Macmillan.

Ellison, N. and Pierson, C. (1998) *Developments in British social policy*, London: Macmillan.

Felstead, A., Ashton, D. and Green, F. (2000) 'Are Britain's workplace skills becoming more unequal?', *Cambridge Journal of Economics*, vol 24, pp 709-27.

Gallie, D. (ed) (1988) *Employment in Britain*, Oxford: Blackwell.

George, V. and Wilding, P. (1994) *Welfare and ideology*, Hemel Hempstead: Harvester Wheatsheaf.

Gooding, C. (1994) *Disabling laws, enabling acts*, London: Pluto Press.

Gregg, P. and Wadsworth, J. (1998) *Unemployment and non employment*, London: Employment Policy Insititute.

Green, F. (2001) 'It's been a hard day's night: the concentration and intensification of work in the late 20th century Britain', *British Journal of Industrial Relations*, vol 39, no 1, pp 53-80.

Hewitt, M. and Dean, H. (2002) *Welfare state and welfare change*, Buckingham: Open University Press.

Jordan, B. (1997) *A theory of poverty and social exclusion*, Cambridge: Polity Press.

Joyce, P. (1987) *The historical meaning of work*, Cambridge: Cambridge University Press.

ILO (International Labour Organization) (2000) *International labour statistics bulletin*, Geneva: ILO.

Lee, G. and Loveridge, R. (1987) *The manufacture of disadvantage*, Milton Keynes: Open University Press.

Levitas, R. (1998) *The inclusive society? Social exclusion and New Labour*, London: Macmillan.

Lewin, K. (1935) *A dynamic theory of personality*, New York: McGraw Hill.

Loney, M. (1983) *The state or the market*, London: Sage Publications.

Lonsdale, S. (1986) *Work and inequality*, London: Longman.

Millar, J. (2003) *Understanding social security*, Bristol: The Policy Press.

Modood, T., Berthoud, R. and Lakey, J. (1997) *Ethnic minorities in Britain: Diversity and disadvantage*, London: Policy Studies Institute.

Northway, R. (1997) 'Integration and inclusion: illusion or progress in services for disabled people', *Disability and Society*, vol 31, no 2, pp 157-72.

O'Bryan, A., Simons, K., Beyer, S. and Grove, B. (2000) *A framework for supported employment*, York: Joseph Rowntree Foundation and York Publishing.

ONS (Office for National Statistics) (2001) *Social trends*, London: The Stationery Office.

ONS (2002) *Social trends*, London: The Stationery Office.

ONS (2003) *Labour Force Survey*, London: ONS.

Oliver, M. (1990) *The politics of disablement*, Basingstoke: Macmillan.

Oliver, M. (1992) 'Changing the social relations of research production', *Disability and Society*, vol 7, no 2, pp 101-14.

Oliver, M. and Barnes, C. (1998) *Disabled people and social policy: From exclusion to inclusion*, London: Longman.

Pahl, R. (1988) *On work: Historical, comparative and theoretical approaches*, Oxford: Blackwell.

Parkinson, M. (1998) *Combating social exclusion: Lessons from area-based programmes in Europe*, Bristol: The Policy Press.

Percy-Smith, J. (ed) (2000) *Policy responses to social exclusion: Towards inclusion?*, Buckingham: Open University Press.

Pierson, C. (1991) *Beyond the welfare state?*, Cambridge: Polity Press.

PMSU (Prime Minister's Strategy Unit) (2004) *Improving the life chances of disabled people: Interim report*, London: PMSU.

PMSU (2005) *Improving the life chances of disabled people: Final report*, London: PMSU.

Rex, J. (1984) 'Social Policy and Ethnic Inequality', Social Administration Conference, July.

Roulstone, A. (2000) 'Disability, dependency and the New Deal for Disabled People', *Disability and Society*, vol 15, no 3.

Roulstone, A. (2002) 'Disabling pasts, enabling futures? How does the changing nature of capitalism impact the disabled worker and jobseeker?', *Disability and Society*, vol 17, no 6, pp 627-42.

Roulstone, A., Gradwell, L., Price, J. and Child, L. (2003) *Thriving and surviving at work: Disabled people's employment strategy*, Bristol: The Policy Press.

Russell, M. (1998) *Beyond ramps: Disability and the end of the social contract*, Maine: Common Courage Press.

Saraga, E. (1998) *Embodying the social: Constructions of difference*, London: Routledge and Open University Press.

SEU (Social Exclusion Unit) (1997) *Social Exclusion Unit: Purpose, work priorities and working methods*, London: HMSO.

Stanley, L. and Regan, S. (2003) *The missing million: Supporting disabled people into work*, London: IPPR.

White, M. (1994) *Unemployment and public policy in a changing labour market*, London: Policy Studies Institute.

Williams, F. (1998) *Social policy: A critical introduction*, Cambridge: Polity Press.

Zadek, S. and Scott-Parker, S. (2001) *Unlocking potential: The new disability business case*, London: Employers Forum on Disability.

Part One:
Work, welfare and social inclusion:
challenges, concepts and questions

ONE

The challenges of a work-first agenda for disabled people

Alan Roulstone and Colin Barnes

... attempts to 'protect' disabled people within a much reduced welfare state have not been effective and have in any case had the unwelcome consequence of increasing the scrutiny and control exercised by professionals....This stands in contrast to the alternative policy agenda articulated by disabled people themselves that stresses autonomy, integration, an end to discrimination, and rights to equal chances in employment, to an adequate level of income, and to services which enhance personal choice and facilitate independent living. (Glendinning, 1991, p 3)

Despite considerable progress, disabled people are still experiencing disadvantage and discrimination, barriers – in attitudes, the design of buildings and policies for example – still have to be overcome by disabled people ... too many services are organised to suit providers rather than being personalised around the needs of disabled people. (Prime Minister Tony Blair, Foreword to PMSU, 2005)

The weight of historical disadvantage experienced by disabled job seekers and workers is now well documented (Barnes, 1991; Burchardt, 2000; DWP, 2001; ONS, 2002a, 2002b; Burchardt, in Millar, 2003, pp 145-66; DRC, 2004a; PMSU, 2004). The principal policy response has been an increased governmental emphasis on 'welfare through work' and 'work-based welfare' (Giddens, 1998).

The focus on paid work as the primary source of social well-being has been further emphasised by New Labour policies (DSS, 1998a; HM Treasury, 2001). The continued rise in sickness and disability benefits from 1997 has been a key driver of policy reform, while the changing rationale for reducing claimant numbers is that of the human cost of long-term absence from the labour market (DWP, 2002, 2004a;

PMSU, 2005). Paid work has become the leitmotiv of New Labour welfare policy and for many, social inclusion the natural corollary of engagement with paid work.

The genesis of disability welfare reform can be traced, however, to much earlier reforms of the Conservative governments of the 1980s and 1990s. This is somewhat paradoxical at first sight. The neoliberal governments of the 1980s did sanction the increase in invalidity benefit (now Incapacity Benefit) by re-designating some unemployment benefit claimants. However, the decade 1980-1990 also witnessed a growing emphasis on rationalising the benefits system for disabled people. These reached their apotheosis in the Fowler reforms of the mid-1980s (Glendinning, 1991) and the 'Way Ahead' document of 1990 (DSS, 1990). To begin to unravel these complexities, it is worth pointing out that welfare retraction was to largely impact income support disability premiums that were deemed expensive and often open-ended. The period 1997-2005 has arguably witnessed the widening of attention on welfare reform to begin to apply the targeting approach favoured by neoliberals to the question of disabled people in receipt of 'out of work' benefits.

There is, however, much debate to be had as to the exact reasons for these policy changes. The political desirability of 'rekindling' the link between rights and responsibilities (Giddens, 1998; Powell, 1999, p 19; White, 2001, p 79; Blair, 2002; Ludlam and Smith, 2001, p 205; Savage and Atkinson, 2001, p 10) has clearly to successfully foster responsibilities of both sides of the labour contract if it is to be successful (Stanley and Maxwell, 2004). That the search for work be matched by the availability of work is a truism but is worth restating at this point as it is susceptible to be overshadowed by the detail of the latest policy intervention. Of note, the question of the perceived relationship between and weight attached to individual effort and social responsibility (Thornton and Lunt, 1995), continue to pervade contemporary debates (Lund, 1999; Powell and Hewitt, 2002). This dialogue is arguably a microcosm of wider ideological relationship between the old rivals of corporatism and market individualism. If disabled people are to take seriously the notion of rights and responsibilities, the latter have to be quantified and be seen to prevail if a rights-responsibilities approach is to be taken seriously.

It is not surprising, therefore, that very different policy interpretations attach to this emphasis on 'work first'. The exact perspective adopted can have a profound impact on wider policy predictions for success in enhancing both disabled people's access to sustained employment (Giddens, 1998, p 125; Roulstone, 2000; Callinicos, 2001, p 59; Ferrera et al in Giddens, 2001, pp 114-33). For example, there is much evidence across the EU nation states that welfare reform and retraction are major themes of the 1980s and 1990s, often driven by the concern that disability spending is a key drain on welfare spending (Aarts et al, 1996; Hogelund, 2003). This emphasis on reducing welfare spending however is not of itself regressive if it is based on a real concern for disabled people's social inclusion (DWP, 2004b; PMSU, 2004, 2005; DWP and IPPR, 2005) and accompanied by a genuine commitment to enhance sustained and suitably rewarded employment opportunities. There is, on the surface at least, evidence of both these concerns in recent social policy.

The mixture of corporatist and neoliberal thinking that characterises New Labour policy is mirrored in a similar policy mix in mainland Europe, its future economic and social direction. European policy shifts are reflected in the move from the more corporatist Essen Actions and Amsterdam Declarations to the Luxembourg Summit's emphasis upon 'employability' and 'entrepreneurship' (DfEE, 1998; European Parliament, 2001; Hillage and Pollard, 1998; Ferrera et al in Giddens, 2001, pp 114-33; Boeri et al, 2002;). It is currently very challenging, therefore, for policy analysts and disability writers and activists to disentangle these exact motivations. Indeed, we still have a lot to understand about the long-term effect of emphasising a work-first agenda. Of note, the very real attempt by subsequent UK governments to reduce the claimant total of working-age disabled people who claim sickness and disability benefits, has not been reflected in substantial benefit claimant reductions. Indeed there was a slight rise in sickness and disability benefit claims between 1998 and 2001 (ONS, 2002). Recent figures point to a reduction in the 'flow' onto sickness and incapacity benefits, but a resilience in the 'stock' of current claimants. That is, despite the efforts to re-engage disabled people with paid work the numbers leaving these benefits and entering paid employment are small (Burchardt in Millar, 2003; PMSU, 2004, 2005; Stanley and Maxwell, 2004).

We do need to understand, therefore, the exact motivations and aspirations of disabled benefit recipients and not assume that these figures are the result of irrational or socially dysfunctional decisions (Levitas, 1998; Dean, 2003). Key changes to Incapacity Benefit, an important benefit for disabled people and a key policy target for spending reduction, have largely been criticised by some commentators as punitive and unlikely to encourage a culture of 'return to work' (Hyde, 2000; Roulstone, 2000). However, Corden (Chapter Eight of this volume) notes some successes in the wider benefit system which help make the movement from work an action motivated by both the push of benefit reform and the pull of employment that pays. It might be argued, however, that the continued conceptual or epistemological confusion at the heart of the 'incapacity principle' will continue to limit disabled people's movement into paid work. Here the inherent contradictory requirement that disabled people be able to prove that they are both fit/unfit for work perpetuates suspicion in both disabled people and potential employers (Mabbett and Bolderson, 2001; Stanley and Maxwell, 2004). Despite this concern and the perceived stigma that attaches to the term 'incapacity', there are defenders of the benefit (TUC, 2004).

Of note, there is also pan-European evidence that despite different disability policy regimes, the levels of success for disabled people entering sustained employment across Europe and wider OECD country membership are consistently poor (see Chapter Nine of this volume; Prinz and Marin, 2003; Marin et al, 2004). Are there structural and deep-seated barriers that transcend the national context? It is important not to take the pan-OECD data on widespread limits to policy change as meaning disability employment policy is failing in general terms. Specific policy and programme successes must be acknowledged if key lessons are to be learned. Recent research in Denmark and the Netherlands, for example, makes quite clear policy suggestions which identify the limits in both welfare regimes, while clearly noting ways in which positive lessons could be gleaned from both countries (Hogelund, 2003).

If, for a moment, we are to look at the underlying changes in policy principles; the increased connection between paid employment and disability are to be welcomed. They represent a transcending of the historical assumption that disability equals social and economic dependence (Finkelstein, 1980; Oliver, 1990; Barnes, 1991). However, any simplistic assumption that disabled people 'can work' has substantial implications for groups who may experience the greatest barriers in gaining and keeping employment (DSS, 1998b; DWP, 2002; Berthoud, 2003; Royal College of Psychiatrists, 2003; Learning Disability Task Force Report, 2004; SEU, 2004, pp 59-70; Roberts et al, 2004). There is also a well-documented risk that the political dictum, 'work for those who can and welfare for those who cannot', although well intentioned, oversimplifies the relationship between impairment disability, and employment, the benefits system and disabled people's diverse constructions of the value and accessibility of paid work (Roulstone, 2000). This has major implications for the future of policy in this area and requires urgent attention.

There is now growing evidence that the target groups of disabled adults within flagship policies such as New Deal for Disabled People are those that may be perceived in cost–benefit terms to be the most easily returned to the labour market, but who may also be the most resistant to paid work (Roulstone, 2000; Arthur et al, 1999). Resistance to paid work among disabled people continues to be attributed in official policy terms to "a culture of dependency and low expectations" (PMSU, 2005, p 9), whereas alternative evidence points to rational appraisals of low employment opportunities in given labour markets (Alcock et al, 2003). Conversely, disabled people who have been out of the labour market or who may never have had work, but who may want paid work, receive little attention in policy terms. Short-term policy objectives here risk leaving longer run disability and employment issues unresolved.

One key factor that is absent from the current appraisal of disabled people and access to the labour market are understandings of disabled women's perceptions of paid work, incapacity, domestic and caring commitments and notions of citizenship (Lonsdale, 1986, 1990). Given that disabled women are more likely to be absent from both paid work and less likely to claim out of work benefits (Martin et al, 1989; Lonsdale, 1990), there is an urgent need to redress this in policy terms. Of note disabled women even when in work continue to earn less than their male counterpart (on average earning £2.31 less per hour) and significantly less than their non-disabled male comparator (£3.54 less per hour) (ONS, 2004). Perhaps the trust required to encourage disabled people to buy into work-first policies more generally would be aided specifically by a policy shift towards valuing paid work for all disabled people who want to work (Stanley and Regan, 2003; DRC, 2004b), regardless of their claimant status.

To date, policy emphasis from the passing of the 1944 Disabled Persons Employment Act has operated with a deficit or supply-side model of employment re-engagement (see Chapter Twenty One of this volume; Barnes, 1991; Roulstone in Barnes and Mercer, 2004, pp 18-34). Here, the role of policy has arguably been to package or rehabilitate the individual to be more work-ready (O' Bryan et al, 2000; Wilson et al, 2003). While this approach may prove useful where dovetailed with good medical rehabilitation and employer activation, it may severely underplay an evaluation of well-documented workplace barriers (Graham et al, 1990; Prescott-Clarke, 1990; Burchardt, 2000; RNIB, 2002; Daone and Scott, 2003). The recent comprehensive report, *Improving the life chances of disabled people* (PMSU, 2005) begins by clarifying that disability is the result of:

> disadvantage experienced by the individual ... resulting
> from barriers to independent living or educational,
> employment or other opportunities. (PMSU, 2005, p 8)

However, the employment chapter of this important report devotes 26 pages to individual activation policies based largely on the perception of disabled people having "pervasive and negative cultural expectations towards working" (PMSU, 2005, p 158). The chapter only devotes five pages to employers, much of which looks at their fears or misapprehensions of disability rather than appraise workplace barriers per se (PMSU, 2005, pp 185-91).

There are many aspects of recent policy that deserve praise. Developments in the form of Disabled Person's Tax Credits (DPTC) and latterly the embedding of DPTC into mainstream tax credits clearly holds significant potential for mainstreaming disability support in a less stigmatising format (Inland Revenue, 2002; Burchardt in Millar, 2003, pp 145-66). Other positive changes have been witnessed in the form of a higher 'earnings disregard' thresholds for Independent Living Fund recipients and an extension of the Incapacity Benefit 'linking rule' period from eight weeks to one year (see Chapter Eight of this volume). Alongside these positive developments are longer run tensions around government policy.

The passing of the Disability Discrimination Act (DDA) 1995, the advent of the Disability Rights Commission in 2000 (DRC Act 2000) and the proposed Draft Disability Discrimination Bill (DWP, 2003; DRC 2004b; Roulstone, 2004) all provide promise in terms of their value in changing attitudes and reducing employment, transport and service barriers, all of which have historically limited disabled people's employment (Zarb, 1995; Burchardt, 2000). However, despite the DDA, DRC, innovative tax credits and latterly job-retention pilots, there is still much evidence that disabled people are excluded from – or are not attracted to – the contemporary labour market (ONS, 2002; Stanley and Regan, 2003). Additionally, key policy potential inhering in the DDA 1995 has arguably been attenuated by the legal construction of the act and the often (if inadvertent) disablist assumptions evident in the application of the DDA (see Chapter Five of this volume; Meager et al, 1999; Hepple et al, 2001; Income Data Services, 2001; Roulstone, 2003; Hurstfield et al, 2004). The low-level of successful recruitment claims under the DDA is particularly concerning given the continued evidence of negative workplace attitudes towards employing certain disabled people (Roberts et al, 2004). The Draft Disability Discrimination Bill (DRC, 2004b) (now the Disability Discrimination

Act 2005) is in part a response to the limits of reactive legislation and attempts to place a proactive duty on employers to action plan and monitor for disabled people's employment. This is a promising development that is currently receiving Parliamentary attention (DRC, 2004b; Roulstone, 2004). A key factor in effective employment monitoring is that, unlike the Race Relations Amendments Act (2000) on whose broad principles it is based, the question of disability and impairment make monitoring more complex. It is to be hoped that the government will embrace a barriers-inclusive approach and that DRC enforcement will include a barriers focus. Only in this way can monitoring transcend a simple headcount of disabled people, an approach that signally failed when applied to the UK employment quota (Thornton and Lunt, 1995).

Active review of disability law, the benefits system around the work-welfare interface and the promise of more seamless policies do offer some promise in the early 21st century. Recent developments include the merging of the former Benefits Agency and Jobcentres into Jobcentre Plus (Chapter Ten of this volume; House of Commons Work and Pensions Committee, 2002), and efforts to make employment a key issue in wider health and social care. The latter is evident both in the recent Green Paper, 'Pathways to Work', its emphasis on health and social care workers making connections with policy and practice stakeholders in the employment field (DWP, 2002; PMSU, 2005, pp 158-64). This emphasis is also evident in the White Paper, 'Valuing People' (DH, 2001), which reassuringly emphasises the right of people with learning difficulties to greater employment opportunities as a key way of affording them enhanced social inclusion. However a closer analysis of proposals to engage health and employment professionals suggests both risks and policy muddle. As policy writers, we have to challenge objectives such as this:

> … the system should aim to enable individuals to … remain in work for longer when sick. (PMSU, 2005, p 160)

In confusing sickness with disability, this statement not only displays the sort of confusion the reports authors claim to transcend (2005, p 8), but is itself clearly inhumane and contravenes virtually every philosophical and moral statement on ill-health from Galen, the Hippocratic Oath through Talcott Parson's famous appraisal of the 'sick role' to the Human Rights Act's assertion of the right not to be treated inhumanely.

The recognition that most disability employment policy has focused upon access to employment and not disabled people's departure from employment has led to Job Retention and Rehabilitation Pilots (see Chapter Seven of this volume; JRF, 2002; DWP, 2003). These pilots aim to address the significant numbers of disabled people who leave the labour market after leaving statutory sick pay schemes (Chief Medical Officer's Update, 2001). This, clearly, is a welcome step in enhancing disabled workers' connection with paid work beyond the age of 50 where they are able to continue working (Martin et al, 1989). Unfortunately, the issues of flexible job and work retention have been overshadowed somewhat by the discourse of reducing sickness absence. What began as a committed attempt to reduce unnecessary early departures from paid work has become a politicised issue focusing on the problems of aggregate numbers of days lost to sickness absence (CBI, 2003; DWP, 2004a). Clearly, trust needs to be present if these promising policy developments are to be maximised. Related to this, the area of employment and job retention point up the need for greater aggregate employer demand for disabled workers. In the absence of this, enhanced job retention for disabled people may simply mean less disabled people are able to enter the labour market.

The development of WORKSTEP, a revised approach to supported employment but which aims to cast off vestiges of links with sheltered employment and dependency, also reflects the energy being placed in disability employment policy (DWP, 2001). It is noteworthy that disquiet remains in some quarters about the loss of intermediate labour market opportunities such as sheltered placements given the perceived weight of barriers to mainstream work (RNIB, 2002).

Despite the significant potential that inheres in the above policy developments, the following chapters help establish unequivocally that a number of important policy barriers remain.

References

Aarts, L., Burkhauser, R. and DeJong, P.R. (eds) (1996) *Curing the Dutch disease: An international perspective on disability policy reform*, Avebury: Foundation for the International Studies of Social Security.

Alcock, P., Beaty, C., Fothergill, S., Macmillan, R. and Yeandle, S. (2003) *Work to welfare: How men become detached from the labour market*, Cambridge: Cambridge University Press.

Arthur, S., Corden, A., Green, A., Lewis, J., Loumidis, J., Sainsbury, R., Thornton, P. and Walker, R. (1999) *New Deal for Disabled People: Early implementation*, DSS Report 106, Leeds: DSS.

Barnes, C. (1991) *Disabled people in Britain and discrimination*, London: Hurst and Co.

Barnes, C. and Mercer, G. (eds) (2004) *Disability policy and practice: Analysing the social model*, Leeds: Disability Press.

Berthoud, R. (2003) *Multiple disadvantage and employment*, York: York Publishing and JRF.

Blair, A. (2002) *Mutual responsibility the key to welfare reform*, Downing Street Press Release, 10 June.

Boeri, T., Layard, R. and Nickel, S. (2002) *Welfare to work and the fight against long-term unemployment*, DfEE Research Brief 206, London: DfEE.

Burchardt, T. (2000) *Enduring economic exclusion: Disabled people, income and work*, York: York Publishing and JRF.

Callinicos, A (2001) *Against the Third Way*, Cambridge: Polity Press.

CBI (Confederation of British Industry) (2003) *The lost billions: 2003 CBI absence and labour turnover survey*, London: AXA PPP Healthcare.

Chief Medical Officer's Update (2001) *Job retention and rehabilitation pilots*, CMO Update 29, London: DH.

Daone, L. and Scott, R. (2003) *Ready, willing and disabled*, London: Scope.

Dean, H. (2003) *Welfare rights and social policy*, London: Pearson.

DfEE (Department for Education and Employment) (1998) *Blunkett welcomes European 'New Deal' agreement on jobs and employability*, DfEE Press Release 563/98, September, London: DfEE.

DH (Department of Health) (2001) *Valuing people: A new strategy for learning disability in the 21st century*, Cm 5086, London: TSO.

DSS (Department of Social Security) (1990) *The way ahead: Benefits for disabled people*, London: DSS.

DSS (1998a) *A new contract for welfare support for disabled people*, Cm 4103, London: DSS.

DSS (1998b) *Radical package of resources to help disabled people to work*, Press Release, 16 July, London: DSS.

DWP (Department for Work and Pensions) (2001) *Strategy for increasing the employment rates for disabled people*, DWP Research Paper, London: DWP.

DWP (2002) *Pathways to work: Helping disabled people into work*, Government Green Paper, London: DWP.

DWP (2003) *The Draft Disability Bill*, (three volumes), Cm 6058, London: TSO.

DWP (2004a) *Whitehall task force announces action to tackle public sector sickness absence*, Press Release, 8 December.

DWP (2004b) *Incapacity Benefit: Quarterly report*, London: DWP.

DWP/IPPR (Institute of Public Policy Research) (2005) 'Fit for purpose: welfare to work and Incapacity Benefit', Speech at University of London, Senate Hall, 7 February.

DRC (Disability Rights Commission) (2000) *Disability Rights Commission Act*, London: TSO.

DRC (2004a) *Disability briefing* (personal correspondence), December, London: DRC.

DRC (2004b) *The Disability Rights Commission's response to the Draft Disability Bill. Report to the Joint Committee on the Draft Disability Bill*, London: DRC.

European Parliament (2001) *European Parliament fact sheets: Employment policy*, (Fact Sheet 4.8.3.), October.

Finkelstein, V. (1980) *Attitudes and disabled people*, New York: World Rehabilitation Fund.

Giddens, A. (1998) *The third way*, Cambridge: Polity Press.

Giddens, A. (ed) (2001) *The global third way debate*, Cambridge: Polity Press.

Glendinning, C. (1991) 'Losing ground: social policy and disabled people in Great Britain 1980-1990', *Disability, Handicap and Society*, vol 6, no 1, pp 3-21.

Graham, P., Jordan, A. and Lamb, B. (1990) *An equal chance or no chance?*, London: Spastics Society.

Hepple, B., Coussey, M. and Choudhury, T. (2001) *Equality: A new framework*, Abingdon: Hart Publishing.

Hillage, J. and Pollard, E. (1998) *Employability: Developing a framework for policy analysis*, DfEE Report RR85, London: DfEE.

HM Treasury and DWP (2001) *The changing welfare state: Employment opportunity for all*, London: HM Treasury/DWP.

Hogelund, J. (2003) *In search of effective disability policy: Comparing the developments and outcomes and Danish and Dutch disability policies*, Amsterdam: Amsterdam University Press.

House of Commons Work and Pensions Committee (2002) Press Notice No 11, Session 2001-02.

Hurstfield, J., Meager, N., Aston, J., Davies, J., Mann, K., Mitchell, H., Regan, S. and Sinclair, A. (2004) *Monitoring the Disability Discrimination Act 1995. Phase 3*, London: DRC.

Hyde, M. (2000) 'Social policy for disabled people of working-age in the UK in the 1990s', *Disability and Society*, vol 15, pp 327-42.

Income Data Services (2001) *Disability discrimination: Adjusting to the legal complexities*, IDS Brief 646, London: IDS.

Inland Revenue (2002) *Disabled Person's Tax Credit Statistics Quarterly*, October, London: Inland Revenue.

JRF (Joseph Rowntree Foundation) (2002) *Job retention: A review of the research*, York: JRF.

LDTF (Learning Disability Task Force) Report (2004) *Rights, independence, choice and inclusion*, Second Annual Report of the LDTF, London: DH.

Levitas, R. (1998) *Social inclusion and New Labour*, London: Macmillan.

Lonsdale, S. (1986) *Work and inequality*, Harlow: Longman.

Lonsdale, S. (1990) *Women and disability: The experience of physical disability among women*, London: Macmillan.

Ludlam, S. and Smith, M. (eds) (2001) *New Labour in government*, Basingstoke: Macmillan.

Lund, B. (1999) 'Ask not what your community can do for you: New Labour and welfare reform', *Critical Social Policy*, vol, 19, no 4, pp 36-43

Mabbett, D. and Bolderson, H. (2001) 'A significant step forward? EU social policy and the development of a rights-based strategy for disabled people', Paper presented to the Annual Social Policy Association Conference, Queen's University Belfast, 24-26 July.

Marin, B., Prinz, C. and Queisser, M. (2004) *Transforming disability welfare policies*, Aldershot: Ashgate.

Martin, J., White, A. and Meltzer, H. (1989) *OPCS surveys of disability in Great Britain: Report No 4: Disabled adults – Services, transport and employment*, London: HMSO.

Meager, N., Doyle, B., Evans, C., Kersley, B., Williams, M., O'Regan, S. and Tackey, N. (1999) *Monitoring the Disability Discrimination Act (DDA) 1995*, DfEE Research Brief 19, London: DfEE.

Millar, J. (2003) *Understanding social security*, Bristol: The Policy Press.

O'Bryan, A., Simons, K., Beyer, S. and Grove, B. (2000) *A framework for supported employment*, York: JRF and York Publishing.

ONS (Office for National Statistics) (2002a) *Social trends*, London: The Stationery Office.

ONS (2002b) *Labour Force Survey: Annual local area statistics digest*, London: ONS.

ONS (2004) *Labour Force Survey*, London: ONS.

Oliver, M. (1990) *The politics of disablement*, Basingstoke: Macmillan.

PMSU (Prime Minister's Strategy Unit) (2004) *Improving the life chances of disabled people. Interim Report*, London: PMSU.

PMSU (2005) *Improving the life chances of disabled people. Final report*, London: PMSU with DWP, DH, DfES and ODPM.

Powell, M. (ed) (1999) *New Labour, new welfare state*, Bristol: The Policy Press.

Powell, M. and Hewitt, M. (2002) *Welfare state and welfare change*, Buckingham: Open University Press.

Prescott-Clarke, P. (1990) *Employment and handicap*, London: Social and Community Planning Research.

Prinz, C. and Marin, B. (2003) *Transforming disability into ability: Policies to promote work and income security for disabled people*, Paris: OECD.

RNIB (Royal National Institute of the Blind) (2002) *Work matters: Enabling blind and partially sighted people to gain and retain employment*, London: RNIB.

Roberts, S., Heaver, C., Hill, K., Rennison, J., Stafford, B., Howat, N., Kelly, G., Krishnan, S., Tapp, P. and Thomas, A. (2004) *Disability in the workplace: Employers and service providers' responses to the Disability Discrimination Act in 2003 and preparation for 2004 changes*, DWP Report 202, London: DWP.

Roulstone, A. (2000) 'Disability, dependency and the New Deal for Disabled People', *Disability and Society*, vol 15, no 3, pp 427-43.

Roulstone, A. (2003) 'The legal road to rights, disabling premises, obiter dicta and the Disability Discrimination Act 1995', *Disability & Society*, vol 18, no 2, pp 117-31.

Roulstone, A. (2004) *The Draft Disability Bill: Employment monitoring and disabled people*, Unpublished Report for the DRC, London: DRC.

Royal College of Psychiatrists (2003) *Employment for all: Assisting people with health problems and disabilities into work. House of Commons Work and Pensions Committee of Inquiry Response*, (www.rcpsych.ac.uk).

Savage, S. and Atkinson, R. (eds) (2001) *Public policy under Blair*, London: Palgrave.

SEU (Social Exclusion Unit) (2004) *Mental health and social exclusion*, London: SEU.

Stanley, K. and Regan, S. (2003) *The missing million: Supporting disabled people into work*, London: IPPR.

Stanley, K. and Maxwell, D. (2004) *Fit for purpose? The reform of Incapacity Benefit*, London: IPPR.

Thornton, P. and Lunt, N. (1995) *Employment for disabled people: Social obligation or individual responsibility*, Social Policy Research Unit Report 2, York: SPRU.

TUC (Trades Union Congress) (2004) *Defending Incapacity Benefit*, London: TUC

White, S. (ed) (2001) *New Labour: The progressive future*, London: Palgrave.

Wilson, A., Riddell, S. and Baron, S. (2003) *The learning society and people with learning difficulties*, Bristol: The Policy Press.

Work and Pensions Committee (2002) *'One' pilots: Lessons for Jobcentre Plus*, First Report, London: House of Commons.

Zarb, G. (1995) (ed) *Removing disabling barriers*, London: Policy Studies Institute.

TWO

The missing million: the challenges of employing more disabled people

Kate Stanley

More disabled[1] people are out of work and claiming disability-related benefits than when the Labour government came to power in 1997 (ONS, 1997, 2003a). At the same time, more disabled people are in work. This is possible because the overall number of people with long-term ill-health or a disability has grown to seven million and the employment rate of disabled people is hovering at just under 50% (ONS, 2002). The scale of the challenge of supporting more disabled people into work must not be under-estimated.

Since 1997, the number of people of working-age claiming benefits relating to unemployment has been on a consistent and sharp downward trend, reflecting the steady improvement in employment across the UK economy. However, the number of people of working-age claiming benefits due to sickness or disability has consistently risen and stood at over three million in May 2003 (ONS, 2003a). Analysis of the Labour Force Survey has suggested that well over one million disabled people want to work but are not working (DWP, 2002): this is the 'missing million'. This figure is contestable but, as disability employment service providers will assert, there is little doubt that many more disabled people would like to work. Given the important impact that being in employment has on reducing poverty and social exclusion, this situation is good for neither disabled people, nor for the wider economy and society.

In this chapter, I assess the scale of the challenge in supporting more disabled people into work. I then seek to establish an understanding of what disability is and use this to consider recent trends in disability and work and how these might have exacerbated the challenge of supporting more disabled people into work. Following this, I examine how the government is attempting to tackle the issues and the prospects for greater numbers of disabled people entering work in the future.

Finally, I suggest what a longer term; more ambitious strategy might look like, describing seven key elements of such a strategy.

The Achilles heel of Labour's welfare to work agenda

In 1998, the Labour government made its first significant attempt to improve the benefits system and move more people into work. It declared that the best way out of poverty for disabled people was through work and that the reformed welfare system would provide the support that would enable disabled people to help themselves. The Department for Social Security Green Paper (DSS, 1998) that set out these plans coined the phrase that has become a mantra for welfare under New Labour:

> Work for those who can, security for those who cannot.

However, six years on, the number of people claiming incapacity benefits stood at more than the combined total of lone parents and unemployed people claiming unemployment benefits (see Table 2.1). Disabled claimants made up over 60% of the total benefits caseload in May 2003.

The overall number of incapacity benefits claimants continues to rise while numbers are falling in every other category. Between May 2000 and May 2003, the number of disabled benefit claimants increased by 150,000 to over three million people (ONS, 2003b). This compares to a drop of 140,000 in unemployed people claiming benefit over the same period. This means that 8.7% of the working-age population were claiming disability-related benefits out of 14.1% of the total working-age population who were claiming benefits. These stark facts beg the question: is the unemployment of disabled people the Achilles heel of New Labour's welfare to work agenda?

Table 2.1: Number of benefit claimants by statistical group and per cent of the working-age population represented by each group (May, 2003)

	Number of claimants (thousands)	% of working-age population
All	4,951	14.1
Sick or disabled	3,052	8.7
Unemployed	883	2.5
Lone Parents	826	2.4
Others	190	0.5

Source: ONS (2003)

It would certainly seem so. A closer look at the trends in disability and the employment of disabled people may give some further indications why disabled people have missed out on the success of the government's welfare to work agenda and parallel improvements in the economy. However, before this can be done, it is essential to establish a clear understanding of disability.

Understanding disability

The 1995 Disability Discrimination Act (DDA) defines a disabled person as someone with "a physical or mental impairment which has a substantial and long-term adverse effect on his ability to carry out normal day-to-day activities". Under this definition, there were seven million people of working-age with a current long-term health problem or disability in the UK in spring 2002 (ONS, 2002). While this is a useful functional definition, we need a more nuanced understanding of disability that helps us to assess the nature of the challenge.

The medical model of disability still holds considerable influence. This model sees disability as being about impairment and focuses on addressing the impairment or the consequences of the impairment, for example, by providing an income to compensate for a lack of ability to work. However, the social model of disability has been influential in the development of disability rights over recent decades. This model sees disability as the product of society's failure to deal with the needs of a disabled person, in part as a result of discrimination; that is, society actively disables a person and efforts should be focused on tackling discrimination.

This chapter is underpinned by an understanding of disability that is influenced by the interactionist model (Howard, 2003). This model emphasises that disability is a dynamic process, not a status, as impairment may be progressive, intermittent or continuous. Similarly, the wider environment in which a person lives is ever changing. This means that if you change the dynamics of the relationship between the individual and the wider social context, you can change the outcomes for disabled people. In this way, disability can be seen as a description of what happens when a person with impairment interacts with their environment over time. This implies that we need to think about the individual, the wider environment and the relationship between them when addressing issues around disability and work.

Possible explanations for the high level of disabled people out of work

If we can better understand the reasons for the consistently high and growing levels of disabled people out of work in Britain, we could better assess the government's responses and the way forward for public policy. I offer four possible explanations here, although there are likely to be many more.

The first is the persistence of a set of myths about disability that have inhibited the ambitions of public policy and the willingness of employers in particular, to bring about significant change. For example, there is a myth that disabled people cannot and do not work. In fact, nearly three-and-a-half million disabled people were in work in 2001 (ONS, 2001). There is a myth that disability is a specialist issue, when in fact it directly affected nearly one in five adults in the UK in 2001 (ONS, 2001). Perhaps most prevalent of all is the myth that disabled people are those with visible physical impairments, when, for example, people with mental health impairments account for a substantial and growing proportion of all disabled people and over one third of Incapacity Benefit claimants (ONS, 2003a). Only when these misleading myths can be replaced with an awareness of the complexity of reality are we likely to make real headway in creating more opportunities for disabled people to work.

The second reason is an increase in the number of people who consider themselves disabled. This is one of the most important and poorly understood trends in the population. Attempts to explain this include recognition of more illnesses and disabilities and forms of disability. In particular, there has been a very substantial rise in the number of people identified as having mental health impairments. We also have an ageing population in Britain and there is an increased prevalence of disability among older people (ONS, 2003b).

Another explanation may be the increased participation of women in the labour market; this has led to more women seeking to replace their lost earnings when they become disabled. While there were 458,000 more men than women claiming incapacity benefits in May 2003 (ONS, 2003a), this can be largely accounted for by the fact that the age range used for the female working-age population is 16-59 years compared to 16-64 years for the male population.

The third reason for the high levels of disabled people who are out of work is that the 'off-flow' from incapacity benefits is very low. That is, the number of people who move off benefits and into work once they have begun claiming incapacity benefits is very low. Between

February 2002 and May 2002, 118,000 people moved off incapacity benefits. This is down on the same period the previous year when 121,000 moved off incapacity benefits (ONS, 2003a). Of those claiming incapacity benefits in May 2003, 77% were claiming benefits two years earlier; this compares to just 8% of those claiming unemployment benefits (ONS, 2003a).

This low off-flow is compounded by a high attrition rate out of work when a person acquires a disability. The majority of people (70%) are in work when they become disabled but evidence seems to show that one in six people lose their job after the onset of disability. This keeps people flowing onto incapacity benefits. Although 'in flows' onto incapacity benefits have begun to go down, the level of in flow remain an issue.

The fourth and final key reason is that the level of unemployment and Incapacity Benefit claims has a complex but close relationship with wider economic trends. This means that we might expect the recent period of economic stability and relatively high levels of employment (of around 75%) to be reflected in higher rates of employment among disabled people and it has been to some extent. For example, the employment rate of disabled people did grow from 45% to 48% between autumn 1998 and autumn 2001 (ONS 2001). However, disabled people have not shared equally in the benefits derived from the strength of the economy.

This is partly due to other economic trends that are also reflected in disability and employment trends. For example, there is a high level of regional variation in the proportion of people claiming benefits due to ill-health or disability from 13.5% of the working-age population in Wales to 5.3% in the South East in May 2003 (see Table 2.2).

These differences reflect regional labour market inequalities (Adams et al, 2003). Disabled people were more likely to be in employment and not claiming incapacity benefits in those regions that experienced a tight labour market in the early 2000s such as the South East and East of England. Whereas, in places such as Wales, disabled people were more likely to be claiming benefits than to be employed.

These four possible explanations begin to explain how disabled people have come to be missing out on Labour's welfare to work agenda and wider economic stability. But there is more to the story. I will now consider whether or not the government's strategy to support more disabled people into work has itself been up to the challenge.

Table 2.2: Percentage of working-age population claiming incapacity benefits (May, 2003)

Region/country	% of working-age population claiming incapacity benefits
South East	5.3
East	6.0
South West	7.1
London	7.2
East Midlands	8.1
West Midlands	8.9
Yorks & Humberside	9.1
Scotland	11.3
North West	11.9
North East	12.8
Wales	13.5

Source: ONS (2003)

Prospects for improvement: public policy strategies

The third attempt in seven years to tackle disability and work issues was published in 2002 with the Green Paper, *Pathways to work* (DWP, 2002). It followed the 1998 Green Paper and reforms made by the Conservative government in 1995. The 1998 Green Paper led to a number of changes, including the revision of the 'All Work Test' so that the assessment provided information about what people could do, as well as what they could not. Incapacity benefits claimants also had to take part in an interview to help them plan a route back to independence. The Green Paper sought to re-frame incapacity benefits by strengthening the link between work and entitlement, so that Incapacity Benefit would be paid only to those who had recently been in work and made National Insurance contributions.

The 2002 Green Paper contained some positive policy reforms to be piloted in six areas, including:

- the creation of a new framework of compulsory work focused interviews within Jobcentre Plus;
- improved referral routes between these interviews and pre-existing employment support;
- the establishment of work focused rehabilitation pilots in conjunction with the NHS.

The intention was to create a 'Choices Package', giving people on incapacity benefits access to a wider range of opportunities. New incentives were also proposed to encourage incapacity benefits recipients into work.

The 2002 Green Paper recognised that the Department for Work and Pensions (DWP) could not tackle this issue alone and that for progress to be made the input of a range of stakeholders would be required. However, there was little in the Green Paper about employers and their responsibilities and how they might be supported in fulfilling them. Similarly, voluntary and private sector organisations and health and rehabilitation services are vital pieces of the jigsaw but received scant attention. The paper also essentially ignored existing incapacity benefits claimants and focused on new claimants.

It was widely felt that the Green Paper did not go far enough to make a marked difference in the employment opportunities of disabled people. However, it is questionable how far a DWP Green Paper could go when the DWP does not have lead responsibility for many of the critical factors in achieving a healthy workforce and social inclusion for all (of course, it does foot the costs of economic inactivity through social security payments). This is an issue where the responsibility for a successful strategy lies within several departments and a crosscutting approach is essential.

Partly as a result of these Green Papers, we have seen the introduction of a variety of tax credits and welfare to work schemes, such as the New Deal for Disabled People, WORKSTEP and supported employment programmes. Further, in 2002 the government separated out the target to achieve increased employment rates for disabled people from similar targets for other groups. This indicated an increased level of priority being awarded to action on disabled people and work. The target was to reduce significantly the difference between the employment rate of disabled people and the overall rate by 2006. It is unlikely that the government will meet this target, notwithstanding the fact that a 'significant reduction' is not defined. This is primarily because the scale of the effort to tackle the unemployment of disabled people is too small to make a significant impact.

I would suggest that the reason for this might be the low level of political priority being awarded to this issue. Take for example, spending on the flagship welfare to work policy, the New Deals. Expenditure on the New Deal for Disabled People for 2002/03 was provisionally estimated at £30 million compared with £80 million on the New Deal for Lone Parents and £270 million on the New Deal for Young People (HM Treasury, 2003). Over two billion pounds was allocated to the New Deal for Young People in 1997 (although only £1,100 million had been spent by 2002) without any pilots being carried out in the UK. Yet all new initiatives with disabled people have been piloted before any substantial financial allocations have been made. There is much to commend the piloting of new programmes before committing substantial funding but this observation does suggest a lack of confidence in relation to disability and work issues that does not appear to arise in relation to other out of work groups. Many commentators, in fact, do argue that we still do not really know what works in supporting disabled people to work and there is truth in this. However, the example of the successful 'Access to Work' in-work support scheme suggests this is not the only reason for a lack of conviction. Evaluations have repeatedly shown that Access to Work is effective (Corden and Thornton, 2002). Of course, it is not suitable to address the needs of all disabled people but is valued by those it does support and could be improved and amended to meet the needs of many more. However, government does not actively promote Access to Work.

There may be a number of other reasons for the lack of a radical agenda for disabled people. Back in the 1980s and early 1990s, when unemployment was higher, it suited government's purposes to move people off unemployment benefits and on to incapacity benefits where they would not contribute to the unemployment figures. Then in the late 1990s, the New Labour government choose to focus its resources on tackling youth employment. This was an easier target and there was more demand for action in this area from the electorate.

It may also be down to an awareness of the sensitivities of trying to move more disabled people into work when there are many for whom work is not a reasonable option. This is tied to issues around eligibility for incapacity benefits that continue to inhibit progress in this area. There is a paradox facing those incapacity benefits claimants who do wish to seek work in that they must demonstrate their incapacity to work in order to be eligible for incapacity benefits while demonstrating to employers their capacity to work in order to gain employment (Howard, 2003). This tension translates into significant risks for disabled people who wish to seek a job or to undertake voluntary or other forms of intermediate work, as their benefits may be put in jeopardy as a result. The effect of this policy confusion is to create fear and a lack of trust in claimants and uncertainty for would-be employers.

As a consequence of disability and work not being made a top political priority, the entrenched issues around benefit eligibility and myths about disability, little, if any, progress has been made to date in moving substantial numbers of disabled people into work. A radical new approach is needed if more progress is to be made in the future.

In the next section, I sketch out what might be some of the components of such a strategy.

A strategy for success

The preceding sections have begun to identify where some of the policy gaps and challenges in supporting more disabled people into employment lie, but there are many more that I have not been able to cover in this short space. This section sketches out the key areas in which steps need to be taken. There is a need for a longer-term, more ambitious strategy to bring about significant change and offer more chance of work for those disabled people who wish to work. This strategy must be underpinned by a greater level of political priority being awarded to the issues of disability and work. This means having a vision for disabled people that includes recognition of the fact that creating greater opportunities for disabled people to work is a social justice issue and success here will impact on success in other areas. For example, the regional differences in rates of Incapacity Benefit claims will have to be addressed if regional inequalities are to be reduced (another government target). Targets for tackling age discrimination and pensions plans are also partly dependent on tackling the number of disabled people who are out of work. Also, and crucially, one in four children in poverty live in a household with at least one disabled adult. Thus, beating child poverty will depend on increasing employment rates for disabled people. Add to this the potential benefits to the economy, reduced costs to the Exchequer and benefits to individual disabled people and the case becomes compelling. I will outline now seven key elements of a strategy that the government and others must pursue.

1. Developing a new account of disability and work

We need to develop a new understanding of the nature of disability. We need to acknowledge and promote the understanding that disability is experienced in diverse ways by different people and at different times. An individual's impairment will interact with the wider environment to produce different impacts. For example, there is a complex relationship between impairment, poverty, poor qualifications and worklessness, which together create complex barriers to work which are difficult to untangle. This means that public policy must gear up to the task of tackling different types and levels of disadvantage as well as tackling multiple disadvantage. The key and most pressing challenge lies in replacing widespread myths about disability with the complexities of reality.

2. Focusing on the role of the employer

Employers must be central to any discussion of disability and work. All employers need to fulfil their obligations under law but it is also in their interests to go further. There is a strong ethical business case to be made here which is a more comprehensive articulation of the traditional business case (Joseph, 2003). The ethical business case recognises that business and social benefits are intrinsically linked. In other words, business concerns are affected by how the company performs in relation to a social agenda. This will include good health management and the prevention of work-related disability as well as efforts to recruit and retain disabled people.

3. Strengthening rehabilitation services

Rehabilitation services when people become disabled are currently highly fragmented, uncoordinated and poorly resourced. The rehabilitation profession is very weak and the health service has largely forgotten that employment is a key element of effective healthcare.

A revived rehabilitation service should be made up of multidisciplinary professionals providing a service that ensures the early identification of people who are disabled or at risk of becoming disabled, and deliver a range of interventions aiming to achieve their return to work through active case management. Government support for the development of a stronger rehabilitation infrastructure, including the establishment of a professional body for rehabilitation professionals, would be an important first step. Further, a re-focused health service should work in partnership with disabled people and rehabilitation services to deliver return to work as a positive treatment outcome for disabled people.

4. Creating more flexible benefits and reducing risks

Disability does not equate to being incapable of work but the policy confusion surrounding this issue sometimes creates that impression. Likewise, Incapacity Benefit does not indicate that a person is incapable of work, but only that the state has deemed it cannot reasonably expect them to work. The benefit system will be less of an obstacle to disabled people entering work if, as discussed in the 2002 DWP Green Paper, there is a change in the language connecting disability with incapacity to work. This should start with a new name for Incapacity Benefit but more is needed. The government must also take more seriously disabled people's fear of losing benefit and diminish the risks associated with moving from benefits into work. For example, review of a disabled person's Incapacity Benefit should be frozen for a fixed period while they are fulfilling a work-focused action plan.

Jobcentre Plus and job brokers must also be enabled to deliver on the expectations created by work-focused interviews. This means providing full information and a range of options and support. Placing additional conditions on benefit receipt is likely to produce positive outcomes only when individuals have the capacity and the right support in place to enable them to fulfil the conditions.

5. Delivering successful welfare-to-work programmes

This can only be achieved through a twin strategy of expanding and enhancing schemes specifically for disabled people and making mainstream programmes accessible to them. There are substantial challenges in developing the range of programmes that are able to meet the needs of disabled people but the New Deal for Disabled People has shown some promise.

6. An ambitious role for Jobcentre Plus

How Jobcentre Plus develops and prioritises its functions in the coming years will be critical to the success of welfare to work for disabled people. A range of welfare-to-work initiatives is needed to reflect the diversity of disabled people's experiences. They must all offer real opportunities for all – from the most job-ready to the least job-ready. To achieve this, Jobcentre Plus will need to be adequately resourced and able to attract high-calibre staff so that it can credibly provide services to both disabled people and employers.

7. Transforming the expectations of all

It seems clear that the expectations of individuals, employers, governmental and non-governmental bodies all need to shift as part of a long-term strategy for engaging more disabled people with the labour market. The best way to stop the flow of people on to incapacity benefits is to shift attitudes within the workplace and to focus on prevention and effective rehabilitation. The best way to reduce the number of people out of work and claiming benefits is to change their expectations of working by delivering welfare-to-work initiatives that ensure that people get the range of support they need to move into work.

Conclusion

The continued growth in the number of disabled people who are out of work and claiming benefits is the Achilles heel of Labour's welfare-to-work agenda. However, there is little chance of this situation changing significantly given the lack of ambition in current policies to address the issues. What is needed is a greater level of political commitment to supporting more disabled people to get into and to stay in work. This commitment must translate into a bolder strategy that tackles the issues at the heart of disabled people's exclusion from work and makes a case for the same level of commitment from employers and disabled people themselves.

Note
[1] Throughout this paper we use the term 'disabled' to refer to people who are either sick or disabled. However, it is important to note that a person may be disabled as a result of ill-health, or they may be disabled as a result of impairment but healthy.

References
Adams, J., Robinson, P. and Vigor, A. (2003) *A new regional policy for the UK*, London: IPPR.

Corden, A. and Thornton, P. (2002) *Employment programmes for disabled people: Lessons from research evaluation*, London: DWP.

DSS (Department for Social Security) (1998) *Ambitions for our country: A new contract for welfare*, London: DSS.

DWP (Department for Work and Pensions) (2002) *Pathways to work: Helping people into employment*, London: DWP.

HM Treasury (2003) *Budget 2003*, London: HM Treasury.

Howard, M. (2003) *An 'interactionist' perspective on barriers and bridges to work for disabled people*, (www.ippr.org/research/healthandsocialpolicy/disabilityandwork).

Joseph, E. (2003) *A new agenda for business*, London: IPPR.

ONS (Office of National Statistics) (1997, 2000, 2001, 2003a) *Client group analysis: Quarterly bulletin on the population of working-age on key benefits*, May 1997, 2000, 2001, 2003a, London: ONS.

ONS (2002, 2003b) *Labour market trends*, May 2002, 2003, London: ONS.

Stanley, K. and Regan, S. (2003) *The missing million: Supporting disabled people into work*, London: IPPR.

Part Two:
The current policy environment

THREE

New Deal for Disabled People: what's new about New Deal?

Bruce Stafford

Introduction

The aim the Labour government's employment policy is "to ensure a higher proportion of people in work than ever before by 2010" (HM Treasury, 2003, para 4.1). For disabled people, this has been translated into a Public Service Agreement target for the Department for Work and Pensions (DWP) of increasing over the three years from 2003 to 2006 the employment rate of people with disabilities and significantly reducing the difference between this rate and the overall employment rate. The New Deal for Disabled People (NDDP) is Labour's main employment programme for people in receipt of a disability or incapacity-related benefit, and, as a member of a 'family' of New Deal programmes, is an important component of the government's welfare to work strategy (Stafford, 2003b). It was piloted and then in 2001 extended nationally.

This chapter discusses both the pilot and nationally extended versions of NDDP. It has three main sections. The first part briefly outlines the main features of NDDP, and the second focuses on some of the key findings that have emerged from published evaluations of NDDP. The final section concludes by arguing that a rigorous evaluation of NDDP should be welcomed by those with an interest in helping Incapacity Benefit recipients into employment.

New Deal for Disabled People: an overview

New Deal for Disabled People aims to help people claiming incapacity-related benefits move into sustained employment. For both pilot and national extension versions, participation in the programme is voluntary and is open to anyone claiming a qualifying benefit (see Table 3.1). The programme is delivered by not-for-profit, private and public sector

Table 3.1: New Deal for Disabled People (NDDP) qualifying benefits (2003)

New Deal for Disabled People Pilots	New Deal for Disabled People national extension
Incapacitated for work for 28 weeks or more and claiming: Incapacity Benefit Severe Disablement Allowance National Insurance credits on grounds of incapacity Programme could also be provided to people in employment and at risk of losing their jobs due to ill-health.	Incapacity Benefit Severe Disablement Allowance Income Support with a Disability Premium Income Support pending the result of an appeal against disallowance from Incapacity Benefit Housing Benefit or Council Tax Benefit with a Disability Premium* Disability Living Allowance* War Pension with an Unemployability Supplement Industrial Injuries Disablement Benefit with an Unemployability Supplement National Insurance credits on grounds of incapacity Equivalent benefits to Incapacity Benefit being imported into Great Britain under European Community Regulations on the co-ordination of social security and the terms of the European Economic Area Agreement.

* Provided it is paid in respect of the recipient herself/himself, and recipient is *not* in paid work of 16 hours a week or more, or getting Jobseeker's Allowance.

Source: Stafford (2003a)

organisations and providers have been encouraged to be innovative so "transforming the way in which the benefits system supports disabled people who want to work" (DWP, 1998, p 3)

Two variants of NDDP were piloted and operated between September 1998 and June 2001:

• Personal Adviser Service (PAS);
• Innovative Schemes.

In the 12 PAS pilot areas, a personal adviser assisted people claiming incapacity benefits to find and retain employment. The then Employment Service ran six of the pilots, and the remainder were operated by partnerships of private and voluntary sector organisations[1]. The Innovative Schemes were established to pilot approaches to tackling disabled people's barriers to work and assisting them into work, which if successful could be replicated. Contracts to run the schemes were awarded to a variety of private and voluntary sector organisations.

In July 2001, NDDP was, using the government's terminology, 'extended' nationally rather than 'rolled out'. Although the pilots informed the design of the national extension, policy makers wanted to 'test' on a national scale further measures to help people claiming incapacity-related benefits move into work. The national extension to NDDP is delivered by around 60 job brokers, who are organisations from the not-for-profit, private and public sectors[2]. These organisations competitively tendered to deliver NDDP initially until March 2004; there have been additional rounds of procurement and the programme has been extended for a further two years to March 2006.

Some job brokers have specific expertise in a 'disability' and others are generalists. Each job broker covers a specific geographical area, some serve single local authorities while others larger areas. People wanting to participate in the programme have to register with a job broker.

There is also a NDDP Gateway at Jobcentre Plus offices. When personal advisers conduct work-focused interviews for new and repeat claimants, they should inform claimants of both the programme and local job brokering services. People registering for NDDP continue to have access to 'mainstream' support programmes, but have to access them through Jobcentre Plus.

Government funding for the national extension is outcome related. Job brokers received a registration fee of £100 per participant and outcome payments for both job entries and sustained employment[3]. The actual amount received by job brokers varies and depends upon what they negotiated as part of the procurement process. Job brokers (and others) have been critical of the funding regime, although there was some support among job brokers for the principle of outcome funding (Corden et al, 2003). The consequences for job brokers vary. In some organisations, the job-broking service was financially integrated and effectively cushioned by other income streams, some job brokers were prepared to tolerate some level of financial loss and some experienced cash flow problems. Some felt that the levels of funding were too low and that job brokers carried too much of the financial risk. Lower than anticipated take-up and greater difficulties than expected in moving some clients into work have exacerbated the funding situation for some job brokers.

Unlike some other New Deals, NDDP does not include an employment option with a subsidy payable to employers. Although some job brokers do offer such payments to employers, it is claimed that the lack of a national subsidy scheme makes NDDP clients less attractive relative to other New Deal clients.

New Deal for Disabled People also operates within a wider policy climate of work incentives, tax changes and employment service initiatives and schemes aimed at specific client groups or geographical areas. It is a supply-side measure, and while it can be seen as part of a wider package of measures, it arguably could be more effectively embedded with other policies that aim to advance the social and employment rights of disabled people.

Key findings from evaluations of NDDP

This section highlights some of the key findings from published evaluations of NDDP. Currently, there is a body of evidence on the implementation and delivery of the pilots and national extension, and a largely descriptive account of the programme's outcomes or impacts. Moreover, at the time writing the findings for the national extension cover only the first 18 months of the programme. The evaluation of the national version of NDDP is on-going and further findings will enter the public domain.

Low take-up of the programme by individuals

Arguably, a feature of the pilots and the national extension is that the take-up of NDDP is relatively low (Loumidis et al, 2001a; Corden et al, 2003; Woodward et al, 2003). The take-up rate for the PAS pilot was 7% (as at November 2000), a total of 18,166 clients; and in addition, nearly 5,200 clients registered for the Innovative Schemes. The estimated take-up rate for the national extension is lower at 1.9% (Stafford et al, 2004). Qualitative research reveals that while the experiences of individual job brokers vary, the take-up of the national programme is less than they had expected (Corden et al, 2003).

The difference in the take-up rates of the PAS and national extension is intriguing. The take-up of the national extension can be expected to increase over time. However, it will be interesting to see whether it ever reaches 7%. Given the similarities between the two versions of NDDP, if the take-up rate for the national extension does not match that for the PAS, then this might be an example of a 'pilot effect', whereby the energy and possibly enthusiasm generated by a pilot cannot be reproduced at national level.

The relatively low take-up of NDDP reflects that (Arthur et al,

1999; Loumidis et al, 2001a; Hills et al, 2001; Corden et al, 2003; Woodward et al, 2003):

- the most common reason given by potential clients for not participating was that they were too unwell;
- providers have been critical of the scale of national marketing and of the materials used (for instance, providers in the PAS pilot and national extension have been disappointed by the content of publicity letters and leaflets sent to the client group by the Department for Work and Pensions);
- the number of referrals from other organisations was lower than anticipated and some of those referred could be judged 'unsuitable' for the programme;
- some people did not identify themselves as 'disabled' and the name of the programme implied that it was not relevant to their needs.

Not surprisingly, levels of awareness of the programme are modest. In the PAS pilot, only a half of surveyed non-participants had heard of NDDP (Loumidis et al, 2001a). Similarly, one year after the national extension was implemented over a half of the eligible population had heard of NDDP and/or a job broker operating in their area (Woodward et al, 2003). Pilot and national evaluations have tentatively identified potential users of NDDP; and Woodward et al (2003) suggest that around 15% of those flowing onto incapacity-related benefits and 7% of existing recipients could use the service.

However, and as pointed out later in this chapter, NDDP was never resourced to address the needs of the entire eligible population and the achieved take-up rates are possibly what would be expected for a voluntary programme aimed at this client group. Moreover, it is debatable whether awareness levels of around a half of the in-scope population are seen as a 'success' or a 'failure' in marketing terms.

Selection of clients by providers

The target population for NDDP is very heterogeneous. While some pilot providers and job brokers worked with people who were a 'long distance' from the labour market, there was a tendency for participants to be closer to the labour market than non-participants (Hills et al, 2001; Loumidis et al, 2001a). Indeed, over time, as the PAS pilot became more focused on employment as the primary programme outcome, only those people closer to the labour market were case loaded by advisers. Although some job brokers did not select at registration and could be opposed to the idea, the funding regime for the national extension did lead some job brokers to prioritise those clients who were more 'job ready'. These clients required less support and were more likely to generate an outcome related payment (Corden et al, 2003). Where work was seen as a longer-term prospect or high levels of support were needed, individuals could be referred to other services or other options like voluntary work, and discouraged from registering for NDDP. Moreover, following changes in job brokers' funding arrangements in late 2003, job brokers are required, under their contract, to ensure that at least 25% of their registrations lead to a job outcome.

Arguably, limited resources and targets that focus on job entries mean some form of selection by providers is inevitable. New Deal for Disabled People was never resourced (£197 million for the pilots and £120 million for the national extension) to meet the needs of the entire eligible population. Whether it should have been is another question. A characteristic of New Deals aimed at their entire in-scope populations, such New Deal for Young People, is that they are mandatory. There is little or no support for a compulsory NDDP, and the selection of participants can be seen as a structural consequence of a voluntary programme. Nonetheless, the NDDP funding regime has been criticised because it cannot provide the intensive support needed for those with significant impairments.

Partnership working is important

Pilot providers and job brokers usually worked in partnership with other organisations (Hills et al, 2001; Loumidis et al, 2001a; Corden et al, 2003). Some partners had a more strategic or advisory role, others a more operational role. Working with others can mean delivering better, more comprehensive services to clients; however, building relationships takes time and resources that were often not available. There was no single model of partnership working in the pilots and over time relationships were fluid. Providers learnt that it was important to manage the organisations' different agendas, to maintain shared objectives and to be clear about respective roles.

The qualitative research with job brokers also highlighted one of the lessons of the pilot, namely, the importance of providers' links with benefit and employment services, as they are a potential source of referrals and provide access to programmes, such as Access to Work[4]. However, pilot providers and job brokers did not always have an easy relationship with benefit and employment services. The number of referrals, for instance, could be fewer than desired, and Jobcentre (Plus) staff could perceive the providers' services as being in competition with their own (Hills et al, 2001; Loumidis et al, 2001a; Corden et al, 2003). There were, however, examples of good relationships (often based on existing contacts or other contracts) (Hills et al, 2001; Corden et al, 2003), and the pilots imply that relationships improve over time.

Frontline staff have a critical role

Although frontline staff have a key role in the delivery of NDDP (Hills et al, 2001; Loumidis et al, 2001a), there is no single model of staff organisation. The pilots also demonstrate that staff delivering NDDP required a wide range of knowledge and skills. Staff needed to have an understanding of the needs of the client group, of disability, of benefit and employment services and of local employers, as well as technical, personal and interpersonal skills. Some pilot providers believed that the competencies required were too diverse and subsequently a degree of specialisation of tasks among staff emerged. The job brokers also seemed to have different models for organising staff, and the extent to which they had generic or specialised roles varied (Corden et al, 2003; McDonald et al, 2004). Generic roles enabled staff to develop an in-depth understanding of the client and their needs; clients only had to give information once and staff welcomed the autonomy it gave them, while specialist roles, such as in job-searching or working with employers, allowed staff to develop expertise and strengthen the service delivered, as well as emphasising team working.

Working with employers is important

Employers' awareness of New Deal, as a brand, is relatively high, but was much lower for the nationally extended NDDP (Aston et al, 2003). Nevertheless, links with employers are important to the success of NDDP. For instance, the evaluation of the Innovative Schemes showed that schemes with good contacts with employers were more successful at finding job opportunities for clients (Hills et al, 2001). Providers' success in engaging employers varied, some employers were committed to employing disabled people others less so (Hills et al, 2001; Loumidis et al, 2001a; Aston et al, 2003). However, working with employers could be a slow process, and providers were not always able to maintain the necessary sizable investment in time and effort (Hills et al, 2001; Loumidis et al, 2001a).

Employers' low level of awareness of NDDP was partly because contacts with employers tended to be made by clients (Aston et al, 2003). This was perceived as beneficial by some employers as it left them in control of their recruitment and selection procedures. For clients wary of being labelled 'disabled', it also meant that employers did not know they were registered on NDDP. This did not prevent job brokers working with clients behind the scenes. However, some clients were disappointed that job brokers did not have more extensive contacts with employers (see later in this chapter) (Corden et al, 2003).

Approaches by job brokers were usually client-driven and in response to an advertised vacancy (Aston et al, 2003). During the first year of the national extension there were few examples of longer-term employer–job broker relationships. Nevertheless, job brokers were planning to develop their links with employers later on (Corden et al, 2003), a pattern of development that was characteristic of the PAS pilot (Loumidis et al, 2001a).

Clients were generally positive about NDDP

In general, clients were positive about NDDP. They valued how services were delivered and actual services provided (Hills et al, 2001; Loumidis et al, 2001a; Corden et al, 2003). Overall, clients held positive opinions about staff and were satisfied with their progression towards employment.

However, it is inevitable that with services aimed at such a heterogeneous user group there are some who were disappointed and dissatisfied with the programme. For some clients the programme did not maintain a sense of progression towards work and/or they were critical of the quality of service provision (Hills et al, 2001; Loumidis et al, 2001a). The early findings from the national extension suggest that dissatisfaction with NDDP arises when clients' expectations are not fulfilled (Corden et al, 2003). Clients contact job brokers with a wide range of aims and aspirations; some are more work-focused than others, while the job brokers service itself offers a diverse range of opportunities. The extent to which clients' expectations were met will depend upon how well they match with a particular job broker's provision. Corden et al (2003) suggest reducing the risk of a poor match requires potential clients to be better informed about what specific job brokers can offer and what is expected of them.

Employment outcomes

Although employment outcomes are not the only possible measure of the success of NDDP, they are central to any assessment of the programme. The original target for the national extension of NDDP was 90,000 job entries over three years (Employment Service, 2000).

Different evaluation designs have been utilised to compare what *did happen* following the introduction of the programme with what *would have happened* in its absence. The latter (known as the counterfactual) is required if estimates of the net impact of the programme are to be made. The evaluation design of the PAS pilot included an 'area' comparison, whereby outcomes for the 12 pilot areas were to be compared against a national survey of the incapacity benefit population (Loumidis et al, 2001b). However, the final report of the independent evaluation did not report any estimate of the net impact of the service. This was mainly because of a poor match between those that participated in PAS and respondents in the national survey. Instead, the then Department for Social Security (DSS) attempted an estimate of the impact of the pilot using administrative data (Redway, 2001). However, due to small sample sizes, it was unable to measure any increase in moves off incapacity benefits by the eligible population in the 12 PAS pilots.

In basic terms:

- by June 2000, 39% of participants in the Tranche 1 Innovation Schemes and 26% in Tranche 2 schemes had moved into work (Hills et al, 2001);
- by November 2000, 26% of participants (4,800) in PAS areas had moved into employment (Loumidis et al, 2001a);
- between July 2001 and June 2004, there were 99,260 registrations with job brokers, of whom 46% (45,390) had moved into employment (DWP, 2004).

However, what is unknown is how many of those moving into work would have done so in the absence of the programme. Whether NDDP has a significant impact on employment outcomes is unproven, therefore. Hopefully, the on-going evaluation of the national extension of NDDP will provide an assessment of whether or not the programme makes a difference.

In-work support

The pilots identified the need for in-work support if former clients were to achieve sustained employment. In-work support is a feature of the national extension and job brokers receive a payment if their clients' employment is sustained. The definition of sustained employment was initially employment lasting for at least 26 weeks out of the first 39 weeks since job entry. Following the extension of job brokers contracts in October 2003, the threshold for sustained employment has been reduced to 13 weeks. This might not seem to be a very long period of time, but it does make NDDP compatible with the definition used for other New Deals.

Qualitative research with employers, clients and job brokers reveals little evidence of active in-work support by job brokers. This might reflect the nascent nature of the service, and levels of in-work provision may increase as more clients move into employment, or it might mean that there is a low demand for in-work services. However, this is unlikely.

Cost effectiveness

There is limited evidence on the cost effectiveness of NDDP. Tentative estimates for the pilots show that the cost per job (Dean and Kent, 2001):

- by end March 2001, for the PAS pilots delivered by the then Employment Service was £2,400 and for the other PAS pilots was £4,100;
- between August 1998 and end May 2000, for the Tranche 1 Innovative Schemes it was £3,700, and between July 1999 and end March 2000 it was £3,100 for Tranche 2 schemes.

These figures are averages, and costs per job did decline over time and vary by pilot location. Furthermore, they do not take account of wider benefits and costs, such as benefit savings, and exclude any additional jobs generated by the pilots. Without a net impact assessment, it is difficult to know if NDDP represents good value for money. The on-going evaluation of NDDP includes a cost benefit analysis. Consequently, whether an NDDP type programme represents good value for money may be known in the future.

Discussion and conclusions

This chapter has reviewed key findings from the published evaluations of NDDP. The scope of the findings to some extent mirror the research designs followed. Thus, there is a body of knowledge emerging on the *process* of implementing and delivering NDDP, but there is limited information on the *impact* of the programme. While the evaluations also incorporate a longitudinal dimension, they do not provide information on the longer-term outcomes of NDDP. Therefore, whether the programme has any lasting impact or if participants and non-participants tend to arrive at the 'same' destination is unknown.

The evaluation of the national extension of NDDP is, at the time of writing, on-going. It was originally conceived as a social experiment, with job brokers' clients randomly assigned to action and control groups. Such a design would have provided policy makers, providers and disabled people with creditable and robust estimates of the net impact and value for money (through a cost-benefit analysis) of NDDP. However, using random assignment with the client group was highly contentious, and government ministers decided not to proceed with an experimental design in December 2001. Hopefully, survey and administrative data will eventually provide an assessment of the impact of NDDP. Such an assessment is important to all those with an interest in disability and employment issues because of the emphasis placed on evidence based policy making by government.

Reassuringly, there is a high degree of consistency between findings from the pilots and the national extension. The pilot findings cover two years, effectively the early and later stages of the pilots, while the findings for the national extension encompass only its 18 months of operation. This similarity is to be expected as the target populations are essentially the same (mainly recipients of Incapacity Benefit) and the services providers are broadly the same (principally caseworkers offering a fairly low-level intervention to people who are relatively close to the labour market). Over time, more significant differences between the pilots and the national extension may emerge. Nonetheless, whatever happens rigorous evaluation of NDDP should be welcomed by those with an interest in helping Incapacity Benefit recipients move into employment, in particular assessing the net impact of employment and other outcomes is vital.

Acknowledgement

The author was a member of the research team evaluating the New Deal for Disabled People PAS pilot and leads the consortium evaluating the national extension. However, the views expressed in this paper are those of the author and do not necessarily reflect those of other team members or the project's sponsors, the DSS and the DfES for the PAS pilot and the DWP for the national extension of NDDP. Thanks are also due to Nicola Selby at CRSP who helped to prepare the manuscript.

Notes

[1] The Employment Service and parts of the Benefits Agency were merged in April 2002 to form Jobcentre Plus, which provides both benefit and employment services for all people of working-age. As part of the rollout of Jobcentre Plus, new and repeat claimants must attend a work-focused interview with a personal adviser.

[2] The NDDP website (www.newdeal.gov.uk/english/unempdisabled) contains a list of all job broker organisations.

[3] In October 2003, the amount of the registration fee was raised to £300. In addition, the re-definition of sustained employment as 13 weeks of employment means that job brokers receive the sustainability outcome payment earlier than under the previous funding regime.

[4] The benefit and employment services for the pilots were the then Employment Service and the Benefits Agency; for the national extension it is Jobcentre Plus.

References

Arthur, S., Corden, A., Green, A., Lewis, J., Loumidis, J., Sainsbury, R., Stafford, B., Thornton, P. and Walker, R. (1999) *New Deal for Disabled People: Early implementation*, DSS Research Report 106, Leeds: Corporate Document Services (CDS).

Aston, J., Atkinson, J., Evans, C. and O'Regan, S. (2003) *Employers and the New Deal for Disabled People: Qualitative research: First wave*, DWP Research Report WAE145, Sheffield: DWP.

Corden, A., Harries, T., Hill, K., Kellard, K., Lewis, J., Sainsbury, R. and Thornton, P. (2003) *New Deal for Disabled People national extension: Findings from the first wave of qualitative research with clients, job brokers and Jobcentre Plus staff*, Sheffield: DWP.

Dean, N. and Kent, C. (2001) *New Deal for Disabled People: An assessment of the cost per job*, DSS In-house Report 82, London: DSS.

DWP (Department for Work and Pensions) (1998) *A new contract for welfare: Support for disabled people*, Cm 4103, London: The Stationery Office.

DWP (2004) www.dwp.gov.uk/asd/asd1/nddp/nddp-june2004.asp.

Employment Service (2000) *New Deal for Disabled People extension invitation to tender*, Sheffield: Employment Service.

Hills, D., Child, C., Blackburn, V. and Youll, P. (2001) *Evaluation of the New Deal for Disabled People innovative schemes pilot*, DSS Research Report 143, Leeds: CDS.

HM Treasury (2003) *Budget Report 2003: Building a Britain of economic strength and social justice*, London: TSO.

Loumidis, J., Stafford, B., Youngs, R., Green, A., Arthur, S., Legard, R., Lessof, C., Lewis, J., Walker, R., Corden, A., Thornton, P. and Sainsbury, R. (2001a) *Evaluation of New Deal for Disabled People Personal Adviser Service Pilot*, DSS Research Report 144, Leeds: CDS.

Loumidis, J., Youngs, R., Lessof, C. and Stafford, B. (2001b) *New Deal for Disabled People: National survey of incapacity benefit claimants*, DWP Research Report 160, Leeds: CDS.

McDonald, S., Davis, A. and Stafford, B. (2004) *Report of the survey of job brokers*, DWP Research Report 197, Sheffield: DWP.

Redway, H. (2001) *New Deal for Disabled People: Using administrative data to access the impact on exits from benefit*, DWP In-House Report 81, London: DWP.

Stafford, B. (2003a) 'In search of a welfare to work solution: the New Deal for Disabled People', *Benefits*, vol 11, no 3, pp 181-6.

Stafford, B. (2003b) 'Beyond lone parents: extending welfare to work to disabled people and the young unemployed', in R. Walker and M. Wiseman (eds.) *The welfare we want? The British challenge for American reform*, Bristol: The Policy Press, pp 143-74.

Stafford, B. with Ashworth, K., Davis, A., Hartfree, Y., Hill, K., Kellard, K., Legge, K., McDonald, S., Reyes De-Beaman, S., Aston, J., Atkinson, J., Davis, S., Evans, C., Lewis, J., O'Regan, J., Harries, T., Kazimirski, A., Pires, C., Shaw, A. and Woodward, C. (2004) *New Deal for Disabled People (NDDP): First synthesis report*, DWP Research Report 199, Sheffield: DWP.

Woodward, C., Kazimirski, A., Shaw, A. and Pires, C. (2003) *New Deal for Disabled People Eligible Population Survey: Wave One*, DWP Research Report, Sheffield: DWP.

FOUR

Disabled people, employment and the Work Preparation programme

Sheila Riddell and Pauline Banks

Introduction

According to Floyd and Curtis (2000), it is the aim of all European governments to increase the economic activity of disabled people. From the government's point of view, there is a perception that the cost of the growth in the number of disabled people claiming long-term disability benefits is unsustainable, but also that non-employment brings financial and health risks to disabled people and their families. From the perspective of the disability movement, exclusion from employment is one of the principal barriers to social inclusion. However, the disability movement is also committed to preserving benefits levels of those who cannot work as a result of their impairment, and wishes to see the emphasis on tackling barriers in the workplace rather than on pressurising disabled people to work. The recent Green Paper, *Pathways to work: Helping people into employment* (DWP, 2002), sets out the case for increasing levels of employment among disabled people, and in particular the measures proposed by the government to help people move from incapacity benefits to work (see later in this chapter for further discussion[1]). Work Preparation is one of the programmes run by Jobcentre Plus (JCP)[2] to help disabled people develop capability and confidence, overcome obstacles and explore alternative employment through short-term workplace trials (Riddell et al, 2002).

This chapter draws on data from a national evaluation of the Work Preparation programme (Banks et al, 2002). The research was intended to identify strengths and weaknesses of the programme as perceived by key stakeholders and to suggest some ideas for its future development. The evaluation brought to light a number of policy tensions in relation to enhancing the employment prospects of disabled people. In this chapter, we first summarise the development of the Work Preparation programme and recent policy developments relating to the employment of disabled people. Subsequently, we present findings from the evaluation of the Work Preparation programme, highlighting different actors' perspectives. Finally, we discuss the findings of the evaluation in relation to the new focus on moving many more disabled people into employment.

The Work Preparation programme and UK government policy on disability and employment

The Work Preparation programme grew out of the job rehabilitation programme, designed to help disabled service men return to work in the aftermath of the Second World War. The programme offered different forms of training, often delivered in residential settings. It was initially seen as highly successful, with 75% of participants finding work. However, during the 1970s, as unemployment increased, the programme was seen as urgently requiring an update (Floyd, 1997). A review of employment services for disabled people (Department of Employment, 1990) was followed by a radical redesign. Placement, Assessment and Counselling teams (PACTs) were established to provide a localised and flexible service. Team managers had the job of procuring and managing employment services, to be delivered by local training agencies, believed to have a thorough knowledge of the local labour market. This was in line with the Conservative government's belief that many public services could be delivered more effectively by private or voluntary sector agencies (Deakin, 1994).

In the mid-1990s, job rehabilitation was renamed Work Preparation and an early review of the new programme was conducted by Lakey and Simpkins (1994). The report noted a number of difficulties, including a shortage of sympathetic employers willing to offer placements, a narrow range of placement opportunities and client dissatisfaction with the short duration of placements (six to eight weeks on average). Action plans drawn up by Disability Employment Advisers (DEAs) were seen as imprecise, quality assurance arrangements weak and clients were rarely visited by the DEA during their placement. A small-scale evaluation of a Scottish voluntary organisation's Work Preparation scheme echoed many of these points (Wilson et al, 2000).

In 1998, the New Labour government published the Green Paper, *New ambitions for our country: A new contract for welfare* (DSS, 1998), which set out the government's position on social security and employment policy. A key feature of the chapter, which remains a constant theme of government policy, is 'work for those who can, security for those who cannot'. In relation to disabled people, the goals were to introduce effective civil rights, remove barriers to work, and provide active help for those wishing to work. Civil rights were to be guaranteed through the extension of the Disability Discrimination Act (DDA) to small employers and previously exempt occupations. In addition, the government expressed a commitment to the reform of incapacity benefits for future claimants. A major new development was the merger of the Employment Service with the working-age parts of the Benefits Agency to form Jobcentre Plus, whose remit was to offer advice on both benefits and work, with the goal of helping unemployed and economically inactive people return to work. Programmes designed to ease the transition into the labour market, such as Work Preparation, became recognised as a key part of the government's reform strategy. However, different perceptions continued to exist in relation to the overall purpose and remit of rehabilitation programmes, and the research described below draws on an evaluation of Work Preparation to illuminate some of these tensions.

Research

The aim of the research, funded by the Department for Work and Pensions (DWP) and conducted between August 2001 and January 2002, was to inform good practice in the structure and delivery of the Work Preparation programme. Practitioners' and service users' views of the programme were obtained through a survey, interviews and focus groups (Riddell, 2002; Thornton, 2002; Banks et al, 2002). We also refer to case studies of Work Preparation service users carried out by Wilson et al (2000).

Purpose of the Work Preparation programme

An internal Employment Service review of Work Preparation, conducted immediately prior to the research, proposed the following new definition:

> Work Preparation is an individually tailored, work focused programme, which enables disabled people to address barriers associated with their disability and prepare to access a labour market, with the confidence necessary to achieve and sustain their job goal.

Drawing on psychological discourses, in order to qualify for Work Preparation, the client should be assessed as requiring support in relation to occupational decision-making behaviours, job-finding behaviours and job-keeping behaviours. Training was not a core element of Work Preparation, but it might include some job-specific instruction. In order to participate in the Work Preparation programme, prospective service users had to be registered on a DEA caseload, regardless of employment or benefit status, have a defined job goal and have at least some of the needs identified earlier in this chapter.

As the government sought ways of getting people more disabled people into work, demand for a place on the Work Preparation programme increased. The Employment Service therefore suggested that, in future, priority might be given to clients most likely to achieve a positive outcome within 13 weeks of completion and those who have not yet undertaken a previous Work Preparation programme in the last two years.

There was broad agreement among practitioners and service providers that Work Preparation was intended to develop and assess users' work readiness, including the extent to which they possessed the basic skills needed for particular types of employment and the ability to cope with the demands of a work routine. Work Preparation was likely to offer a more relaxed environment than a disabled person might encounter if they moved straight into a paid job, but it still provided an opportunity for the disabled person to test themselves in a real rather than simulated workplace. The role of Work Preparation in job retention was mentioned by DEAs, but more emphasis was placed on developing the employability of people who had never worked or had not worked for some time. Data from the baseline study indicated that Work Preparation was only rarely used as a means of helping people retain a job if they became ill while in employment. In all three regions, less than 1% of outcomes was to retain the service user in employment. In the 2002 Green Paper, the government indicated its intention to use Jobcentre Plus programmes to retain people in employment. There may be a need to develop further this aspect of the Work Preparation programme's remit if this objective is to be fulfilled.

Professionals and contractors placed more emphasis on increasing employability rather than getting a client into work. However, Wilson et al (2000) reported that service users often believed that the purpose of Work Preparation was to get them into a job and were disappointed when this outcome was not achieved. Many of the case-study individuals had extensive training histories, often spread over many years, involving a range of work placement and training programmes. They often felt impatient with protracted periods of employment and wanted a proper job. One woman, aged 30 with mild learning difficulties, had spent 12 years training with a voluntary organisation without obtaining any qualifications or employment. She commented that she felt "trained enough for a catering job", but at the end of her placement was referred back to the DEA. Employers, who were interviewed as part of this study, were somewhat alarmed when they discovered that some service users were hoping for a job at the end of the placement, and demanded that the voluntary organisation explain that the placement was a work experience opportunity and should not be regarded as a route into employment. Some regions have been attempting to deal with these conflicting expectations by developing 'project-led' recruitment programmes. In these programmes, employers are involved from the start in specifying the standards required to meet their recruitment requirements. Disabled people are recruited to project-led schemes on the understanding that, if they meet the specified standards, they may be selected for the job.

Target group for the Work Preparation programme

Different views emerged about the appropriate target group for the programme. On the one hand, it was acknowledged by Disability Service Team (DST) managers and contract managers in the focus groups that in the past the programme may have lacked focus, and it should now be recognised that Work Preparation was not for those wishing to 'get out of the cold' for 13 weeks, but should be targeted much more systematically on those close to the labour market. However, it was also recognised that there was a moral imperative to work with anyone who requested help in finding a job and those with significant impairments should not be turned away. It was clear that DST managers tended to adopt a pragmatic approach, ensuring that a range of service users were given the opportunity to participate, some of whom might be "months and maybe a year plus away from work". Those who required less support were counterbalanced by those who use Work Preparation as "a stepping stone onto the next rung of the ladder".

It was suggested that two programmes might be developed, one focused on people who were nearly work-ready, and another, offering more intensive support, on people who were unlikely to find work in the immediate future. In relation to the benefits status of clients, the same dichotomy arose, with some respondents asserting that claimants of incapacity benefits should have the greatest call on the programme, since they were likely to have been out of work for some time and therefore needed more support in returning to the labour market. Others felt that Jobseeker's Allowance claimants should have first call on the programme, since they were likely to have recent work experience and therefore could be helped back into work relatively easily.

Disability Employment Advisers, Occupational Psychologists (OPs) and external stakeholders also concurred with the view that the Work Preparation programme should accommodate people who were almost ready for employment, and those who needed longer term support. Questions of target group are also closely related to those of programme length. DST managers and contractors pointed out that for people with higher support needs, such as those with head injuries and significant mental health problems and learning disabilities, even a 13-week programme did not allow them to 'dip their toe in the water'. If these individuals were to be helped into employment, much longer-term support would be required. Work-Based Learning for Adults (England) and Training for Work (Scotland) offer skills-based training, but it is not always possible for individuals to obtain places on these programmes.

Although the Work Preparation programme was ostensibly open to all disabled people, it was evident that filtering processes operated. One OP commented that some service providers who claim to deliver a generic service in fact "reject clients they think they cannot deal with". Disability Employment Advisers were aware of the way in which their client profile reflected characteristics of the local labour market and work cultures. For example, one DEA pointed out that over two thirds of Work Preparation participants in the local area were men, reflecting the fact that "it's a very big working class area where traditionally a lot of women haven't worked".

It was evident, therefore, that despite the reported all-embracing focus of the Work Preparation programme, clear patterns of uptake were discernible, reflecting the characteristics of disabled people initiating contact with DEAs, patterns of onward referral and of acceptance by a service provider. As noted earlier in this chapter, the Employment Service suggested that the focus should shift towards those closest to the labour market, and the government is prioritising current and prospective incapacity benefits claimants. Professionals delivering the programme did not entirely concur with the proposal that there should be a tighter focus on people who are almost ready for work, preferring to hold on to the view that it should be open to all seeking help with finding a job.

Outcomes

The baseline study provided important information on the outcomes of participants in Work Preparation programmes in the three regions. On average about 20% of clients starting the programme were in some sort of employment 13 weeks after the end of the programme. The destination of about 52% of clients in the baseline study was unknown. There was some regional variation in outcome, but this may, in part, reflect the extent to which service providers submitted information on service user status at the required time. Table 4.1 provides information about the proportion of service users attaining particular outcomes. There was no association between nature of impairment and type of outcome (although, as noted earlier in this chapter, some service users were unable to access the programme in the first place).

Informants in the research were asked their views about how well the system for gathering information about outcomes should be assessed, and different views emerged. The DSTs and contract managers in the focus groups agreed that the reporting of outcomes was unsatisfactory and therefore the data were unreliable. One DST manager commented that outcome data would be more reliable if gathered by Employment Service rather than service provider staff because, "there's not much incentive for the providers to go chasing people thirteen weeks after. By that time they've had their money …".

On the other hand, DEAs felt that their local systems worked well, although many acknowledged that they had little knowledge of success rates in other regions or in relation to particular impairment groups. Occupational Psychologists, on the other hand, believed that the recording of outcomes could be improved and the 13-week outcome data were not very robust. It was suggested that providers should be given tighter guidelines, and a proportion of the final payment should be dependent on outcomes.

With regard to how outcomes should be assessed, all respondents agreed that the proportion of clients getting a job should be measured. However, other outcomes, including increased confidence, should also be taken into account, because these might be important milestones on the way to achieving employment and required a significant input on the part of the DEA and service provider. One DEA commented:

Table 4.1: Classification of Work Preparation outcomes and proportion of clients achieving each in three regions

Outcome	Criteria	%
Employment	Mainstream and supported employment	18.5
Further/higher education	Further/higher education (full-time or part-time)	2.2
Training	Training, including Work-Based Training for Adults (England), Training for Work (Scotland)	5.1
Further Employment Service (ES) programme	Further ES programme, for example, WORKSTEP	5.1
Retention	Remain with employer in current position or alternative more appropriate position	0.5
Referred back to DEA/looking for work further support, or looking for jobs	Sometimes written on provider's final report – suggested client not yet 'work ready' and might require	11.7
Other, including voluntary work	A number of clients were involved in voluntary work, sometimes hoping paid work could be achieved in the future	1.5
Sick	Deterioration in condition – no longer able to seek employment	4.1
No recorded outcome	Outcome not recorded in either client's file or provider returns, but client still in contact with DEA at some level	23.7
Unknown	No information apart from start and finish dates	27.7

Note: Data are for 2,823 clients in three regions, starting Work Preparation from April 2000 to March 2001. Outcome data recorded 13 weeks after end of placement.

> If you're talking about motivation and confidence building – you could have improved a person no end, but there's still no 'outcome'.

Problems with assessing soft outcomes were also acknowledged. In the words of one DEA:

> It's on a person's say-so, as to whether he thinks some one's improved motivation-wise or confidence-wise, it would be quite subjective. But it would be helpful to try and measure it.

It was recognised by informants that clients' and employers' views of the effectiveness of particular schemes were often missing. A DST manager commented that evaluation data from clients was gathered routinely, but was not collated and acted upon. A DST manager noted that information "just gets put back into the client files and nobody collates it .... So if there's any trends appearing, nobody looks for them".

In other European countries and the US, there are debates about which outcomes should be measured and 'incentivised'. There are concerns that vocational rehabilitation services do not appear to have great success in moving disabled people, particularly those on long-term disability benefits, back into work (Bloch and Prins, 2001). This leads to suggestions that employment should be prioritised as a desired outcome, and funding to providers should be contingent on the proportion of clients moved into work. At the time of the research, the Employment Service had committed itself to results-based funding, and the recent Green Paper (DWP, 2002) also emphasises the goal of moving people from long-term incapacity benefits into employment. However, it is also acknowledged that some service users may take some time to achieve this goal, and progress should be recognised. A number of feasibility studies have explored the possibility of measuring soft outcomes (Jackson, 1999; Denison et al, 2000). These studies have pointed out the importance of gathering information on client progress over time, but also the difficulty of quantifying soft measures.

Delivery of the Work Preparation programme

As noted earlier in this chapter, the creation of the Work Preparation programme in the 1980s was informed by the view that the private sector should have a major role in the delivery of vocational rehabilitation services, since local companies were likely to have a better knowledge of the local labour market and could respond more flexibly to employers' and service users' needs. Interviews indicated that DEAs, supported by OPs, interviewed and assessed clients before preparing an action plan and referring the client to a service provider who would deliver the action plan and report back. Some DEAs visited clients in their work placement, but others left this to the service providers. Disability Employment Advisers also interviewed clients as soon as possible, and certainly within 15 days, after the end of the work placement to decide on future action. However, it was reported that service providers' reports had not always been received at this point, which meant that the meeting was less useful. In addition, the reports were sometimes rather vague, and as a result the DEA did not always have a clear idea of what aspects of the placement had been successful. There were also differences in the extent to which DEAs were pro-active in following-up and maintaining client records after the end of the work placement. Some DEAs felt that they would like to be more involved in working with employers and service users during the work placement.

Disability Service Team managers also had some critical comments to make about service providers' performance and contractual arrangements. There was a tendency, they felt, to use standard placement options for clients instead of 'going out there and getting fresh provision'. Work Preparation funds can be used to provide a wide range of services, such as counselling, confidence building modules or support for self-employment, but in reality the majority of clients (about two thirds) undertook a six-to-eight week work placement.

Managers were also concerned about the time taken to place a client. Only 60% of clients were placed within 20 working days of referral, whereas the regulations stipulated that this should happen in 95% of cases. Problems were generally solved through negotiation rather than using financial sanctions because, "if we took a big stick to them we'd end up with half the providers being dismissed if you like, and we wouldn't be able to offer anything to our clients".

Service providers also had suggestions about how the working relationship with DEAs and DST managers could be improved. They felt there was a need for more contact and joint working between providers and DEAs/DST managers, better communication of information about the client from the DEA to the provider including assessments and OP's reports, less and more simplified paperwork, increased, more regular referrals and better funding. The use of 'call off' contracts was seen as particularly problematic, so that the service provider felt that they were bearing a disproportionately high level of risk. Many of these points echo the findings of Lakey and Simpkins (1994), who pointed out that the funding per case was inadequate to allow service providers to invest in service development.

At a Jobcentre Plus seminar held to discuss the future of Work Preparation (Thornton, 2002), the lack of effective interface between social work, health and employment services was noted, with professionals having little knowledge of each other's sphere of work. Future programmes might receive joint funding from the Department of Health (DH) and the DWP. English Welfare-to-Work Joint Investment Plans (JIPs) were seen as a positive development in terms of improving joint understanding, promoting networking and raising awareness of the work of Jobcentre Plus. However, the effectiveness of the JIPs might be limited because of the lack of an independent budget.

The role of employers in the delivery of Work Preparation was also seen as problematic. As a result of the short nature of work placements, DEAs and service providers felt that employers did not fully understand the purpose of the programme and engage with clients, a finding supported by the earlier Scottish study (Riddell et al, 2002). Participants at the seminar felt that employers might be more sympathetic to people with learning difficulties, because providing a work placement for this group was seen as 'doing good'. However, clients with brain injury, who might have unpredictable behaviour, were seen as much more difficult to include in the workplace. Employers are encouraged to participate in the Work Preparation programme on the grounds that there is a business case, as well as a social obligation, to promote diversity in the workforce. If natural supports are to be drawn upon in the workplace, then some degree of financial incentive may be required.

Clearly, there are some operational issues to be resolved if programmes such as Work Preparation are to work effectively. There is clearly a need for better inter-agency working and closer cooperation between DEAs and OPs. External contracting of service delivery had not been entirely unproblematic. Particular points of tension appeared to lie at the end of the work placement, where communication between the DEA, the service provider and the service user sometimes fell down. If there is a wish for more Work Preparation clients to move into employment after a work placement, then responsibility for pursuing this objective needs to be more clearly assigned. At the moment, the service user ceases to have responsibility for the client at the end of the work placement, but the DEA may not have the necessary information to be sure about appropriate next steps. As noted in the report of a seminar on 'Good Practice in Work Preparation' (Thornton, 2002), sustained employment might be encouraged by specifying an after-care element in providers' contracts and making a payment after the client had been in work for a specified number of weeks. Alternatively, the DEA remit could be expanded, with targets for sustained employment. Other pressing service delivery issues include the need for much closer engagement with employers.

Discussion and conclusion

What specific and wider lessons may be learnt from the development of the Work Preparation programme? Although relatively small-scale, the rationale for the programme was to help disabled people into employment, but, like other programmes such as WORKSTEP, a relatively small number of people progressed into the open labour market. Service users often saw Work Preparation as a stepping-stone into work and were disappointed when a paid job did not follow a work placement. By way of contrast, service providers and Employment Service professionals emphasised that work was only one valid outcome; deciding to work on a voluntary basis, or not to work at all, should be seen as equally valid options. Providers and Employment Service workers pointed out that, if achieving paid employment was heavily 'incentivised' within funding regimes, then there was pressure on service providers to reject clients who needed greater support for a longer period of time. Outcome measures focusing on progress towards employment would encourage providers to work with clients with greater levels of need.

There was general agreement among service providers, DEAs and service users that there was a need for greater continuity and flexibility of support, and that the present structure of Jobcentre Plus programmes might not facilitate this. Blurring the boundaries and funding streams attached to particular programmes, including the New Deal for Disabled People, job broker services, Work-Based Learning for Adults, WORKSTEP, and the Work Preparation programme, might help DEAs and service providers to deliver the longer-term support required by some clients. A greater range of services, in addition to short-term work placements, might also be provided.

Discussion about the appropriate purpose and target group for vocational rehabilitation programmes is taking place in many industrialised countries. In the US, there has always been a commitment to prioritise the vocational rehabilitation needs of disabled people with the most significant impairments. However, commentators such as Berkowitz (1996) have argued that vocational rehabilitation programmes have not yielded positive outcomes in relation to the amount of money invested, and greater priority should be given to people closest to the labour market. In Australia, an attempt has been made to differentiate between employment and welfare orientated programmes, with different funding streams and expected outcomes associated with each (see Riddell, 2002, for further discussion). In the UK, it is evident that there is still debate about whether the target group for programmes like Work Preparation should be those with the greatest needs, or those closest to the labour market. The Green Paper (DWP, 2002) states clearly that those who are at risk of losing their jobs through accident or illness should be given high priority in the allocation of vocational rehabilitation resources. This is in line with the Jobcentre Plus view of the future target group for Work Preparation, namely those who are likely to be able to access employment following a brief period of assessment and development of work-focused skills.

Debates about the rationale of Work Preparation are also linked to discussion of outcome measurement. Some commentators emphasise that investment in programmes should be in line with their ability to procure savings to the Treasury by moving people from benefits into work (Berkowitz, 1996). Others, while recognising employment as the desirable ultimate goal, recognise that some people require support over time to make progress towards employment. If this is the case, it is argued that soft as well as hard outcomes should be measured. The Green Paper commitment to evaluating the outcomes of the pilot NHS/Jobcentre Plus programmes indicates the importance attached to developing a firmer evidence base in this area. There is clearly further conceptual and operational work to be done here.

The Green Paper is explicit about its desire to promote active labour market policies in relation to disabled people. Throughout the western world (Berkowitz, 1996; Bloch and Prins, 2001) concern at the expansion of the number of people claiming incapacity benefits is apparent. However, there continue to be debates about the correct balance to be struck between supply side measures, which require disabled people to equip themselves for work and find jobs, and demand side measures, which require employers to remove barriers and employ greater numbers of disabled people. The success of the government's plan to promote active labour market policies for disabled people will depend, at least to some extent, on the adequacy of employment support services. At the moment, it appears that employment programmes for disabled people are not succeeding in assisting the majority of participants to find employment. However, for them to become more effective, they perhaps need to be viewed in a wider context. As Bauman (1998) has noted, if more people at the margins, including disabled people, are to find and keep paid work, then work incentive measures and training programmes must be accompanied by adequate support and financial rewards for those wishing to enter the labour market. Otherwise, higher rates of employment may be accompanied by a greater sense of insecurity and exclusion.

Notes

[1] The views expressed in this chapter are the authors' own and do not necessarily reflect those of Jobcentre Plus or the DWP.

[2] Jobcentre Plus delivers the services formerly provided by the Employment Service and the Benefits Agency. From 1 April 2002,

employment services for disabled people have been provided by Jobcentre Plus. These include the New Deal for Disabled People, Job Broker Services, WORKSTEP and the Work Preparation programme.

References

Banks, P., Riddell, S. and Thornton, P. (2002) *Good practice in work preparation: Lessons from research*, WAE Research Series, Sheffield: DWP.

Bauman, Z. (1998) *Work, consumerism and the new poor*, Buckingham: Open University Press.

Berkowitz, M. (1996) 'Improving the return to work of social security beneficiaries', in J.L. Mashaw, V. Reno, R.V. Burkhauser and M. Berkowitz (eds) *Disability, work and cash benefits*, Kalamazoo (MI): W.E. Upjohn Institute for Employment Research.

Bloch, F.S. and Prins, R. (eds) (2001) *Who returns to work and why?*, New Brunswick and London: Transaction Publishers.

BSRM (British Society of Rehabilitation Medicine) (2000) *Vocational rehabilitation: The way forward*, London: BSRM.

Deakin, N. (1994) *The politics of welfare*, Brighton: Harvester Wheatsheaf.

DE (Department of Employment) (1990) *Evaluation of special schemes for people with disabilities*, London: DE.

DSS (Department of Social Security) (1998) *New ambitions for our country: A new contract for welfare*, London: The Stationery Office.

Denison, S., Eccles, J., Tackey, N.D. and Jackson, A. (2000) *Measuring soft outcomes and distance travelled: A review of current practice*, Research Report 219, London: DfEE.

DWP (Department for Work and Pensions) (2002) *Pathways to work: Helping people into employment*, London: DWP.

Floyd, M. (1997) *Vocational rehabilitation and Europe*, London: Jessica Kingsley.

Floyd, M. and Curtis, D. (2000) 'An examination of changes in disability and employment policy in the UK', *European Journal of Social Security, (Special Issue: Disability Policy in European Countries)*, vol 2, no 4.

Jackson, A. (1999) *Soft indicator study: A literature review*, Bath: Annabel Jackson Associates.

Lakey, J. and Simpkins, R. (1994) *Employment rehabilitation for disabled people: Identifying the issues*, London: Policy Studies Institute.

Riddell, S. (2002) *Work preparation and vocational rehabilitation: A literature review*, WAE Research Series, Sheffield: DWP.

Riddell, S., Banks, P. and Wilson, A. (2002) 'A flexible gateway to employment? Disabled people and the Employment Service's work preparation programme in Scotland', *Policy & Politics*, vol 3, no 2, pp 213-30.

Thornton, P. (2002) *Good practice in work preparation*, Report of seminar held by Jobcentre Plus, Manchester, 15–16 May, Sheffield: DWP.

Wilson, A., Lightbody, P. and Riddell, S. (2000) *A flexible gateway to employment? An evaluation of Enable Services' traditional and innovative forms of work preparation*, Glasgow: Strathclyde Centre for Disability Research.

FIVE

Legislating for equality: evaluating the Disability Discrimination Act 1995

Nigel Meager and Jennifer Hurstfield

Introduction

This chapter presents selected findings from some recent studies of the workings of the Disability Discrimination Act (DDA) (see Hurstfield et al, 2004). In particular, it focuses on the third of a series of studies, which looked at the Act's implementation through in-depth case studies of participants in cases and potential cases[1], although we also incorporate some findings from the first two studies (Leverton, 2002; Meager et al, 1999a)

The DDA came into force in December 1996. Under the employment provisions (Part Two of the Act), it is unlawful to treat a disabled employee less favourably than a non-disabled employee for a reason related to their disability, without justification. The Act also requires an employer to make 'reasonable adjustments' where the person concerned is at a substantial disadvantage compared with non-disabled people (failure to make such adjustments, without justification, is counted as discrimination).

This chapter focuses on the findings that relate to the employment provisions (Part Two) of the DDA, although the study also covered cases which were taken under the DDA provisions relating to goods and services (Part Three).

Patterns in DDA cases

Before outlining our in-depth qualitative findings from our most recent study, it is worth briefly summarising some quantitative findings from the two earlier studies.

The earlier studies showed that the number of cases registered under the employment provisions has steadily increased since the Act's inception, as follows:

1997: 115 cases per month
1998: 187 cases per month
1999: 244 cases per month
2000 (first eight months): 292 cases per month.

More recent data from the Employment Tribunals Service, compiled on a slightly different basis (Employment Tribunals Service, 2004) show further growth, although with evidence of some recent stabilisation:

2000/01: 386 cases per month
2001/02: 439 cases per month
2002/03: 442 cases per month
2003/04: 471 cases per month

Disability Discrimination Act cases are now running at a higher annual rate than race discrimination cases, and at between a third and a half of the annual rate of sex discrimination cases.

The two previous monitoring studies identified several patterns in DDA cases.

Characteristics of applicants in DDA cases

• At 61%, men are over-represented among DDA applicants, compared with their representation among disabled people in employment, and among disabled people in the population of working-age.
• The commonest impairments among applicants in DDA cases are: 'problems connected with the back or neck', 'depression, bad nerves or anxiety', and 'problems connected with the arms or hands'.

Types of cases

A significant minority (a quarter) of cases involve more than one of the four main sub-jurisdictions of the DDA. These sub-jurisdictions relate to whether the case involves:

• dismissal;
• recruitment;

- (failure to make a) reasonable adjustment; or
- 'other detriment' (including other aspects of employment discrimination, such as victimisation).

Table 5.1 summarises the sub-jurisdictions of cases recorded during the first two DDA monitoring studies. It is unfortunate that more recent data are not available, but some striking patterns are evident.

First, over two thirds of cases involve individuals claiming that they have been dismissed for a reason related to their disability. Second, nearly a third of cases involve a claim that an employer failed to make a reasonable adjustment. This proportion has increased over time, which may imply an increasing understanding of the notion of reasonable adjustment and its application. Just over one in six cases involve 'other detriment', a proportion that has remained stable over time. Finally, and most notably, only 9% of cases involve a claim that a disabled person has been discriminated against in recruitment, and this proportion has fallen slightly over time.

It is clear that the vast majority of those taking DDA cases are already in employment (or have recently lost their job). Fewer than one in ten cases involve non-working disabled people who are trying to get a job (and this proportion may be even lower than shown in the table, as some of those taking recruitment cases are already in employment, and changing jobs).

Table 5.1: DDA (Part Two) cases by sub-jurisdiction

DDA sub-jurisdiction	Cases lodged: Dec 1996 to 9 July 1988 (phase 1 study) % of cases	Cases lodged: 10 July 1988 to 1 September 2000 (phase 2 study) % of cases	All cases lodged up to 1 Sept 2000 Number	% of cases
DDA1 – dismissal	68.5	68.5	6,105	68.5
DDA2 – other detriment	16.9	17.7	1,555	17.5
DDA3 – recruitment	10.8	8.2	794	8.9
DDA4 – reasonable adjustment	26.3	35.1	2,914	32.7
Total no of cases (excluding missing cases)	2,454	6,454	8,908	

Note that column totals exceed 100% as some individual cases had multiple sub-jurisdictions

Source: IES Database of DDA cases; Leverton (2002)

This finding is particularly noteworthy when set alongside disabled people's reports of their experiences of discrimination. Thus, for example, a national household survey in 1996 (Meager et al, 1999b) asked economically active disabled interviewees whether they had ever been discriminated against in a work context as a result of their disability. The answers suggested that the most common experiences of discrimination occurred in the recruitment process. It would seem that the distribution of types of DDA cases does not reflect the patterns of discrimination reported by disabled people. Other things being equal, we would expect to observe many more recruitment cases in the early caseload. (It is also notable that the incidence of recruitment cases is much lower, and the incidence of dismissal cases much higher, than in the early years of sex and race discrimination legislation.)

Our earlier qualitative case-study research (Meager et al, 1999a) suggested reasons for this under-representation of recruitment cases, including:

- *The greater difficulty in meeting the burden of proof in recruitment cases.* Typically, if a disabled job applicant is rejected in the recruitment process, it can be extremely difficult to obtain the necessary evidence about the other candidates, and the criteria used in selection. Equally, it can be straightforward for an employer to defend a recruitment discrimination claim by citing evidence of 'better-qualified' candidates.
- *Lack of access to support and advice for potential applicants in recruitment cases* (compared with those in dismissal or reasonable adjustment cases, for whom trade union or other support may be more easily accessed).
- *A lower willingness of legal advisers to take recruitment cases*, compared with cases under other sub-jurisdictions, because of a perception that such cases involve large workloads and low probabilities of success at tribunal. Our earlier research showed that people taking recruitment cases were significantly less likely to have legal representation than were people taking cases under other sub-jurisdictions.

Types of employers involved in cases

The two earlier studies showed that the public sector is over-represented in DDA cases, with the incidence of claims in the public sector being some three times higher than might be expected on the basis of its share of employment. This does not imply, however, that the incidence of discrimination is higher in the public sector. Rather, it is likely to reflect a greater prevalence of equal opportunity and disability policies in the public sector (with a higher level of awareness of their rights among the workforce), alongside more active trade union representation, and possibly a lower level of fear among employees that taking a case might damage subsequent career prospects.

DDA cases as multiple jurisdiction cases

The previous research showed that over half of DDA cases also involve claims under one or more other jurisdictions of employment law, most commonly unfair dismissal. A common pattern was for the applicant to have sought advice about an unfair dismissal claim, and for an adviser to have suggested that because the case involved issues concerned with sickness absence, for example, a DDA claim might also be appropriate. It might have been expected that the proportion of such 'double-barrelled' cases would diminish over time as the Act became better established; in practice, however, the incidence of these claims has tended to increase over time.

Withdrawals and settlements

Most DDA employment cases are settled or withdrawn without a tribunal hearing. The previous research showed that only 19% of 'concluded' cases went to a tribunal hearing, and nearly all of the others were withdrawn or settled (Table 5.2). The withdrawal/ settlement rate has been increasing over time, and more recent data from the Employment Tribunals Service (ETS, compiled on a slightly different basis) suggest further decline in the proportion of cases reaching tribunal. Thus, of the 4,030 cases that were 'disposed of' in the year 2002/03, only 17% were heard at tribunal.

These findings raise the question of whether the high rate of withdrawals or settlements reflects 'positive' factors (for example, successful conciliation or mediation via the Advisory, Conciliation and Arbitration Service) (Acas) or 'negative' factors (for example, pressure from employers, fear of the tribunal process, fear of impact on the applicant's labour market chances, and so on). Here, we present some evidence from our recent qualitative work which throws some light on these issues.

Table 5.2: Outcome of concluded DDA (Part Two) cases

Outcome	Cases concluded by 9 July 1998 % of cases	Cases concluded 9 July 1988 to 1 September 2000 % of cases	All cases concluded by 1 September 2000 Number	All cases concluded by 1 September 2000 % of cases
Heard at tribunal	22.0	17.9	1,165	18.8
ACAS conciliated settlement	40.8	39.4	2,456	39.7
Withdrawn/private settlement/stayed	33.7	38.9	2,335	37.8
Struck out/disposed of/other	3.5	3.7	227	3.7
Total (all concluded cases)	1,403	4,780	6,183	

Source: IES Database of DDA cases, Leverton (2002)

Representation and support in cases

The earlier studies, which pre-dated the creation of the Disability Rights Commission (DRC), showed that just over a fifth of applicants in cases going to a tribunal hearing were un-represented. A further third were legally represented, and the remainder represented by advice organisations, trade unions or friends and relatives. Disability organisations were a rare source of advice and representation.

Respondents (that is, employers against whom cases are taken) were much more likely than applicants to have legal representation; this imbalance is rather greater than that found in other jurisdictions of employment law.

Outcomes of cases

The success rate of DDA cases is very low, but the proportion of cases heard at tribunal decided in favour of the applicant rose slightly between the first two studies, from 16% to 20%. A key question is whether the growing success rate reflects:

- improvements in support available (for example, because of the advent of the DRC, or because legal advisers are now more experienced in supporting cases); or
- a growing tendency for 'weaker' cases not to be taken to tribunal.

If we take account of the growing rate of withdrawal of cases (discussed earlier in this chapter), however, there has actually been very little change in the 'real success rate' over time. In both of the earlier studies (and according to more recent ETS data) the proportion of registered cases leading to a 'successful' outcome for the applicant was only 4%. The ETS data suggest that of all the employment jurisdictions heard at employment tribunals, only race discrimination cases have (slightly) lower success rates than DDA cases.

Our earlier study included multivariate statistical analysis that showed that the following factors significantly affect the chances of a case succeeding, after controlling for other features of the case:

- *The applicant's impairment:* applicants with physical/mobility problems are least likely to succeed; those with sensory impairments or impairments relating to internal organs are most likely to.
- *Legal representation:* legally represented applicants are more likely to succeed than applicants who represent themselves. However, it may not just reflect the importance of legal representation in influencing the outcome of case; it might also reflect an unwillingness of lawyers to represent 'weaker' cases. Legal representation of the respondent: applicants are less likely to win their case should the employer be legally represented by an external lawyer. (Interestingly, however, applicants are more likely to win if the respondent is represented by an in-house lawyer.)
- *The nature of the job:* cases brought against employers in manufacturing, primary, construction and 'other services' are most likely to succeed. Cases involving unskilled occupations have higher success rates than those involving managerial and professional or skilled manual occupations.

Experiences of taking a DDA case

In this section, we present findings emerging from our qualitative research with parties (disabled applicants, employer respondents, legal representatives and advisers for both sides) involved in cases.

We also review evidence of changes over time. A key general conclusion is that, contrary to expectation, the major barriers facing disabled people in achieving access to justice under the Act had not reduced or been overcome in the period between the two studies (which took place in 1997/98 and 2002/03). These barriers included: lack of knowledge of the DDA; cost barriers in obtaining representation and in funding cases; and an unwillingness to take a case because of a reluctance to be labelled 'disabled'.

Origins and early stages of cases

The case-study research shows a low level of prior awareness of the DDA among applicants and potential applicants, with most cases being initiated by someone other than the applicant (solicitor, advice centre, trade union, and so on). Even where applicants had prior awareness of the Act, their understanding of the Act and the meaning of its detailed provisions were generally very limited. A key issue for applicants in taking cases was whether or not their condition/impairment was a 'disability'; many did not see themselves as disabled, until an adviser mentioned the DDA, and many were reluctant to label themselves as 'disabled' by taking a DDA case.

Applicants were rarely motivated by financial concerns in taking cases. Rather, issues of justice or fairness dominated their views, as did a wish to publicise their case (sometimes tempered by a concern not to jeopardise future employment prospects by being labelled a 'trouble maker'). Employer respondents were also often unaware of the DDA and its detailed provisions. The obligation to make reasonable adjustments, in particular, was one that many respondents had yet to grasp. Even in large organisations with high levels of awareness in the personnel department, it was common for levels of awareness elsewhere (for example, among line managers) to be lower.

Advice and representation

The research shows not only that applicants often do not have legal representation, but also that, when represented, disabled applicants commonly rely on legal aid, or *pro bono* support. The cost of representation is a key barrier preventing many potential applicants from taking cases, and where cases are taken, it is also a reason why a significant minority of applicants choose to represent themselves.

The definition of 'disability' and other legal issues

The DDA defines a disabled person as someone with:

- a physical or mental impairment which has a substantial and long-term adverse effect on his/her ability to carry out normal day-to-day activities.

Further important features of the definition in place at the time of the research are that:

- mental health conditions must be 'clinically well recognised' to be covered;
- a person who had, but no longer has, a disability covered by the definition, is still covered by the legislation;
- a person with a progressive impairment such as multiple sclerosis does not have to show that the condition *currently* has a substantial effect. It must, however, have *some* effect on day-to-day activities[2].

Our case studies showed that this definition of 'disability' was widely seen as complex and difficult to interpret. Particular problems centred on the following:

- Confusion regarding the coverage of *'mental impairment'*, despite statutory guidance on this issue. Indeed, in the most recent study, many legal representatives felt that case law on the meaning of mental impairment in the Act had added to rather than reduced confusion.
- The focus on *normal day-to-day activities*, which gave rise to individuals (particularly those whose impairment affected them at work) who might commonly be regarded as disabled, failing the test because their condition was not judged to affect normal day-to-day activities.
- The effects of *medical treatment*, which were not being discounted in some cases, as required by the law and despite statutory guidance.
- *Progressive conditions*, which were not always being treated as required under the act.
- The role of *medical evidence*, which represents a major barrier for many applicants in establishing their status under the act. Tribunals rely heavily on such evidence, the cost and difficulty of obtaining which is a disincentive for many (potential) applicants. There is a particular difficulty in cases where applicants incur expense and stress establishing that they are 'disabled' under the Act, only for their case to fail on some other part of the Act.
- *Employers' strategies in defending cases.* Some respondents, aware of the difficulties and cost for disabled applicants in proving that they met the definition, adopt a deliberate strategy of challenging the applicant on the definition, expecting that this would pressurise the applicant to settle or withdraw the case. Case studies suggested that this practice may have become more widespread over time, as

employers (and their legal representatives) learned that this could be an effective strategy in defending a case.

Overall, our research suggests that the burden of proof on the disabled applicant to establish that they are covered by the definition of disability remains a major barrier for (potential) applicants. A further legal issue, over which both applicants and respondents were confused, relates to the notion of 'justification' in the DDA. The Act defines 'discrimination' as being less favourable treatment (for a reason related to a disability) which *cannot be justified* (or a failure to make a reasonable adjustment, which cannot be justified)[3]. It differs in this respect from other anti-discrimination legislation (such as that relating to race or sex). Applicants and their representatives often found this approach in the DDA hard to understand; respondents were equally confused about the grounds on which they could justify unfavourable treatment of a disabled person.

Case outcomes

Settled, withdrawn and conciliated cases

We noted earlier in this chapter the high rates of withdrawal and settlement prior to tribunal, among DDA employment cases, and low rates of success at tribunal. Our case studies looked at factors underlying these observations, and suggested that the likelihood of a case being withdrawn or settled was influenced, first, by the costs of legal action. Applicants were concerned that, even if successful, any award or remedy would not compensate for the cost and stress of taking a case.

Another issue related to Acas involvement in helping parties to settle a case. While people taking cases often regarded this positively, some applicants reported that they had felt pressurised by Acas to settle and that, having agreed to settle, they subsequently felt frustrated at 'being denied their day in court'. Equally, some legal representatives argued that potentially important cases which might clarify points of law were not coming to tribunal for reasons of cost, or the stress of taking the case, rather than the merits of the claim. The lack of expertise and/or experience among advisers and legal representatives was an important factor in DDA success or failure. While the position had improved since the earlier research, many of those from whom advice was sought (particularly non-specialists, such as trade union officers, Citizens' Advice Bureaux, and so on) lacked a good understanding of the Act, and were sometimes wary of its legal complexities.

The experience of taking a DDA case is easily overlooked. However, stress on applicants was a major factor. Many cases fell by the wayside en route, because the process of taking the case, gathering evidence, or entering into conflictual relationships with (former) colleagues was extremely stressful. Many applicants reported that the stress of taking the case had worsened the condition or impairment underlying the (alleged) discrimination.

Employers' fear of adverse publicity often led them to settle cases, even where they were confident of winning at tribunal. (A common practice was for employers to impose confidentiality clauses when settling, reducing the likelihood of damage to the employer's reputation.)

Factors affecting outcomes of tribunal cases

Looking at cases which went to tribunal, the case studies found that the chance of a case succeeding was affected by the availability and quality of legal representation, and, related to this, the availability and quality of evidence (especially medical evidence), and the credibility and expertise of witnesses. The attitudes of the tribunal chair and members were also key in shaping the DDA outcomes. These varied enormously in terms of both their general awareness of disability issues, and the specific adjustments they made to the tribunal process for disabled applicants. Many applicants had not anticipated how formal and legalistic the tribunal process would be. Again there was an important asymmetry here between applicants and employer respondents. Respondents were often able to rely on their representatives to mediate the process and deal with legal technicalities, while many applicants, in contrast, were represented by themselves or by people with little legal expertise or experience of DDA cases.

The duration of the process (the time between the alleged discrimination and the case being heard, as well as the length of the case per se) could affect the outcome, because longer-lasting cases tended to put more stress on applicants, and meant that parties could often not accurately recall what happened.

Impact of DDA cases

A key outcome of a DDA case is not simply whether it is successful, but the direct and indirect impacts that taking the case has on the disabled person, and on the employing organisation against which the case was taken.

As discussed earlier in this chapter, the process was particularly stressful for applicants. Some said that the negative experiences of taking a case outweighed the positive outcomes, even in successful cases. A few reported that taking part in a case had damaged relationships with (ex) colleagues, or deterred a prospective employer from taking them on.

Among employers, the impact varied. There was some evidence of DDA cases having led to a revision of employer policy and practice, whether or not they were successful at tribunal. Examples of impact included: a greater concern to understand causes of employee absence and to improve rehabilitation and return-to-work support; a greater perception of a need to generate medical reports and evidence; and efforts to raise disability/equality awareness among staff. However, a minority of employers claimed a perverse impact from their experience, arguing that experience of a DDA case would make them more wary of recruiting disabled people in future. (Indeed, some were clearly aware that the likelihood of a recruitment case being taken under the DDA by a potential employee was less than the likelihood of a case being taken by an existing employee or ex-employee.)

Policy issues

The research findings raise several important policy issues. Wider and more detailed awareness of the Act among both disabled people and employers would be desirable, both to make disabled people (and people covered by the Act who do not see themselves as disabled) more aware of their rights; but also to discourage poorly founded cases from being taken.

The differences between disabled applicants and employer respondents in the quality and availability of representation and advice, and the heavy reliance of disabled applicants on charitable and free sources of advice and representation, raise questions about whether and how (potential) applicants might be better supported in taking cases.

More specifically, the relative lack of recruitment cases suggests that the Act is doing a better job of supporting disabled people already in the labour market than it is in supporting those who are outside and trying to get in. There is a strong case for more resources to be devoted to tackling discrimination at the point of recruitment, and establishing cost-effective mechanisms to support disabled people in taking recruitment cases.

The cost and difficulty of providing medical evidence is a barrier in many DDA cases, and may prevent potential cases from being taken. The tendency for some employers to challenge applicants on the definition of disability, and the need to seek medical evidence in response, reinforces this difficulty. Progress might involve clearer guidance about when and how medical evidence should be used; or the establishment of independent (and cheap) sources of medical advice for DDA cases. A related point is whether it would be appropriate in DDA cases to establish whether discrimination had occurred (on the assumption that the applicant is disabled) before testing whether the applicant is disabled under the Act. This process might avoid expensive and time-consuming medical evidence being collected for cases that will ultimately fail under other aspects of the Act.

The tribunal setting and the legal process are a major barrier for many disabled people. There is a stigma attached to the disabled label and many disabled people are reluctant to discuss intimate personal detail in the semi-public setting of a tribunal. The research suggests that tribunals and officials are often insufficiently aware of disabled people's access needs, and of how the legal process itself can disproportionately disadvantage disabled people.

Despite the DDA having been in place for nearly eight years, our research reveals many concerns about inconsistency within the system in the application of the law. Some relate to the inconsistent use of directions and preliminary hearings as a means of clarifying issues in a case, before (or instead of) of launching into a full tribunal hearing; and the varying weight placed on medical evidence in different tribunals. Others relate to a wider awareness of disability issues; and raise the question of whether employment tribunals hearing DDA cases should also include a disabled person.

Has the DDA had an impact on employment?

Our research focused on the experiences of participants in actual and potential DDA cases. We found that there has been little easing over time of the barriers affecting the implementation of the DDA employment provisions, and that many of these barriers disproportionately disadvantage disabled applicants.

The scale of labour-market disadvantage still facing disabled people is reflected in the fact that 81% of non-disabled people were in employment in summer 2003, compared with 49% of disabled people. It is not surprising that statistical evidence of recent trends in the employment of disabled people shows little evidence of significant improvement; Labour Force Survey data show a small increase in the employment rate of long-term disabled people from 45.1% in summer 1998 to 49% in summer 2003. ('Long-term disabled' includes everyone with a work-limiting disability and/or a disability covered by the DDA.) However, using the definition of 'work-limiting' definition of disability (a long-term health problem or disability that affects the *amount* or *type* of work a person can do), the rise in the employment rate has been much less marked, from 38.1% to 41% over the same period[4].

The employment rate is the single, starkest indicator of the extent of labour market disadvantage faced by disabled people. In the absence of a reduction in the massive differential between the employment rates of disabled people and those of non-disabled people, it would be difficult to argue that legislative interventions such as the DDA, or policy measures such as the New Deal for Disabled People have yet done much to dent that disadvantage.

Notes

[1] 'Potential cases' were situations involving an apparent breach of the Act, but which did not lead to a case being taken.

[2] Since this research was undertaken, a Disability Discrimination Bill has begun its passage through the UK Parliament, one which includes proposed amendments to the definition which will bring people with certain progressive illnesses into scope of the DDA at an earlier stage of their illness.

[3] Since the research was undertaken, important changes to the Act have been introduced which define a new concept of 'direct discrimination', for which no defence of justification is admitted.

[4] For a discussion of definitions of disability statistics, see Tibble (2004).

References

Employment Tribunals Service (2004) *Annual report of the Employment Tribunals Service, 2003/4*, London: TSO.

Hurstfield, J., Meager, N., Aston, J., Davies, J., Mann, K., Mitchell, H., O' Regan, S. and Sinclair, A (2004) *Monitoring the Disability Discrimination Act 1995: Phase 3*, London: DRC.

Leverton, S. (2002) *Monitoring the Disability Discrimination Act 1995: Phase 2*, DWP In-house Report 91, London: DWP.

Meager, N., Doyle, B., Evans, C., Kersley, B., Williams, M., O'Regan, S. and Tackey, N. (1999a) *Monitoring the Disability Discrimination Act (DDA) 1995*, DfEE Research Report RR119, London: DfEE.

Meager, N., Bates, P., Dench, S., Honey, S. and Williams, M. (1999b) *Employment of disabled people: Assessing the extent of participation*, DfEE Research Report RR69, London: DfEE.

Tibble, M. (2004) *User's guide to disability estimates and definitions*, London: DWP.

SIX

Disability frameworks and monitoring disability in local authorities: a challenge for the proposed Disability Discrimination Bill

Ardha Danieli and Carol Woodhams

Since the implementation of the Disability Discrimination Act (1995) (DDA), employers have increasingly put in place policies and practices designed to shape their disability management practice (EOR, 2003; IRS, 2003; Hurstfield et al, 2003). The amendments to the DDA in the form of the Disability Discrimination Bill (DDB) (now the Disability Discrimination Act 2005) are likely to increase such activities. While all employers are required to ensure that they comply with the legislative requirements, in the public sector the replacement of Compulsory Competitive Tendering (CCT) with 'Best Value' has placed further requirements on Local Authorities (LAs) to improve their service provision and their corporate employment policies and practices in order to ensure the social inclusion of different groups within their local community. These initiatives are being given further impetus via the DDB which includes a disability equality duty on public authorities to have due regard to:

> ... the need, where opportunities for disabled persons are
> not as good as those for other persons, to promote equality
> of opportunity between disabled persons and other persons
> by improving opportunities for disabled people. (DRC,
> 2003, p 7)

Equality, therefore, has become a mainstream issue in local government and is evidenced in *The equality standard for local government*, which aims to "combat the institutional processes that lead to discrimination and which form part of the culture and administration of governance in Britain" (LGEO, n.d., p 1). Mainstreaming equality according to Speeden (2004, p 1) means:

> ... making equality a central consideration of all aspects of employment and service delivery .... In practice this means looking at services and practices in a different way to the past – moving away from a uniform approach to service management towards one that recognises difference. Needs within the local community are shaped by race, ethnicity, gender, disability, religious belief, sexuality and age: mainstreaming should ensure that these aspects of community life are taken into consideration in employment and in the delivery of services.

As part of achieving Best Value and mainstreaming equality, central government has provided indicators to be used in auditing progress on equality and social inclusion in the form of Best Value Performance Indicators (BVPIs). The disability rights movement and the Disability Rights Commission (DRC) have of course made the social inclusion of disabled people a central issue and it has been argued that this requires a fundamental shift in how disability is conceptualised and therefore how discrimination can be removed. Central to this has been a call for a shift from medical to a social understanding of disability. Stone (2001, p 7) has argued:

> The social model is essential if the duty to provide best value and demonstrate continuous improvement is to be fulfilled.

In a similar vein it could be argued that the requirement of individual disabled people to challenge acts of discrimination after the event under the DDA encourages an individualistic approach to disability, and that the DDB shifts the onus from the individual to the collective responsibility of service providers and public sector employers to remove any potential discrimination before it occurs. As such, a more socially based model of disability is implied in the DDB than in the DDA.

A central aspect of demonstrating continuous improvement for disabled people is the monitoring of the current position and existing practices in order to plan for further improvement. This chapter deals with the concept of workplace equality monitoring and discusses the findings of an exploratory study into disability monitoring with the local government sector. Using quantitative and qualitative data, we will demonstrate that monitoring activities are connected to models and definitions of disability. We will argue that while many local authorities claim to base their disability management on a social model of disability, in practice, monitoring procedures are conducted as required by the government's BVPIs, support a medical model of disability as enshrined within the DDA. We suggest that this is in part a result of the difficulties of implementing the social model for monitoring purposes and that while monitoring on the basis of a social model may be desirable, the requirement to demonstrate progress by for example increasing the number of disabled employees becomes problematic for organisations.

Monitoring disability: some differences

It is one of the well-established features of a comprehensive approach to equality management that organisations should have a monitoring procedure in place to analyse their workforce for group representation. As part of a broader workforce audit, that includes perceptions of equality, employee satisfaction, and so on. An analysis of internal employee monitoring data might include a breakdown of job, grade, site, length of service, qualifications, skills levels, promotion history, type of contract, turnover, take up of training courses, appraisals, sickness records, and so on (Cameron, 1993), which are then cross-tabulated by employee profile characteristics (sex, age, ethnicity, sexual orientation, religion, disability, and so on).

In reality, only the most simplistic analysis of the data is performed and is not uniformly executed for all disadvantaged groups. A recent IRS survey (2004) confirmed that both private and public sector organisation carry out monitoring exercises on ethnic groups for example, but that disability monitoring was carried out by only 47% of their sample. How might this be explained? Unlike other disadvantaged groups, monitoring for disabled representation, requires that the feature of group membership is first described, a task that is complicated by a number of variables.

First, the group is notoriously unstable in membership. Many employees will pass in or out of this group during their working lives. This implies that monitoring for this group will need to be carried out at regular intervals for changes in status. Second impairments are frequently hidden and thus perceived to be personal 'property'. The more personal and invisible characteristics become, the less easy it is to gather data on. To draw comparisons with another group with hidden status, Stonewall, a professional lobbying group for equality on the basis of sexual orientation states, "many organisations would like to monitor sexuality, they simply don't know how" (Anon, 2004). This is problematic because it complicates the process and weakens the motivation to monitor.

Third, there is no necessary link between impairment and disability. In other words, while someone may have an impairment, they may not be see themselves as disabled. Employees with impairments can find their disability status shaped by the accessibility of their environment, the impact it has on their choice of occupation, their age, even their sex (Woodhams and Corby, 2003). The implication here is that unless the context of job, workplace, building, the perceptions of others, environment, and so on, is constant, monitoring becomes meaningless. This introduces a significant, and as yet largely unexplored, area of the complications of monitoring disability, which focuses on the different ways that disability is defined.

Defining disability for monitoring purposes

Broadly speaking, there are three methods used in the employment context to define disability. The most frequently used method of disability definition relies on the use of medical criteria and is referred to as a 'medical model' (Oliver, 1990). By explicitly connecting medical impairment and their consequences –that is, limitations in functional abilities – this model underpins the UK's DDA (Gooding, 1996).

The appeal of this method of definition lies in its apparent objectivity; that is, evidence can be provided in the form of someone either having or not having an impairment which impacts on their abilities. As such, access to additional resources and adaptations need only be granted to those who qualify within these definitions. Within organisations, these 'objective' decisions are usually taken by doctors or occupational health specialists who provide 'evidence' that without the additional resources the disabled individual will be disadvantaged by their impairment. Each case is dealt with individually and judged on its own merits.

The second method of definition leaves classification within the control of the individual and is referred to as 'self-classification'. Manifesting the personal nature of the category, and the individualised use of the 'disabled' label, definition is left entirely to the discretion of each employee. In other words, even if individuals would qualify as 'disabled' within a medical model, if they do not wish to classify themselves as 'disabled' they are allowed to make that choice. Within this definition, employers would not expect to have corroborating evidence for the claimed status as disabled and any extra resources should automatically be provided.

The third method of definition is based on the 'social model' of disability (Oliver, 1983; Barton, 1989; Barnes, 1991; Finklestein, 1993; Oliver and Barnes, 1991). From this perspective disability does not emanate from the individual and their impairment, but rather from an environment that is designed to favour those who have no impairments. As such, the experience of disability becomes collectivised and the territory of 'correction' becomes society and the environment, rather than the person with the impairment. Under this model, monitoring is based on an audit of physical, economic and social barriers (see Zarb, 1997), suppressing enquiry relating to type, severity or duration of an individual's impairment. Thus, the measurement indicators of a workplace-based social model audit would include aspects of workplace and job design, methods and criteria for job success, and so on. After elaborating on our research methods, the rest of this chapter examines the models of disability that underpin monitoring procedures in UK LAs.

Research methods

Data on broad aspects of disability management including the frequency of monitoring initiatives within the LA context was collected within two questionnaire surveys (using identical research questions and samples) issued in 1995 (see Woodhams and Danieli, 2000) and followed up in 2003. Questionnaires were sent to named human resource (HR) managers in all UK LAs. The response rate was 262 (50%) of LAs in 1995 and 171 (37%) in 2003[1]. The data for 1995 and 2003 were investigated for differences in size and geographic region and no significant differences were found. It was assumed, therefore, that findings from each survey were comparable.

In addition, organisational data, in the form of publicly available documents, were collected and a supplementary interview programme was conducted in 2003 among LAs investigating issues of disability management, including monitoring. Interviews were carried out with human resources, equality or disability officers of ten selected LAs that were chosen on the basis that they employed above average proportions of disabled employees and we might therefore expect that monitoring had played a significant part in this. Interviews were recorded and transcribed.

Disability monitoring and the local authority context

By 2003, 90% of local authorities (LAs) who responded to the survey claimed to be monitoring for disability during the recruitment phase and 75% stated that they conducted subsequent monitoring of their existing workforce. Thirty-seven percent of respondents then used this information to suggest targets for the following year's employment of disabled employees. Unsurprising, given the implementation of the DDA in 1996 and the introduction of BVPIs, that in 2003 each of these activities were performed by a higher proportion of LAs to an extent that is highly statistically significant (see Table 6.1).

While this data is interesting and encouraging, it sheds little light on the monitoring processes and models that lie behind the statistics. Interviews were performed in order to investigate these issues in more depth. The interview data is analysed here according to a number of themes which emerged, all of which explore different aspects of the models used by LAs for monitoring, namely the espoused model of disability management, the actual models in use and the tensions this generates and finally innovations and the future of monitoring after the implementation of the DDB.

The espoused model of disability management

An examination of the LAs' public documents and press releases suggests that the social model does shape their employment practices so for example, LA1 claims:

> [Name of council] has adopted the social model of disability and is working towards removing or altering as many barriers as possible to disabled people. Barriers have nothing to do with individual disabled people's bodies; they are created by people which means it is possible to remove

Table 6.1: Disability employment monitoring survey results: 1995 and 2003

Element	1995	2003	Statistical significance (χ^2)
Monitor disability *at* recruitment	(197) 64%	(154) 90%	$\chi^2 = 37.21$, p<0.001***
Monitor disability *after* recruitment	(150) 39%	(128) 75%	$\chi^2 = 16.34$, p<0.001***
Set disability employment targets	(39) 13%	(64) 37%	$\chi^2 = 39.47$, p<0.001***

them. You can take a social approach to disability by identifying and getting rid of the disabling barriers which are within your control such as; management practices, the way work is organised, or building design. (LA1 website, 18 June 2003)

Furthermore, LA2 claims:

[Name of council] continually promotes the social model of disability – which says that people are disabled not by their impairment, but by a society. (LA2, Press Release, 29 November 2001)

However, during interviews, respondents were frequently unsure, or at least not very good at expressing the differences between the medical and social model:

I think the medical one is very like, use the medical terminology, and the social one is more geared towards the attitudes and the general public which sort of fits in well with everybody's lifestyles. (HR service manager, LA2)

There was also little recognition of the way that a social model might impact on monitoring practice. The HR adviser at LA2 did define disability as a function of other people's negative perceptions, suggesting that the LA should:

… regard disability as a function of discrimination, if you get discriminated against because of it, then I think it's a disability. If you don't, then I don't think it is.

The disabilities officer at LA3 added other factors that would need to be taken into account in an audit of the way that employment may disable employees:

People may be disabled in their home but not at work or vice versa, the nature of disability is that if you put the medical issue aside and … ask people whether they feel they are excluded or discriminated against, for example, are you restricted by the way in which your environment impacts on your impairment. We need to be thinking like this.

Despite an acknowledgement of the importance of the social model, interviewees often reverted to terminology consistent with an understanding of disability as an 'individual tragedy' when discussing monitoring. For example, the equalities officer at LA4 stated she believed that:

> ... employees don't declare their disabilities if they feel they can manage and if they don't need adaptations they will not want to draw attention to themselves. ... They often need time to personally adjust to having a condition.

The reference to people feeling they can 'manage', not wanting to 'draw attention to themselves' and needing time to 'adjust' are all indicative of a view of disability as a personal, individual phenomenon and that admitting to being disabled stigmatises the individual.

We will return to the problem of stigmatisation in due course. Nevertheless, while there was some commitment to using a social model at both corporate and individual level, there was also some recognition that this did not necessarily inform practice:

> We have as an organisation got a piece of paper that we take down and take the dust off and say 'look we have ascribed to the social model of disability' but at the end of the day ... if there is an issue, people always come down to case law, always come down to the medical model. (Equalities manager, LA1)

In the following section, we consider why the medical model is seen as a solution to issues or 'problems' that may arise.

The actual models in use and tensions

The implications of the previous section of this chapter are that, when it comes to actual practice, in contrast with their ideological commitment, LAs are using a monitoring procedure underpinned by a medical model of disability. To a large extent, respondents reported that this is driven by the imposition of a reporting system by central government that uses the DDA definition:

> We are required to use the DDA model. There are Best Value Indicators that Local Authorities are required to report on. And they have definitions that, for consistency, we have

to follow. And the definition the government had given us is the medical model definition. ... But in terms of our work towards disability, our preference is to use the social model. (HR service manager, LA2)

The ability to use both models was sometimes judged to be helpful. The HR manager at LA5, for example, reported that the LA has sent out two monitoring questionnaires in the last three years. The first survey was informed by a self-declaration definition. However, believing this to have produced inaccurate data, the second survey used the DDA definition to:

> ... help employees who may have thought they did not have a disability to identify that in actual fact they did. (HR manager, LA5)

The exercise reportedly resulted in an increase in the percentage of employees declaring disabilities and receiving support. However, this also demonstrates the uncertain identity of the category 'disabled'. The disability officer at LA6 shared a similar experience:

> We attach a flowchart to help them ascertain whether they have a disability or not and it has the DDA definition ... since we have been doing that, more of our employees have indicated that they are disabled.

Nevertheless, there were also issues relating to the use of medical criteria and the DDA definition that limited its perceived usefulness. The disabilities officer at LA3 hoped that the council would not use the DDA definition in a soon-to-be-conducted monitoring activity. He felt the definition is "too complex and confusing and it may mislead people, it is too medical". Similarly the disability officer at LA6 stated that although the authority used the DDA definition during the monitoring process, "Whether people understand it is another matter", a view echoed by LA4's equalities officer who, despite issuing additional advice on the DDA definition, thought the definition, "helps some people, but it is difficult for others, and some managers as well, it is hard to get hold of the concept".

Apart from the complexity of applying the DDA definition, the issue of the stigma associated with the category disabled was a recurring theme in the data. There was generally a fear that it would be used against the individual often mentioned and this impacted on the ability of organisations to acquire accurate monitoring data:

> Many employees do not declare their disability as they are frightened that they are going to be singled out, I think that is one of the prime reasons, they think that the council will think that they can't cope. (Personnel manager, LA7)

> We have got people who I think most people would regard as having a disability but choose not to be classed as disabled …. I think because they don't like to think that they have a disability, they want to be regarded on their abilities and don't want to be labelled in effect. (Disability officer, LA8)

While LAs may espouse a commitment to the social model, clearly for monitoring purposes the medical model is dominant in terms of an individual's willingness to identify as disabled, despite the problems of complexity, individualism and stigmatisation. Nevertheless, there was a great deal of dissatisfaction with basing monitoring procedures on the medical model and some organisations were trying to resolve this.

For some of our organisations, the solution lay in a statement of self-declaration that did not rely on either social or medical guidance. This took the form of statements such as: 'Do you consider yourself to be disabled?', or 'Do you have a disability?'. On one level, this method of data gathering appeared to be satisfactory and seemed to be responsible for much less interviewee anxiety so that the disability officer at LA6 simply stated that, "we ask people to self declare and we take that as being correct". However, as we discussed earlier, at LA6 employees were 'helped' to identify as disabled by providing additional information based on the DDA definition. For most of our organisations, self-declaration alone was deemed insufficient so that the majority (seven out of ten) were concurrently using two methods of defining and monitoring. The disability officer at LA7 illustrated this:

> We started issuing questionnaires to employees, asking them if they would like to declare themselves disabled – plus we do use and have always used the DDA definition.

The HR manager at LA5 reported a similar practice. The most recent monitoring process required individuals to identify themselves, first without guidance and second using DDA criteria:

> There was no resistance to that. We sent a covering memo to explain what the details would be used for, in that it would purely be for statistical information and that it would not be used against them if they declared themselves.

While the response rate to their survey was nearly 100% of course this is not an ideal situation. Organisations may find themselves with two different sets of statistics – one based on the DDA and medical definition and another based on self declaration – a situation unlikely to occur with other disadvantaged groups and which has policy implications which we will return to in due course.

Moving forward: innovations and the future

It is likely that the public sector duty within the DDB will come into force in December 2006. It is also likely that one of the by-products of this piece of legislation will be the increase of monitoring initiatives. Local Authorities are even more likely, for example, to monitor their internal employment practices for equal access to training and promotion opportunities, proportionate representation within discipline and grievance hearings and within senior levels of management, and so on. When looking to the future, our data revealed some innovative suggestions for improving monitoring practice, but none of them suggested a change to the frameworks within which disability was identified and 'counted'. The personnel manager at LA8 felt that the solution lay in setting the right climate and tone for the monitoring exercise:

> I think it is working well, we say "We are not being intrusive", "This is why we're asking you", and, "It's going to be held confidentially and this is why we need it". I think if you take time to explain people are more likely to provide the information.

Going one step further, LA9 employed an external agency which used a campaign of pre-monitoring publicity combined with a self-declaration approach and a list of example impairments that are not always seen as disabling, such as asthma, diabetes, depression, epilepsy.

Five per cent of employees self-declared, an increase of almost a third over the previous year.

LA8 was also working on improvements to their processes. The equalities adviser reported:

> Now that we need the information for our BVPI, … we have been working with our IT people to try and make the process easier for people to fill in so we get more of these forms back.

Finally, the disabilities officer at LA3 presumably had his tongue firmly in his cheek when looking forward to a monitoring exercise that the organisation was about to undertake in the next two weeks which he anticipated would be as unsuccessful as the last attempt:

> I think we should send the questionnaire out saying, "We will presume you are black, female and disabled, unless you tell us otherwise", as one American company did and got almost 100% return.

Discussion

In this chapter, we have sought to report on the difficulties of monitoring disability. We have argued that the monitoring of disabled employees is underpinned by particular definitions of disability and that while in recent years, LAs have espoused a commitment to a social model of disability our data suggests that such a commitment is not being implemented in organisational monitoring practices. How might we explain this? In order to answer this question, we need to briefly consider why local authorities monitor.

The necessity to monitor progress for the achievement for equality would be difficult to dispute in any context. Clearly, within the local government environment, the motivation for monitoring also stems from the requirement of LAs to report the proportion of disabled people in their employment to central government for best value purposes. This requires the use of the DDA definition and this, as we have discussed, is underpinned by a medical model of disability. However, we would suggest that even if they did not have to fulfil this requirement, given that organisations generally operate on the basis of economic rationality, 'objective' criteria are required. The medical model underpinning the DDA are assumed to provide such criteria, but the associated complexity and the stigma perceived to be associated with the category 'disabled', reduces the number of people willing to apply such definitions to themselves.

While a stigma continues to exist, it can be seen as evidence of a *lack* of progress on changing perceptions of disability from a medical to social model. This is exacerbated by government's requirement that monitoring is conducted according to BVPIs which are based on the medically based DDA definitions. We would argue that this is unlikely to be altered by the implementation of the DDB which, while extending protection to people with forms of impairments previously not included within the DDA, does not suggest that the government is likely to require organisations to adopt workplace equality monitoring using a social model definition of disability. Thus, while the DDB suggest a shift in terms of locating the removal of disability discrimination as a responsibility of service providers and employers rather than the individual disabled person, it leaves undisturbed medial definitions of disability.

However, there are other problems with applying the social model for monitoring purposes. Given the heterogeneity of disability, achieving a fully enabling environment is equally problematic because what may be an enabling environment for someone with a particular impairment may be a disabling environment for someone with a different impairment. For those charged with the implementation of monitoring, the social model is not only difficult to implement in practice for the reasons discussed above, there is a more paradoxical problem with the implementation of the social model for monitoring purposes.

If the social model actually informed the management of disability in the workplace, monitoring would shift from the individual to the social and environmental aspects of the organisation. Any aspects of these which were found to cause people with impairments to experience their impairments as disabling and so, ultimately as discriminatory, would need to be changed. This might include redesigning all jobs, ensuring that promotional criteria did not indirectly discriminate against people with impairments and ensuring that all employees understand and operate according to a social model of disability in their day-to-day activities. However, if this were to be achieved, any subsequent monitoring of individuals would reveal very few if any disabled people employed. In other words, the organisation would become a victim of its own success. For reporting purposes, both internal and external, local authorities need to demonstrate that they employ disabled people and are increasing their proportions within the workforce but the model of disability they wish to be seen to be supporting does not enable them to be seen to be achieving this.

It is perhaps then not surprising that local authorities are either using the medical model or combining it with a self-declaration procedure which is used as a surrogate for the social model for monitoring purposes. The co-existence of both forms of monitoring does of course create a dilemma for those organisations that have two sets of statistics relating to the number of disabled employees. They then have a choice as to which they use for different audiences with no guarantees that either figure is accurate. As we have demonstrated, from our study, the majority of our sample appear to be using the figures produced using the DDA definition and as long as progress is monitored mainly on the basis of quantifiable indicators this is unlikely to change.

Note
[1] The number of LAs decreased in 2003 from 526 to 463 due to local government reorganisation.

References

Anon (2004) 'Employers failing to monitor all groups', *Personnel Today*, 4 May, p 51.

Barnes, C. (1991) *Disabled people in Britain and discrimination*, London: Hurst and Co.

Barton, L. (1989) *Disability and dependency*, London: Falmer Press.

Cameron, I. (1993) 'Formulating an equal opportunities policy', *Equal Opportunities Review*, no 47, Jan/Feb, pp 16-20.

DRC (Disability Rights Commission) (2003) *Draft Disability Discrimination Bill: Initial briefing by the Disability Rights Commission*, (www.drc- gb.org/newsroom/newsdetails.asp?id=602&section=4).

EOR (Equal Opportunities Review) (2003) 'More disabled people in work since DDA', *Equal Opportunities Review*, November, p 4.

Finklestein, V. (1993) 'The commonality of disability', in J. Swain, V. Finkelstein, S. French and M. Oliver (eds) *Disabling barriers, enabling environments*, London: Sage Publications/The Open University Press.

Gooding, C. (1996) *Blackstone's guide to the Disability Discrimination Act 1995*, London: Blackstone Press.

Hurstfield, J., Allen, B., Ballard, J., Davies, J., McGeer, P., and Miller, L. (2003) *The extent of use of health and safety requirements as a false excuse for not employing sick or disabled persons*, Norwich: HSE Books.

IRS (2003) 'Managing disability 2003: a progress report', *IRS Employment Trends*, no 785.

IRS (2004) 'No longer a minority pursuit – monitoring the workforce', *IRS Employment Review*, no 800, 21 May.

Local Government Employers Organisation (n.d.) *The Equality Standard for Local Government Report by the Employers' Organisation for Local Government*, Layden House, 76–86 Turnmill Street, London EC1M 5LG.

Oliver, M. (1983) *Social work with disabled people*, London: Macmillan.

Oliver, M. (1990) *The politics of disablement*, Basingstoke: Macmillan.

Oliver, M. and Barnes C. (1991) 'Discrimination, disability and welfare: from needs to rights', in I. Bynoe, M. Oliver and C Barnes (eds) *Equal rights for disabled people – The case for a new law*, London: IPPR, pp 7–16.

Speeden, S. (2004) 'Mainstreaming equality', *Equalities Newsletter*, Local Government Information Unit (LGIU), 7 June, (www.lgiu.co.uk).

Stone, V. (2001) *Quality and disability: Equality in the best value regime*, London: DRC.

Woodhams, C. and Corby, S. (2003) 'Defining disability in theory and practice: a critique of the British Disability Discrimination Act 1995', *Journal of Social Policy*, vol 32, no 2 pp 1–20.

Woodhams, C. and Danieli, A. (2000) 'Disability and diversity – a difference too far?', *Personnel Review*, vol 29, pp 402–16.

Zarb, G. (1997) 'Researching disabling barriers', in C. Barnes and G. Mercer (eds) *Doing disability research*, Leeds: The Disability Press, pp 49–66.

SEVEN

Job retention: a new policy priority for disabled people

Geof Mercer

Introduction

The New Labour government elected in 1997 stressed its commitment to promote social inclusion, and prioritised a broad programme of 'welfare-to-work' initiatives to move people out of unemployment and dependence on social security benefits and into paid work (DSS, 1998). While the primary focus has been on 'pathways to work' issues (DWP, 2002), this chapter concentrates on the extension of this policy agenda to 'job retention' and sustained employment.

The discussion begins by outlining the interest in job retention and then consider the different programmes directed at disabled people. In practice, the design of employment support policies and the development of 'good practice' in the workplace have followed the implementation of the Disability Discrimination Act (DDA) 1995. An immediate issue is their impact on workplace attitudes and practices. The chapter concludes by illustrating the potential for involving organisations of disabled people, and a comprehensive, 'disabling social barriers' perspective in the development of employment support policies.

Job retention issues

Throughout the last quarter of the 20th century, campaigns by organisations of disabled people against social and environmental barriers included calls for a redirection of employment policy to address exclusionary workplace structures, attitudes and practices (Barnes and Mercer, 2003). These anti-discrimination struggles had a growing impact on how policy makers viewed disabled people's participation in the labour market. Employers, too, began to consider their responsibilities to disadvantaged groups, while also examining the 'business case' for taking positive action on disability (Zadek and Scott-Parker, 2001).

Over this period, the unemployment rate of disabled people remained at twice that of non-disabled people, with only 49.1% economically active in spring 2003 compared with 72.5% of the non-disabled population (ONS, 2003). While the first policy task was to support unemployed people into work, interest then focused on 'job stability' or the length of time an individual remained with an employer. This was further distinguished in some accounts from 'job retention', although its meaning has varied. One approach expanded the definition:

> staying with the same employer, with the same or different duties or conditions of employment. (Thornton, 1998, section 1.3)

Another perspective linked job retention to individual level changes:

> employees who remain in their job when their own circumstances change, such as the onset of sickness or disability or having a child. (Kellard et al, 2001, p 9)

In practice, most analyses of UK data have been restricted to the number staying in post with the same employer, although longitudinal studies (such as the British Household Panel Survey) allowed a more 'dynamic' picture to be explored (Burchardt, 2000, 2003). The main variation on this theme has been the performance indicator for 'welfare-to-work' programmes. Thus, one outcome measure of the New Deal for Disabled People (NDDP) equated it with how many recipients remained in work for 26 weeks without a return to benefits (Kellard, 2003, p 96).

A central finding from these studies has been that the return to paid work was for many short term. Up to a half of those who moved from unemployment to work returned to economic inactivity within a year (Teasdale, 1998). Of those transferring from Jobseeker's Allowance, 25% left work within 12 weeks, but thereafter the departure rate fell to under 5% (Trickey et al, 1998). These data replicated general labour market research findings that the early weeks in post were critical (Mercer, 1979), although stability rates varied across jobs and sectors (Ashworth and Liu, 2001). For a significant minority, there was a repeated cycle of movement between short-term spells of work and periods of unemployment (Kellard et al, 2001, p 8). Instead of achieving sustained employment, disabled people were over-represented in the emerging 'flexible' workforce, which was both short-term and low paid, with few prospects of career advancement (Kellard, 2003; White and Forth, 1998). Additionally, those who acquired impairment in employment were over twice as likely to leave work within a year as their non-disabled counterparts (Burchardt, 2003).

However, studies have been slower to generate insights into how far stability and retention rates diverged between disabled and non-disabled people or within the disabled population according to such factors as age, gender, and level of qualifications (Burchardt, 2000; Kellard, 2003). There was broader agreement that the decision to stay in post or leave was the outcome of a complex process more often than a one-off event. Individuals weighed the relative 'costs and benefits' of alternative destinations (another job or employer, early retirement, or out of work altogether). Hence, the choice was not always directly related to levels of satisfaction with the employer or job (Kellard et al, 2001, p 15).

Quite clearly, the evidence-base for designing policies has been incomplete. Viewed from a 'social barriers' approach, impairment was not a necessary or sufficient reason for leaving work. Instead, attention was directed at employer attitudes and practices, workplace relationships generally, and wider obstacles to inclusion in society at large.

Developing employment support

The Green Paper, *Pathways to work* (DWP, 2002), restated New Labour's primary objective of moving a significant proportion of the (then) 2.7 million Incapacity Benefit (IB) claimants into (sustained) paid work. Government thinking distinguished between the most 'severely disabled' who could not participate in the competitive labour market, and those with 'common health problems' (Waddell and Burton, 2004). The intention was to enable as many individuals as possible in the latter category to return to, or continue in, paid work. This was reinforced by evidence that up to 40% of claimants considered their 'health' was not the major reason for being unemployed, but rather 'external' obstacles such as financial disincentives, employer and workplace discrimination (DWP, 2002, p 13).

The new thinking was embedded in major organisational changes leading to the merger of the advice, training and financial (benefits) support functions of the Employment Service and the Benefits Agency into Jobcentre Plus. This paralleled a series of 'New Deal' programmes, including the NDDP, covering job entry and retention issues, led by job brokers and personal (Disability Employment) advisers. A

WORKSTEP programme matched disabled workers with both 'supported' and 'competitive' employment opportunities. In addition, the introduction of the Disabled Person's Tax Credit in 1999, re-invented as Working Person's Tax Credit in 2003, brought improved incentives to stay in work. Its targets included people forced to move to a less well-paid job. Moreover, the Access to Work scheme offered reimbursement for part of the extra costs incurred by disabled workers, such as travel, and funding some personal assistance, special equipment and adaptations.

Overall, approaches to employment support encompassed sheltered workshops, supported employment, social firms, train and place models, individual placement and support, and Intermediate Labour Market (ILM) projects (ODPM, 2004, pp 56-7). Across these initiatives, the balance was shifting from traditional 'supported' to 'open' employment. A significant marker of this trend was the White Paper, *Valuing people* (DH, 2001), covering people with the label of learning difficulties which promoted the transfer of more people from day care into either 'open' (with full market wages) or 'subsidised' employment.

How far then was this new emphasis translated into the design of policies and the role of other key stakeholders such as employers, trade unions, insurers and General Practitioners (GPs)?

Policy design

While there has been no shortage of suggestions for policies to encourage job retention, no consensus exists on what works, with whom and why (Walker and Kellard, 2001). Major issues have been the character and timing of support programmes. The standard division has been between pre-employment (work-preparation) services and post-employment initiatives, although in practice these often overlap. Pre-employment programmes have concentrated on job specific and 'soft' skills (teamwork and communication) training, financial and benefits advice, and counselling. In contrast, post-employment services revolved around induction training and support, occupational health, mentoring, emergency support (and special payments or incentives) and 'external' services such as childcare, and transport (Kellard et al, 2001).

Currently, the favoured method has been a comprehensive, preventive case management package that integrates post-employment services with pre-employment programmes:

Examples include employer-focused interventions, intensive work-readiness training and specific retention support, particularly to tackle practical problems that may arise in employment, including transport and childcare problems, financial difficulties and workplace disagreements. (Kellard, 2003, p 95)

The Department for Work and Pensions (DWP) has strongly promoted an in-work vocational rehabilitation strategy. Traditionally, rehabilitation started after the initial medical treatment ended, but the current emphasis has been on early action to identify 'vulnerable' workers allied to prompt and better coordinated workplace rehabilitation. The DWP also developed a sickness-absence package for use by smaller firms and pressed for monitoring of the process and outcomes of these rehabilitation policies (James et al, 2003; Waddell and Burton, 2004). Larger organisations were encouraged to develop their own rehabilitation teams, while 'NHS Plus' was established to offer occupational health expertise to smaller firms. However, the calls for greater worker representation in this process and more emphasis on dismantling social and environmental barriers had less priority.

In addition, seven Job Retention and Rehabilitation Pilots (JRRPs) were set up to evaluate best practice. These recruited their first clients in April 2003, with a total of 7,500 planned for March 2005. Eligibility for entry to a JRRP was restricted to employed and self-employed people in one of the pilot areas who have been off work because of 'sickness, injury or disability' for between six and 26 weeks, and were at risk of losing their job. A 'quasi-experimental' trial has been designed with participants randomly assigned to either a control group that receives existing services, or one of three treatment groups that receive one of the following packages:

- enhanced support from pilot staff that concentrated on workplace issues and improved advice for employers;
- extra NHS-based support including occupation health advice and services; or
- a mixture of the two schemes.

The design of vocational rehabilitation has been stimulated by criticism of the readiness of GPs to certify incapacity for work without considering other options, such as recommending workplace adjustments. A reformed rehabilitation service would comprise a multidisciplinary team that could address the diverse obstacles to job retention and offer continuing assessment, advice and support. Furthermore, proposals were made for an on-line advice system on 'job retention' options directed at GPs, as well as extending responsibility for issuing sick notes to other healthcare specialists more familiar with employment issues.

Another innovative approach has entailed developing a Code of Practice with solicitors to moderate the number and level of injury compensation claims (against employers) by encouraging clients to consider medical rehabilitation as a first resort. At the same time, attempts have been made to persuade private insurance companies of the value of reaching early settlements where this might facilitate an individual's rehabilitation and increase the likelihood of staying in work.

An instructive illustration of the contrasting standpoints in the timing and design of employment support is provided in research with mental health service users. The traditional ('clinical recovery model') emphasis was on achieving psychosocial rehabilitation before moving into employment ('place and train'), but this has been reversed in a 'social recovery' approach. This placed individuals in employment before they received individual support and training 'on the job' in tandem with modifications to the job and working practices (Secker at al, 2002). The emphasis was on 'natural supports', fostering a positive workplace culture and relationships with colleagues, linked with training and support to learn, as well as confronting discriminatory practices and attitudes so as to make the disabled employee feel accepted and valued (see Chapter Fourteen of this volume; ODPM, 2004; Secker and Membrey, 2003, p 210).

It has been claimed that this 'place and train' strategy has been more effective than traditional pre-vocational training programmes in keeping mental health users in competitive employment (Crowther et al, 2001), although North American studies have stressed their labour intensive character (Kellard, 2003). Again, few programmes have been systematically evaluated, including their cost-effectiveness (Kellard et al, 2002).

This has led to further questions. Should employment support services be targeted at specific individuals or groups? Who should be involved in delivering post-employment service support? At present, a number of large charities, such as the Royal National Institute of the Blind (RNIB, 2002), MIND (National Association for Mental Health) and the Multiple Sclerosis Society have explored ways to enhance their role in assisting disabled people to remain in work (Paschkes-Bell et al, 1996; Barnes et al, 1998). Nevertheless, in general, the participation of disabled staff and user-led organisations has been underplayed in the design and implementation of most support schemes.

Workplace perspectives: employers and employees

Employers and workplace practices have been key targets for policy interventions. Despite a series of surveys reporting that employers expressed broadly inclusive attitudes towards disabled staff (Morrell, 1990; Honey et al, 1994; Dench et al, 1996; Meager et al, 1998; Goldstone with Meager, 2002; Roberts et al, 2004), critics complained that these were not commonly translated into everyday workplace practice (Barnes et al, 1998, p 36). For example, half of the employers who agreed with the principle of making appointments solely on merit anticipated difficulties in retaining someone who acquired an impairment (Roberts et al, 2004). Employers also acknowledged that they differentiated between impairments, and were less willing to employ people with a visual impairment, with learning difficulties and mental health system users, or considered them only suitable for unskilled, routine jobs (Dench et al, 1996). And yet organisations that employed a disabled person expressed more inclusive views (Goldstone with Meager, 2002; Roberts et al, 2004).

Around two thirds of organisations said they had made workplace adjustments for disabled employees and this figure increased to three quarters when the interviewer asked about specific examples (Goldstone with Meager, 2002). The most frequently mentioned were special equipment, making the workplace more accessible (for example, hearing loops, wheelchair lifts, adjustments to counters and sills, parking spaces for disabled drivers), and more flexible working hours and relationships. Size of organisation mattered insofar as two thirds of those with over a hundred employees made adjustments for an employee who became disabled compared with only a fifth of firms with less than six employees (Roberts et al, 2004). Yet despite widespread fears of the likely costs, particularly among smaller organisations, only a third of organisations making adaptations reported incurring direct financial costs (Meager et al, 1998).

For their part, disabled people have remained critical of employers for their slowness to recognise the social and environmental barriers to inclusion, and the diversity of their support needs. Disabled people identified a range of discriminatory attitudes and practices, including unwillingness to make workplace adaptations, lack of sympathy to requests for more flexible hours, being passed over for promotion, and pressured into early retirement or redundancy. They also lamented the lack of coordination across the various employment support schemes (Grewal et al, 2002; Molloy et al, 2003). Nonetheless, despite the incomplete and uneven shift in disability at work, disabled people have developed a variety of strategies to assert their support needs and rights in employment (Roulstone et al, 2003).

Even so, a significant minority of disabled workers previously held 'totally different' jobs but felt forced to change because of their impairment (Grewal et al, 2002, p 154). Likewise, more than a quarter of disabled people who left employment complained that the possibility of making workplace adaptations was not raised (Meager et al, 1998). Such findings underscored government action to persuade employers to change by disseminating examples of 'good practice', job retention guidance, and generally raising employer awareness of disability and challenging prejudices – as with the anti-stigma campaign to promote employment of mental health system users (Johnson, 2002; ODPM, 2004; Kellard et al, 2001). Conversely, financial incentives to reward employers for their job retention performance have not been encouraged.

Indeed, rather than develop a formal policy, many employers preferred dealing with job retention issues on an *ad hoc* basis (Goldstone with Meager, 2002; Roberts et al, 2004, p 55). This was reinforced by uncertainties about exactly who was covered by the DDA or what constituted 'reasonable adjustments' (Roberts et al, 2004). Nevertheless, despite employer concerns (even before the extension of the employment provisions of the DDA to small and large firms alike), disabled employees have been reluctant to embark on legal action (Meager et al, 1999; Roulstone et al, 2003).

A user-led case study

A notable aspect of employment support policies has been the failure to exploit disabled people's knowledge and experience of disabling barriers. Hence, the significance of recent initiatives by user-led organisations that have a strong commitment to challenging disabling social and environmental barriers and promoting the social inclusion of people with impairments. As an illustration, the Centre for Independent Living in Glasgow (CILiG) obtained EU funding to develop a specialist housing information, advice and advocacy service for disabled people: the Glasgow Disabled Person's Housing Service (GDPHS); that became operational in mid-2000 (Carson and Spiers, 2004). The GDPHS developed an Intermediate Labour Market (ILM) project to assist unemployed disabled people to find permanent work, backed up by positive assessments that such projects nationally had achieved a six-month retention rate of over 90% – well above that of New Deal adult training programmes (Marshall and Macfarlane, 2000).

Twelve full-time, one-year work placements were negotiated with local housing associations. Each provider contributed towards the cost of the project, while wage rates ensured disabled participants were better off than if they had stayed on welfare benefits. The selection of the first cohort targeted individuals who received the Disability Living Allowance at the medium or higher level. Every applicant underwent rigorous checks to match their skills and work experience to the requirements of the placement organisation.

Very different work placement experiences emerged, despite a common plan covering access, support mechanisms and staff training (Carson and Spiers, 2004, pp 42-6). The contrasts were vividly illustrated in the case of Sasha, a young female "from an Asian family, Deaf and never been in paid employment" (Carson and Spiers, 2004, p 42). In her first placement, she was expected to 'fit in' with existing work routines, and not given formal feedback about her performance. Instead, the management decided that her presence created 'problems' and Sasha was transferred to more menial tasks. She began to despair about moving into long-term employment. Her second placement proved an altogether more positive experience. From the outset, there was close cooperation with the project team, while senior staff demonstrated considerable sensitivity to the issues and barriers facing a disabled employee and treated the employment project as a development opportunity for existing staff as much as Sasha.

From the first intake, seven individuals who obtained full-time jobs were still in post one year later. In addition, the GDPHS proved good value for money with its costs more than outweighed by the reduction in welfare benefits and housing adaptations, and the higher income from rents and Council Tax, income tax receipts and national insurance contributions (Carson and Spiers, 2004, p 47).

This user-led Employment Project demonstrated not only the potential impact of involving disabled people and organisations controlled by them but also illustrated wider arguments located in a social barriers approach. Structural action, such as improving the accessibility of workplaces, was complemented by policies directed at disabled individuals. There was also abundant evidence that exclusion affected individual self-esteem and confidence such that disabled people began to believe the criticism that they were 'not up to the job'. In these circumstances, support from a peer group (or user-led organisation) was crucial in helping to diagnose the problem, and explore alternative remedies (Carson and Spiers, 2004, p 48).

Conclusion

At the present time, the concern with job retention has been stimulated by New Labour's aim to reduce the numbers on incapacity benefit, and manage the sickness absence of disabled (and other) employees. The DWP has increased support for job stability and retention by providing a range of services and financial incentives, reinforced by legislation to promote workplace inclusion and disabled people's civil rights. The policy mantra has shifted to awareness of what disabled people can do, with support, rather than what they cannot do. Yet despite the growing policy interest, robust evaluation evidence of the impact of the various initiatives and investment of resources has been in short supply. Aside from the low take-up of programmes such as NDDP, data collection has been inconsistent across projects. Hence, the impact on job retention (as opposed to entry to work) has been far from clear.

Equally significant, the apparent lower job stability and retention among disabled people has not been matched by effective measures to confront disabling barriers and introduce enabling practices into the workplace. Much remains to be done to challenge prevailing analyses of work, welfare and disability and develop policies to support disabled people into sustained employment, with realistic prospects of career advancement the next policy goal.

References

Ashworth, K. and Liu, W.C. (2001) *Jobseeker's Allowance: Transitions to work and early returns to JSA*, DWP In-house Report 80, London: DWP.

Barnes, C. and Mercer, G. (2003) *Disability*, Cambridge: Polity Press.

Barnes, H., Thornton, P. and Maynard Campbell, S. (1998) *Disabled people and employment: A review of research and development work*, York: York Publishing Services.

Burchardt, T. (2000) *Enduring economic exclusion: Disabled people, income and work*, York: Joseph Rowntree Foundation.

Burchardt, T. (2003) *Employment retention and the onset of sickness or disability: Evidence from Labour Force Survey longitudinal datasets*, DWP In-house Report 109, London: HMSO.

Carson, G. and Spiers, J. (2004) 'Developing a user-led project: creating employment opportunities for disabled people within the housing sector', in C. Barnes and G. Mercer (eds) *Disability policy and practice: Applying the social model*, Leeds: The Disability Press, pp 35-50.

Crowther, R.E., Marshall, M., Bond, G.R. and Huxley, P. (2001) 'Helping people with severe mental illness to obtain work: a systematic review', *British Medical Journal*, vol 332, no 7280, pp 204-7.

Dench, S., Meager, N. and Morris, S. (1996) *The recruitment and retention of people with disabilities*, Report 301, Brighton: Institute for Employment Studies.

DH (Department of Health) (2001) *Valuing people: A new strategy for learning disability for the 21st century*, Cm 5086, London: DH.

DSS (Department of Social Security) (1998) *New ambitions for our country: A new contract for welfare*, Cm 3805, London: The Stationery Office (TSO).

DWP (Department for Work and Pensions) (2002) *Pathways to work: Helping people into employment*, Cm 5690, London: TSO.

Goldstone, C. with Meager, N. (2002) *Barriers to employment for disabled people*, DWP In-house Report 95, London: HMSO.

Grewal, I., Joy, S., Lewis, J., Swales, K. and Woodfield, K. (2002) *'Disabled for Life?' Attitudes towards, and experiences of, disability in Britain*, DWP Research Report 173, Leeds: Corporate Document Services (CDS).

Honey, S., Meager, N. and Williams, M. (1994) *Employers' attitudes towards people with disabilities*, Brighton: Institute of Manpower Studies.

James, P., Cunningham, I. and Dibben, P. (2003) *Job retention and vocational rehabilitation: The development and evaluation of a conceptual framework*, Health and Safety Council Research Report 106, Norwich: HMSO and Health and Safety Executive Books.

Johnson, A. (2002) *Job retention and advancement in employment: Review of research evidence*, DWP In-house Report 98, London: DWP.

Kellard, K. (2003) 'Job retention and advancement in the UK: a developing agenda', *Benefits*, vol 34, no 10(2), pp 93-8.

Kellard, K., Adelman, L., Cebulla, A. and Heaver, C. (2002) *From job seekers to job keepers: job retention, advancement and the role of in-work support programmes*, DWP Research Report 170, Leeds: CDS.

Kellard, K., Walker, R., Ashworth, K., Howard, M. and Liu, W.C. (2001) *Staying in work: Thinking about a new policy agenda?*, DfEE Research Report 264, London: DfEE.

Marshall, B. and Macfarlane, R. (2000) *The intermediate labour market: A tool for tackling long-term unemployment*, York: York Publishing Services for the Joseph Rowntree Foundation.

Meager, N., Bates, P., Dench, S., Honey, S. and Williams, M. (1998) *Employment of disabled people: Assessing the extent of participation* DfEE Research Report 69, London: DfEE.

Meager, N., Doyle, M., Evans, C., Kersley, B., Williams, M., O'Regan, S. and Tackey, N.J. (1999) *Monitoring the Disability Discrimination Act (DDA) 1995*, Brighton: Institute for Employment Studies.

Mercer, G. (1979) *The employment of nurses*, London: Croom Helm.

Molloy, D., Knight, T. and Woodfield, K. (2003) *Diversity in disability. Exploring the interactions between disability, ethnicity, age, gender and sexuality*, DWP Research Report 188, Leeds: CDS.

Morrell, J. (1990) *The employment of people with disabilities: Research into the policies and practices of employers*, Research Paper 77, London: Department of Employment.

ODPM (Office of the Deputy Prime Minister) (2004) *Mental health and social exclusion*, London: Social Exclusion Unit, ODPM.

ONS (Office for National Statistics) (2003) *Labour market trends*, September, London: ONS.

Paschkes-Bell, G., Da Cunha, S., and Hurry, J. (1996) *Adapting to change: When an employee becomes disabled*, London: RNIB.

RNIB (Royal National Institute of the Blind) (2002) *Work matters: Enabling blind and partially sighted people to gain and retain employment*, London: RNIB.

Roberts, S., Heaver, C., Hill, K., Rennison, J., Stafford, B., Hawat, N., Kelly, G., Krishnan, S., Tapp, P. and Thomas, A. (2004) *Disability in the workplace: Employers' and service providers' responses to the Disability Discrimination Act in 2003 and preparation for 2004 changes*, DWP Research Report 202, Leeds: CDS.

Roulstone, A., Gradwell, L., Price, J. and Child, L. (2003) *Thriving and surviving at work. Disabled people's employment strategies*, Bristol: The Policy Press for the Joseph Rowntree Foundation.

Secker, J. and Membrey, H. (2003) 'Promoting mental health through employment and developing healthy workplaces: the potential of natural supports at work', *Health Education Research*, vol 18, no 2, pp 207-15.

Secker, J., Membrey, H., Grove, B. and Seebohm, P. (2002) 'Recovering from illness or recovering your life? Implications of clinical versus social models of recovery from mental illness for employment support services', *Disability and Society*, vol 17, no 4, pp 403-18.

Teasdale, P. (1998) 'Incidence of and repeat spells of unemployment: an analysis using claimant data', *Labour Market Trends*, November, vol 106, no 11, pp 555-62.

Thornton, P. (1998) *International research project on job retention and return to work strategies for disabled workers*, Geneva: International Labour Organization.

Trickey, H., Kellard, K., Walker, R., Ashworth, K. and Smith, A. (1998) *Unemployment and job seeking: Two years on*, DSS Research Report 87, London: DSS.

Waddell, G. and Burton, A.K. (2004) *Concepts of rehabilitation for the management of common health problems*, London: TSO.

Walker, R. and Kellard, K. (2001) *Staying in work: Policy overview*, DfEE Research Report 265, London: DfEE.

White, M. and Forth, J. (1998) *Pathways through unemployment: The effects of a flexible labour market*, York: Joseph Rowntree Foundation.

Zadek, S. and Scott-Parker, S. (2001) *Unlocking potential: Disability and the business case*, London: Employers' Forum on Disability.

EIGHT

Benefits and tax credits: enabling systems or constraints?

Anne Corden

In rebuilding the welfare state to enable 'Work for those who can, security for those who cannot' (DSS, 1998), New Labour saw the need for a radical joined-up strategy in order to include disabled people in the general policy shift towards work. The central elements of the new government's overall reform strategy for long-term sick and disabled people were active tailored help and encouragement for those who want to move into work; removing disincentives in the benefit rules and system; ensuring that work pays, and tackling discrimination and promoting change in the workplace. Thornton (2000) has discussed the strengths and weaknesses of these elements, and some of the inconsistencies and issues still to be resolved.

Within this broad programme of welfare reform, New Labour also sought reduction in expenditure on incapacity benefits (DSS, 1998). Despite reforms designed to tighten access to the main contributory benefit in 1995, the number of working-age recipients of Incapacity Benefit had continued to climb. There was a sharp reduction in the number of new recipients but a lengthening average duration of claim (Kemp and Thornton, forthcoming). Thus, embedded within policies to reduce poverty and social exclusion lay determination to move some current recipients off Incapacity Benefit; to tighten access for new potential recipients by changes in the rules, and to offer advice and services to help people take routes other than those leading to long-term benefit receipt.

There was considerable challenge here for the new government, whose guiding principle for support for disabled people within the philosophy of 'welfare to work' was that, "Those who are disabled should get the support they need to lead a fulfilling life with dignity" (DSS, 1998, p 2). Any tightening of access to incapacity benefits would be highly sensitive. Experience of the earlier Benefits Integrity Project showed the strength of feeling against social security developments perceived as 'an attack on disabled people' (Drake, 2000). There were also increasing concerns about the deepening of inequality. It would be important that any benefit changes designed to encourage disabled people to do paid work were seen quickly to lead to positive outcomes.

Fundamental changes were required to achieve a benefits system that encouraged paid work. As structured and administered in 1997, the disability benefits system could be seen as rewarding 'incapacity' and punishing attempts to do paid work. However, in a complex social security system, it can be hard to introduce changes designed for improvement without also creating some perverse incentives or negative outcomes that undermine the policy intention and maintain social exclusion. It can also take considerable time for people to learn about so-called 'incentives' designed to influence their behaviour, and to train and equip professional advisers who might help them understand and respond.

This chapter traces the government's attempts to remove structural barriers and disincentives to work within the disability benefits system itself, and to provide financial incentives to do paid work. We look at the intention and mechanism of various new structural and administrative arrangements, and what evidence there is about the outcomes. We find that there have been advantages and new opportunities for some people, but conflicts and tensions remain.

In-built constraints

Many of the structural constraints had roots in the 'all-or-nothing' approach to entitlement for Incapacity Benefit and/or the administrative dividing line between people considered to be 'in work' and those 'not working'. It is useful to explain this further.

In the UK, entitlement to Incapacity Benefit is decided on an 'all-or-nothing' basis, and there is no concept of partial incapacity. Categorising people as incapable of work by reason of some 'specific disease or bodily or mental disablement' and therefore entitled to benefit has a long history, dating from the introduction of sickness benefit in 1948. The distinction was carried through into the development of a long-term invalidity benefit in 1971 (Brown, 1984). When this was replaced by Incapacity Benefit in 1995, a new test, the 'All Work Test', was devised. This was designed to distinguish people who should not be expected to work at all because of their medical condition and were therefore entitled to claim Incapacity Benefit from those who were expected to look for work in return for Jobseeker's Allowance. The All Work Test was designed to focus only on the effects of a medical condition, taking no account of other factors such as age or availability of work. The test was developed from established clinical measures of impairment and standard psychometric principles and focused on a range of activities of daily living considered relevant to capacity for work. Government medical advisers and consultants saw advantages in the test in having high validity and being "relatively simple, quick and cheap to administer" (Waddell et al, 2002, p 161).

Categorisation of people as either fit or unfit to seek work does not reflect the reality of people's circumstances, however. Being able to work is not an 'all-or-nothing' concept (Berthoud, 1998) and a measure of functional impairment does not reflect capacity to work. How to apply the test to people with fluctuating conditions has been a continuous problem (CPAG, 1999). Some Incapacity Benefits recipients can do some kinds of work, for some periods of time. Some people with impairments would be able to do some kinds of work with the right kind of conditions or support.

However, the idea that incapacity benefits recipients were not able to work was reinforced by strict monitoring and control by local benefits offices of those small amounts of work that were allowed, voluntary work and so-called 'therapeutic work'. People who were found working outside the rules faced loss of benefits. In the 'all-or-nothing' context, some people feared that any move in the direction of work, such as doing voluntary work or even expressing interest in work, might lead to reassessment of their capacity for work and loss of benefits (Davis, 1996; Arthur et al, 1999). Some people believed that loss of incapacity benefits meant a likely reduction of income as they returned to lower value unemployment benefits and had to wait to requalify for Incapacity Benefit. Such fears extended to loss of Disability Living Allowance (DLA), which is of considerable value to some disabled people. Doing paid work does not, in itself, affect entitlement to DLA, but having a job might be interpreted as an indication of a lower need for supervision and care during working hours, which might result in loss of DLA or reduction in level of payment. There is little evidence of the extent to which this happened, but there is evidence that knowing about such a possibility raised concern for some disabled people (Beyer et al, 2000) and some of their partners and parents whose own entitlement to carers' allowances might also be affected (Corden, 1997).

The incoming Labour government identified the All Work Test and the expectations and assumptions it created as a significant problem. The all-or-nothing test effectively "writes off as unfit for work people who might, with some assistance, be able to return to work, perhaps in a new occupation" (DSS, 1998, p 54). The government wanted a new approach which focused on what disabled people could do, rather than what they could not, encouraging a more positive identity for the people concerned, and greater recognition of their potential among advisers and those concerned in benefits administration. At the same time, changes in the rules were required to allow and encourage Incapacity Benefit recipients to try working without fear of penalty.

When Incapacity Benefit recipients are asked directly about barriers in returning to or trying work, they most commonly report barriers related to their health (Loumidis et al, 2001a, 2001b). Perceived financial implications, in terms of potential low earnings and financial insecurity, and practical effects of changes in income sources, such as the impact on housing costs, are also reported as obstacles. Leaving Incapacity Benefit or trying work can bring people up against constraints within the benefits system associated with the '16 hour' administrative benchmark. Working for longer than 16 hours weekly generally brings people out of entitlement to the main out-of-work benefits. Those who need financial support to boost their earnings then come within the scope of tax credits and in-work benefits. Making the transition from out-of-work income to earnings can be financially risky. The problems associated with the transitional period are now well known and affect disabled and non-disabled people (Shaw et al, 1996). They include problems in meeting housing costs and household bills while waiting for wages, and the fear of debt (Loumidis et al, 2001a).

Problems perceived go beyond the transitional period. Being unable to earn enough money on a regular basis is reported as a barrier by some incapacity benefits recipients when they think about working (Loumidis et al, 2001a). People who fear being unable to sustain work, including people with fluctuating conditions or recurring symptoms, see particular risks in leaving the security of incapacity benefits (Corden et al, 2003). The nature of some people's health condition or impairment may mean that they would prefer working only part of the day or week, resulting in relatively low earnings. Unless they can reach 16 hours work, they are not entitled to tax credits for working people. Even with in-work financial support, some people are still unable to achieve an income sufficient to meet their living expenses, including some people who use means-tested personal assistance funding or live in supported accommodation (Howard, 2002; O'Bryan et al, 2000).

The following section explores these perceived financial risks, and recent policy measures to address them within the benefits system itself.

Reducing the barriers

Accumulating evidence of the financial risks and traps perceived in moving towards work from Incapacity Benefit has led to recent policy development across a number of government departments, and a flurry of pilot measures and changes in benefit rules. They fall generally into three kinds: measures to 'ease' the transition towards work; measures to boost low incomes and make work pay; and what might be called 'anchor-lines' or 'safety-nets' for people who need to return to benefit after trying work.

Easing the transition to work

One of the first measures was to remove restrictions on the amount of voluntary work which Incapacity Benefit recipients might do. Until 1998, no more than 16 hours voluntary work was allowed. There is now no limit to the amount of work that may be done as a volunteer, although permission should be sought from the Jobcentre. The belief that taking part in a voluntary activity can act as a stepping stone towards paid work is embedded in the government's active labour market policies. There is evidence from a number of studies involving disabled people and those who advise them that this does sometimes happen, as volunteers gain skills and expertise, and rebuild confidence (Corden and Sainsbury, 2001; Corden and Ellis, 2004; Davis Smith et al, 2004).

For those who do want to try paid work new opportunities were created when the 'therapeutic work' provision in Incapacity Benefit was replaced in April 2002. The so-called therapeutic work provision allowed some Incapacity Benefit recipients to undertake small amounts of work on medical advice, with a view to helping to improve, prevent or delay deterioration in medical condition, or as part of hospital treatment or sheltered work. It was hard for people whose condition was unlikely to change to use this provision, for example, people with learning disabilities (Simons, 1998). Outside institutional environments, the measure was probably not widely used (Corden and Sainsbury, 2001). However, there was evidence from studies of people claiming other out-of-work benefits that small jobs of less than 16 hours weekly could boost working prospects (Iacovou and Berthoud, 2000).

The therapeutic work provision was replaced by 'Permitted Work' rules which currently allow four kinds of paid work to be done while claiming Incapacity Benefit. Some of the rules variously maintain the concept of work as 'therapy', are designed to help people unlikely to progress towards full employment in the near future, but who have found particular opportunities to increase incomes and promote their social inclusion, and people who can work part-time with ongoing and regular support. One kind of permitted work, however, is specifically designed as a bridge between benefit and full-time work, and may help people to try work without loss of the financial security of long-term benefits, and without medical surveillance or interventions by third parties. This is called permitted work (higher limit) and allows Incapacity Benefit recipients to do work of less than 16 hours weekly for up to 26 weeks at earnings of up to £72 per week. It can be extended for another 26 weeks if there is evidence that this will improve capacity to undertake full-time work. In practice, DWP will expect the person seeking an extension to have the support of a job broker (see Chapter Three of this volume), personal adviser or disability employment adviser.

Evaluation of permitted work has been undertaken (Dewson et al, 2004). By July 2004, some 14,000 people were undertaking permitted work (higher limit). The measure creates some inequity, as only £20 of the permitted earnings is disregarded in the benefit assessments for income support and housing benefit. People who receive these means-tested benefits, with a disability premium, may find that their permitted work reduces their income support and increases the rent they must pay.

Further measures to ease the transition to work include extensions to housing benefit and council tax benefit for the first four weeks of work. This may help people meet basic living costs while they wait for the first wages. A Jobfinder's Grant of £200 was piloted from April 1999 for people moving off incapacity benefits, designed to offset some of the initial expenses that people may face when starting work, such as buying suitable clothes. Qualitative evaluative research (Corden and Sainsbury, 2001; Loumidis et al, 2001a) showed that the lump-sum grant was welcome and did ease some household budgets. However, availability of the grant was not a strong influence on decisions about taking work. The grant was replaced in 2001 by the general Job Grant of £100, available to a range of people including those moving off Incapacity Benefit. Job Grant will be increased to £250 for people with children, from October 2004.

The latest addition to measures designed to ease financial transitions to work is the return to work credit (DWP, 2002) introduced in 2003 in seven pilot areas. This is a payment of £40 per week for the first 52 weeks of a move off Incapacity Benefit into work of 16 hours or more at gross earnings of £15,000 or less. The payment is made through

Jobcentre Plus offices, where advisers explain its availability, and it may act both to reduce financial anxieties about moving to work and provide a valuable additional boost to low earnings.

The next section discusses further measures introduced to make paid work financially worthwhile.

Boosting low incomes and making work pay

New tax credits launched in October 1999 had a pivotal role in the government's determination to help people move away from out-of-work benefits and towards greater financial independence through the labour market. Working Families Tax Credit (WFTC) and Disabled Person's Tax Credit (DPTC) were designed to make work pay, alongside the minimum wage (HM Treasury, 2000).

The design of WFTC and DPTC built on that of Family Credit and Disability Working Allowance (DWA), which were in-work benefits administered by the Benefits Agency for the Department of Social Security (DSS). While Family Credit had some success in raising living standards and encouraging parents to work, in particular lone parents (Marsh and McKay, 1993), DWA was generally considered a failure, with very low take-up (Rowlingson and Berthoud, 1996).

The two new tax credits represented a fundamental change in the way in-work support was provided. Disabled Person's Tax Credit provided more generous help than DWA and was available to more people. Administration by the Inland Revenue and payment through the payroll wherever possible would, it was hoped, underline the link with earnings, emphasise the financial rewards of working and remove some of the stigma attached by some people to association with the benefit system. A 'fast track' gateway was further introduced in October 2000.

Evaluative research on DPTC commissioned by the Inland Revenue included a survey of recipients in summer 2001 (Atkinson et al, 2003) and a two-phase qualitative study (Corden and Sainsbury, 2003). The survey found that almost 80% of respondents found their DPTC either essential or very helpful. Among those who said it had helped, one fifth had found that DPTC made it financially more worthwhile to work or made it possible to work. Another 7% said it allowed them to live on lower wages than they could otherwise afford, in some cases because they could work fewer hours than otherwise obliged. In terms of its impact as an incentive, only 28% of respondents were not working when they first found out about DPTC, but among these people, most said DPTC had been an influence on their decision to start work. One quarter said DPTC had influenced their working time by allowing them to work fewer hours. The researchers identified a 'high impact' group, of 23%, who said they would not be doing their present job without DPTC. This was more common among women, older people, self-employed people, and particularly, lone parents.

The qualitative findings confirmed that DPTC did help some people move off incapacity benefits, and met a range of policy objectives among some recipients, enabling them to do work that suited them, making work pay, raising living standards, helping parents afford good quality child care and increasing flow of resources towards children, where parents lived apart. Findings from other studies also showed that DPTC was important in encouraging some people claiming incapacity benefits to try or return to paid work (Corden and Sainsbury, 2001; Loumidis et al, 2001a).

The qualitative evaluation of DPTC also threw light on some of the constraints on achieving the policy objectives. Tax credits were new concepts, and some people made wrong assumptions about entitlement. Disabled Person's Tax Credit was perceived as having a complex structure, and levels of understanding of the rules were generally low. It was hard to relate poorly understood rules to hypothetical work situations without direct personal advice from informed professionals or advisers. The involvement of employers in paying DPTC was disliked by some people and, importantly, some people in the target population just did not perceive themselves as 'disabled' while some did not want to be categorised within a group in society who may be perceived as stigmatised and excluded.

There was never any measure of take-up of DPTC. By October 2002, there were 35,150 recipients in Great Britain, of whom some 23,000 were single people, but it was likely that low take-up meant that the full potential of DPTC was not met. The fast track component was little used. Despite its popularity with many recipients, DPTC was not particularly successful in increasing the financial rewards from work. Government figures (DWP, 2002) showed that only about 25% of people receiving Incapacity Benefit would have been at least £25 better off per week if they moved into a job of 30 hours at the minimum wage. Some would have been worse off.

As the government moved rapidly through its reform agenda in relation to modernising the tax and benefit system, the 'next generation' of tax credits came on stream. In April 2003 the Working Tax Credit (WTC) replaced the adult elements of WFTC and DPTC, and the employment credit element of New Deal 50+. This development was presented as part of a coherent strategy for promoting work and tackling poverty, in combination with the minimum wage and the New Deal programmes providing personalised help (HM Treasury, 2002). The WTC brought disabled workers into mainstream in-work support.

In April 2004, there were 76,100 disabled workers in households benefiting from the disability element of WTC (Inland Revenue, 2004). It is hoped that WTC will increase the numbers of those receiving an Incapacity Benefit who would be better off in work (30+ hours) to 55% (DWP, 2002). However, the introduction of WTC has been marred by administrative delays and errors (House of Commons, 2004). The Inland Revenue is making major investments in staff training and increased helpline capacity to improve the situation. Other problems that are emerging relate to the recovery mechanism and its effect, for example the way reduced payments are treated for housing benefit (CPAG, 2004).

'Anchor-lines' and 'safety-nets'

Fear of being unable to sustain work is one of the barriers perceived when people think about moving off incapacity benefits. The fear may be well founded, as relatively high proportions of people moving into work have been shown to return to incapacity benefits (Arthur and Zarb, 1997; Dorsett et al, 1998). There has been a 'linking rule' within Incapacity Benefit since October 1998, specifically to reduce financial risk and uncertainty perceived by people who face the possibility of recurrence of symptoms, or fluctuating health conditions.

The linking rule enables people to return to the same level of Incapacity Benefit they were receiving before they started work, if they become incapable again within the following 52 weeks. Evidence from small-scale evaluation showed that knowing about this rule could be a powerful incentive (Corden and Sainsbury, 2001), although this effect was reduced by lack of awareness of the rule, or belief that and/ or experience that the rule is hard to access.

Changing perceptions of 'incapacity'

An earlier section described the problems in the All Work Test as identified by the in-coming Labour government (DSS, 1998) and the need to shift some of the expectations and assumptions it created. In addition, there had been some suggestions that Incapacity Benefit was perceived by some older people, their GPs and benefits staff, as appropriate in circumstances of declining health, ageing and scarcity of work (Ritchie et al, 1993; Beatty and Fothergill, 1999; Kemp and

Thornton, forthcoming).'Incapacity for work', it was suggested, might be substituting for alternatives of 'retirement' or 'unemployment'.

Despite the perceived need for change, there has not been radical reform of the All Work Test. Although the test was replaced by a Personal Capability Assessment in 2000, this was effectively a renaming of the existing test of functional capacity. The problems associated with using measures and indicators of functional impairment to assess capacity for work remain. An additional component was introduced in certain parts of the country where labour market reintegration programmes aimed at incapacity benefits recipients have been or are being piloted. Here, the examining medical doctor conducting a medical examination as part of a Personal Capability Assessment writes a separate 'Capability Report' providing information about work-related activities the person might be able to do and what help might be required to do them. This medical information may be passed to other organisations and agencies involved in rehabilitation.

Qualitative evaluation of this initiative (Legard et al, 2002) found the Capability Report passed to the personal adviser of people taking part in NDDP and ONE pilot programmes was of limited use. The policy intention now (DWP, 2002) is to develop the Capability Report further and to achieve greater coordination with work-focused interviews. Particular attention is being paid to the timing of the availability of the Capability Report. The scope for applying the Capability Report is limited, however. Around 20-25% of people claiming incapacity benefits have 'very severe medical conditions' and are exempt from the Personal Capability Assessment (DWP, 2002) and only around one third of those who do have the assessment are asked to take part in a medical examination with an approved doctor.

Rather than looking to move away from the current test of functional impairment, policy makers' recent interest has focused on finding ways of improving the quality and efficiency of the process of gathering and reporting medical evidence for the Personal Capability Assessment (Sainsbury et al, 2003).

It remains to be seen how far people's own perceptions of their capacity to work have been influenced by changing the name of the All Work Test, or knowing that the doctor who examined them has written a report about them in terms of what work they might do. Recent interviews with both new and experienced incapacity benefits recipients (Sainsbury et al, 2003) showed that people attached strong importance to the need for full medical evidence, to show the effect of their condition or 'how ill' they were, in the belief that this demonstrated their entitlement. Evaluation of the Incapacity Benefit reform pilots (DWP, 2002) will provide further evidence of people's conceptualisation of capacity and incapacity for work[1].

Discussion

This chapter has focused on the disability benefits system. It is important to re-emphasise that most incapacity benefits recipients describe health-related barriers as the main reason for their not doing paid work. Economic security and lack of financial risk are also important to many.

There is considerable evidence from research cited above that the government's package of benefit and tax credit reform has enabled some people with impairments or long-term health conditions to take opportunities to work in ways that suit their capacity and the opportunities available to them. A number of different ways of trying work without loss of benefit are now allowed, indeed encouraged; with a raft of different measures for reducing financial risks. In-work financial support for people working at least 16 hours is now available through tax credits to more people than previously. Those who work fewer hours now have more opportunities for reaping financial rewards. For some people, the measures do enable moves towards paid work and help sustain work that is financially worthwhile.

It is difficult, however, from the evidence available, to quantify such impacts. There are some important gaps in information here, for example lack of tax credit take-up measures among disabled people.

Significant constraints within the benefits/tax credit system remain for some disabled people who must use these systems. In complex systems that interact and overlap, it is hard for people to understand their own position and the options available. People without access to informed advice or help, and those less able to use the technologies of the new information environment may face increasing disadvantage. Administrative errors and delays continue to affect what happens to people using benefits and tax credits. As regulatory systems become more complex and increasingly computerised, so citizens may need more help to access the systems, and face increasing risk of systems error or failure.

Structural aspects of means-tested in-work support mean that significant numbers of disabled people will still not be better off financially in work. It is very hard to eliminate poverty traps altogether from means-tested systems. Low take-up and administrative problems effectively increase the constraints or perverse incentives. In so far as disabled people experience such constraints, then policy effectiveness is also undermined.

Note

[1] The government introduced Incapacity Benefit reforms for new claimants in three pilot areas in 2003, and four more areas in 2004. Key features of the reforms include mandatory work-focused interviews in Jobcentre Plus, new specialist teams of Incapacity Benefit personal advisers and a package of interventions to support return to work.

References

Arthur, S. and Zarb, G. (1997) *Evaluation of the recent changes to disability working alllowance*, Social Research Branch In-house Report 25, London: DSS.

Arthur, S., Corden, A., Green, A., Lewis, J., Loumidis, J., Sainsbury, R., Stafford, B., Thornton, P. and Walker, R. (1999) *New Deal for Disabled People: Early implementation*, DSS Research Report 106, Leeds: Corporate Document Services (CDS).

Atkinson, J., Meager, N. and Dewson, S. (2003) *Evaluation of the Disabled Person's Tax Credit: A survey of recipients*, Inland Revenue Research Report 6, London: Inland Revenue.

Beatty, C. and Fothergill, S. (1999) *Incapacity Benefit and unemployment*, Sheffield: Centre for Regional Economic and Social Research, Sheffield Hallam University.

Berthoud, R. (1998) *Disability benefits: A review of the issues and options for reform*, York: Joseph Rowntree Foundation.

Beyer, S., Grove, B., Leach, S., O'Bryan, A. and Simons, K. (2000) *Ideas for developing supported employment*, Manchester: National Development Team.

Brown, J. (1984) *The disability income system*, London: Policy Studies Institute.

Corden, A. (1997) *Supported employment: People and money*, Social Policy Report 7, York: Social Policy Research Unit, University of York.

Corden, A. and Ellis, A. (2004) 'Volunteering and employability: Exploring the link for incapacity benefits recipients', *Benefits*, vol 40, no 12.2, pp 112-18.

Corden, A. and Sainsbury, R. (2001) *Incapacity benefits and work incentives*, DSS Research Report 141, Leeds: CDS.

Corden, A. and Sainsbury, R. (2003) *Evaluation of the Disabled Person's Tax Credit: Views and experiences of recipients*, Inland Revenue Research Report 5, London: Inland Revenue.

Corden, A., Harries, T., Hill, K., Kellard, K., Lewis, J., Sainsbury, R. and Thornton, P. (2003) *New Deal for Disabled People national extension: Findings from the first wave of qualitative research with clients, job brokers and Jobcentre Plus staff*, Sheffield: DWP and Pensions Research Management.

CPAG (Child Poverty Action Group) (1999) *Welfare rights bulletin*, 7–9 August, London: CPAG.

CPAG (2004) *Welfare rights bulletin*, 7–8 April, London: CPAG.

Davis, A. (1996) 'Users' perspectives and problems: what the research tells us', in G. Zarb (ed) *Social Security and mental health: Report on the SSAC workshop*, Social Security Advisory Committee Research Paper 7, London: HMSO, pp 24-34.

Davis Smith, J., Ellis, A., Howlett, S. and O'Brien, J. (2004) *Volunteering for all? Exploring the link between volunteering and social exclusion*, London: Institute for Volunteering Research.

Dewson, S., Davis, S. and Loukas, G. (2004) *A stepping-stone to employment? An evaluation of the Permitted Work Rules – Wave 2*, Brighton: Institute for Employment Studies.

Dorsett, R., Finlayson, L., Ford, R., Marsh, A., White, M. and Zarb, G. (1998) *Leaving Incapacity Benefit*, DSS Research Report 86, Leeds: CDS.

Drake, R.F. (2000) 'Disabled people, New Labour, benefits and work', *Critical Social Policy*, vol 20, no 4, pp 421-49.

DSS (Department of Social Security) (1998) *New ambitions for our country: A new contract for welfare*, Cm 3805, London: The Stationery Office (TSO).

DWP (Department for Work and Pensions) (2002) *Pathways to work: Helping people into employment*, Cm 5690, Norwich: TSO.

HM Treasury (2000) *Tackling poverty and making work pay – Tax credits for the 21st century*, (The Modernisation of Britain's Tax and Benefit System, no 6), London: HM Treasury.

HM Treasury (2002) *The Child and Working Tax Credit*, (The Modernisation of Britain's Tax and Benefit System, no 10), London: HM Treasury.

House of Commons (2004) *Inland Revenue: Tax credits*, House of Commons Committee of Public Accounts, Report of Session 2003/04, HC89.

Howard, M. (2002) *Not just the job*, York: Joseph Rowntree Foundation.

Iacovou, M. and Berthoud, R. (2000) *Parents and employment*, DSS Research Report 107, Leeds: CDS.

Inland Revenue (2004) *Child and Working Tax Credits quarterly statistics*, April, London: Inland Revenue.

Kemp, P. and Thornton, P. (forthcoming) 'Disguised unemployment? The growth in incapacity claims in Britain', in B. Bakker, P.A. Kemp and A. Sunden (eds) *Sick societies? Trends and disability benefits in post-industrial welfare states*, New Brunswick: Transaction Publishers.

Legard, R., Lewis, J., Hiscock, J. and Scott, J. (2002) *Evaluation of the Capability Report: Identifying the work-related capabilities of incapacity benefits claimants*, DWP Research Report 162, Leeds: CDS.

Loumidis, J., Stafford, B., Youngs, R., Green, A., Arthur, S., Legard, R., Lessof, C., Lewis, J., Walker, R., Corden, A., Thornton, P. and Sainsbury, R. (2001a) *Evaluation of the New Deal for Disabled People Personal Adviser Service pilot*, DSS Research Report 144, Leeds: CDS.

Loumidis, J., Youngs, R., Lessof, C. and Stafford, B. (2001b) *New Deal for Disabled People: National survey of incapacity benefits claimants*, DWP Research Report 160, Leeds: CDS.

Marsh, A. and McKay, S. (1993) *Families, work and benefits*, London: Policy Studies Institute.

O'Bryan, A., Simons, K., Beyer, S. and Grove, B. (2000) *A framework for supported employment*, York: Joseph Rowntree Foundation.

Ritchie, J., Ward, K. and Duldig, W. (1993) *GPs and Invalidity Benefit*, DSS Research Report 18, London: HMSO.

Rowlingson, K. and Berthoud, R. (1996) *Disability, benefits and employment*, DSS Research Report 54, London: TSO.

Sainsbury, R. and Corden, A. (2003) *Medical evidence and Incapacity Benefit appeals: Evaluation of a pilot study*, DWP In-house Report 129, London: Social Research Division, DWP.

Sainsbury, R., Corden, A. and Finch, N. (2003) *Medical evidence and Incapacity Benefit: Evaluation of a pilot study*, DWP Research Report 189, Leeds: CDS.

Shaw, I., Walker, R., Ashworth, K., Jenkins, S. and Middleton, S. (1996) *Moving off Income Support: Barriers and bridges*, DSS Research Report 53, London: HMSO.

Simons, K. (1998) *Home, work and inclusion: The social policy implications of supported living for people with learning difficulties*, York: Joseph Rowntree Foundation.

Thornton, P. (2000) 'Work for those who can, security for those who cannot? Welfare reform and disabled people', in H. Dean, R. Sykes and R. Woods (eds) *Social Policy Review 12*, Bristol: The Policy Press, pp 112-32.

Waddell, G., Aylward, M. and Sawney, P. (2002) *Back pain, incapacity for work and Social Security benefits*, London: Royal Society of Medicine Press.

NINE

Challenging the disability benefit trap across the OECD

Mark Pearson and Christopher Prinz[1]

Introduction

Increasingly, disability benefits have become a trap for potential recipients who, once on benefit, typically stay there until retirement age. They are equally a trap for policy makers, who face – and, by and large, have failed to address – a choice between spending both political and financial capital in reforming what in nearly every country are patently seriously flawed policies, or 'letting sleeping dogs lie'. Unfortunately, there appear to be few votes to be gained by reforming disability policies. Only when policy begins to collapse under the weight of its own contradictions do governments summon up the courage to introduce change. And these contradictions are legion: a policy designed for permanent disability having to cope with medical conditions which may be temporary; a benefit policy designed for those who cannot work yet in practice many or most recipients wish to work, and so on.

This chapter briefly describes the magnitude of the dilemma across the Organisation for Economic Co-operation and Development (OECD), arguing that current policies are both expensive and yet fail to achieve satisfactory outcomes for people with disabilities themselves. It then discusses the primary causes driving current outcomes. Subsequently, it looks at disability policy trends in OECD countries since around the mid-1980s before turning to some very general policy conclusions. The chapter heavily relies on a 20-country comparative analysis published in early 2003 (OECD, 2003). The chapter concludes that no other area of social policy has been as ineffective in meeting the new challenges and in achieving its stated objectives as disability policy.

The first problem: growing levels of benefit receipt

At the turn of the 21st century, incapacity-related public cash spending across the OECD was as high as 2.3% of GDP, 2.6 times higher than unemployment-related spending (Figure 9.1). Only in Denmark was the latter higher than the former, and in Belgium, France and Canada cash spending on the two programmes was at the same level. In several countries, on the contrary, including the Czech Republic, Hungary, Iceland, Norway, Switzerland and the UK, incapacity-related cash spending was six to 12 times higher than unemployment-related cash spending[2]. In the light of this, the strong focus of social policy and research on unemployment rather than disability issues seems unjustified. There is an increasingly pressing need to move to address the problems of the present and future, not those of the past.

Accordingly, a large proportion of the population relies on disability benefits, typically 6% of the working-age population, but close to 9% in Nordic countries and the Netherlands and more than 10% in Poland (Figure 9.2). There is also significant cross-country difference in the composition of benefit recipients as to the nature of benefits (contributory, earnings-related insurance benefit or non-contributory, flat-rate benefit, with or without means-testing). The UK is very close

Figure 9.1: Public incapacity- and unemployment-related social expenditure (2001)

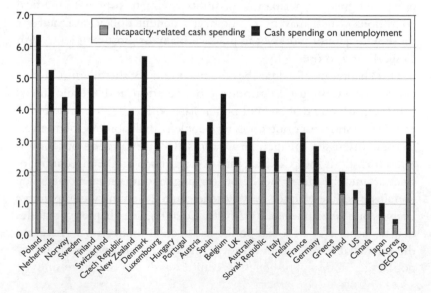

Source: OECD (2004)

Figure 9.2: Disability benefit recipiency rates (% of age group 20-64) (1999)

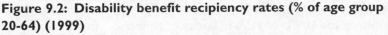

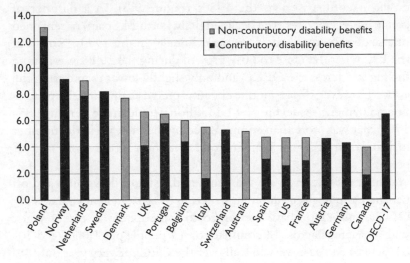

Source: OECD (2003)

to the OECD average in terms of both incapacity-related public expenditure and disability benefit receipt as a share of the working-age population.

Cross-country variation in disability benefit receipt is essentially explained by three factors:

- differences in the share of the population with reduced work capacity (see Figure 9.9 for an estimate on self-assessed disability);
- differences in the design of the disability benefit programme itself (see Figure 9.8);
- differences in the role of disability benefits within the entire social protection system.

The last point is particularly important. Comparing disability benefit programmes without looking at other social protection programmes is insufficient, because people with reduced work capacity will be found on other benefits to a degree which varies sharply across countries. This is particularly true for early retirement programmes, and to a lesser extent also for unemployment and social assistance schemes[3].

Changes in disability benefit receipt growth can therefore only be assessed fully in combination with information on trends in other, partly competing partly complementary, benefit programmes. From a cross-country angle, disability benefit receipt rates have continued to grow over the 1990s, but in a majority of countries growth has slowed down in comparison to the 1980s (Figure 9.3). In a number of countries, receipt rates even declined (Italy, Portugal, Spain) or remained unchanged (Netherlands, Denmark, France) in the 1990s. Not so in the UK, where, at close to 60%, growth during the 1990s was among the highest across the OECD and only slightly lower than during the 1980s. However, this result must be interpreted against the steep fall in unemployment – a decline (by 1.1 million people in the period 1985-1999) that was more than compensated by the increase in the number of people on disability benefits (of 1.3 million in the same 14-year period).

Benefit receipt levels are the combined result of flows onto and off benefit. Despite a very different structure by age and gender across the OECD, *inflow* rates have converged to some extent in recent years, with an average across 18 countries of 6.7 people per 1,000 aged 20-64. Benefit *outflow* is very low all over the OECD. Every year only 1% of the stock of benefit recipients leaves disability benefit due to recovery or work resumption. Disability benefit receipt is pretty much a life sentence. The UK is an exception in this regard, with much higher rates of inflow as well as outflow than elsewhere. The resulting higher turnover in the UK implies that disability benefits are less of a trap (outflow rates stand at around 5% annually), but also that a much larger group of the population is at risk of long-term benefit receipt if

Figure 9.3: Disability benefit recipiency growth in the 1980s and 1990s (% change)

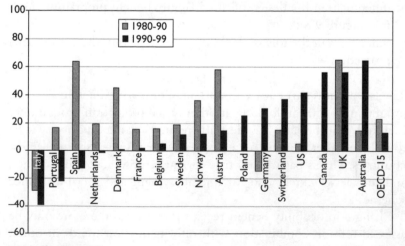

Source: OECD (2003)

policy goes wrong. The exceptional position of the UK can be explained by a combination of factors, including a different split between sickness and disability, with a larger share of people with temporary incapacity on disability benefits.

The second problem: exclusion

If outcomes for people with disabilities were adequate, maybe policy makers and ultimately taxpayers and voters, would accept the high levels of expenditure and growing rates of benefit receipt described earlier in this chapter. However, it is difficult to argue that this is the case. Rather than come up with a long list of indicators of the quality of life of people with disabilities, this section focuses on the two main outcomes which policy is attempting to attain: achievement of an adequate income, and social integration.

Comparing the absolute level of income across countries is rarely free of problems, and so in an international context, it is preferable to look at the income of people with disabilities relative to those without. Figure 9.4 suggests that in a majority of countries the economic status of those with disabilities is little different from the population as a

Figure 9.4: Relative average income of disabled and non-disabled people: Equivalised income of households with a disabled person relative to households with no disabled person, and personal income of persons with a disability relative to those without a disability (late 1990s)

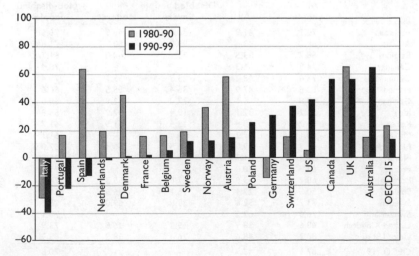

Source: OECD (2003)

whole, though the same cannot be claimed of, for example, the UK and the US.

Of course, such averages hide an underlying variation that may be of concern. No information is available on a cross-national basis that gives poverty rates of people with disabilities, for example. Furthermore, some groups may be particularly disadvantaged, such as those with 'severe disabilities'.

A high level of economic well-being can be achieved through high levels of benefits or high levels of employment. The position of different OECD countries in Figure 9.4 suggests that benefit systems play a crucial role. Countries with earnings-related disability benefits with high replacement rates are found at the top, while those where means-tested benefits are important are found at the bottom. In turn, this finding could indicate that employment rates are low or that income from work is relatively low, or both. The Organisation for Economic Co-operation and Development (2003) concluded that low employment rates are the key problem, not low earnings for those disabled people who are in work.

Employment is not synonymous with social integration, but it comes close, generally ensuring social interaction and social status. While it is possible to think of exceptions, in general higher employment of people with disabilities means that their social situation has improved, in addition to the probable improvement in their financial situation. Table

Table 9.1: Employment rates of OECD disabled and non-disabled people aged 20-64 years by severity of disability (late 1990s)

	All people	Disabled people All	Disabled people Severe	Disabled people Moderate	Non-disabled people
Australia	72.1	41.9	31.4	46.9	76.6
Austria	68.1	43.4	23.9	50.2	71.8
Belgium	58.7	33.5	21.1	40.0	61.7
Canada	74.9	56.3	–	–	78.4
Denmark	73.6	48.2	23.3	55.1	79.4
France	63.6	47.9	36.4	55.5	66.6
Germany	64.8	46.1	27.0	52.9	69.0
Italy	52.2	32.1	19.4	37.9	53.8
Korea	61.2	45.9	13.4	51.5	61.7
Mexico	60.1	47.2	–	–	61.1
Netherlands	61.9	39.9	26.5	46.4	67.0
Norway	81.4	61.7	–	–	85.8
Poland	63.9	20.8	–	–	71.2
Portugal	68.2	43.9	27.6	55.3	74.0
Spain	50.5	22.1	15.1	26.5	54.2
Sweden	73.7	52.6	33.8	69.0	75.8
Switzerland	76.6	62.2	–	–	79.1
United Kingdom	68.6	38.9	19.3	46.8	73.9
United States	80.2	48.6	26.4	58.8	83.9
OECD (19)	67.1	43.9	–	–	70.8

Source: OECD (2003)

9.1 shows the employment rates of people with disabilities. These generally are clustered between 40% and 50%, with high rates in Canada, Norway and Switzerland[4]. The UK does somewhat poorly, though Belgium, Italy, Spain and Poland have a worse record[4].

While the absolute employment rate of people with disabilities is the target of policy, it is arguable that it can give a misleading view of the impact of *disability policy*. After all, the top performers listed in Table 9.1 have high employment rates in the population as a whole, whereas most of those performing poorly have relatively low employment rates. One lesson might be that healthy labour markets more generally also benefit those with disabilities. However, it may also be revealing to look at *relative* employment levels, which may tell us something about the effectiveness of disability policy. In the late 1990s, across 19 OECD countries employment rates of disabled people were, on average, as much as 40% below those of their non-disabled peers, with large differences by severity of disability (Figure 9.5). At that time, the UK performance (in terms of relative employment rates) was significantly below OECD average, especially among people severely hampered by their health problem. Switzerland was the top-performing country for all disabled persons taken together; France for those with a 'severe disability'; and Sweden for those with a 'moderate disability'. Poland, followed by Spain, showed by far the poorest outcome on that indicator.

Figure 9.5: Relative employment rates of disabled persons aged 20-64 years and non-disabled persons by severity of disability (where available, late 1990s)

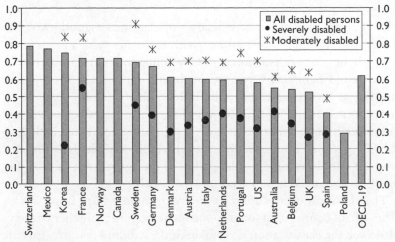

Source: OECD (2003)

Understanding the issue

Despite large cross-country variation, disability benefits have become a key challenge for policy makers in virtually all OECD countries. In terms of problems underlying the process, three groups of countries can be distinguished:

1. *Countries in which disability benefits have become the benefit of last resort.* In these countries, typically unemployment rates are low. Social policies in recent years are characterised by an increasing focus on work-testing in the unemployment and/or the social assistance programme. Pathways into early retirement have also often been closed off. The result is increasing pressure on the disability benefit programme. Lacking comprehensive reform of the latter, disability benefit receipt has increased significantly over the 1990s. Australia, the UK, the US and Switzerland all belong to this group of countries.
2. *Countries in which disability benefits have become an early retirement pathway, be it instead of, or in addition to, other early retirement options.* In these countries, in particular, ongoing and further pension reforms, especially those affecting access to early retirement, will lead to increasing pressure on the disability benefit scheme. Austria, Portugal, Sweden, Denmark and Germany are examples of that group.
3. *Countries in which disability benefits serve as a benefit of last resort and as an early retirement pathway.* Norway, Poland and the Netherlands belong to this group, and as a result have the highest rates of disability benefit receipt in the OECD.

The age structure of the beneficiary population is a good proxy for the classification into these groups, with countries with a particularly young beneficiary population generally falling into Group 1 and those with an old beneficiary population into Group 2 (Figure 9.6). In Austria, as an extreme example, inflow into disability benefits is concentrated at age 50-60, with very low receipt rates below this age group but high receipt rates at ages 55+. In other countries, including the UK, on the contrary, inflow into disability benefits is as high for younger people as it is for older people, if the age pattern of disability prevalence was taken into account (see OECD, 2003).

The classification of countries to any of these groups is not always clear-cut, of course, with some countries belonging to neither of them. However, the classification is useful in understanding country-specific reform needs. In all three cases, the *permanent* nature of disability benefits

Figure 9.6: Age-specific disability benefit recipiency rates (per 1,000 of population) (1999)

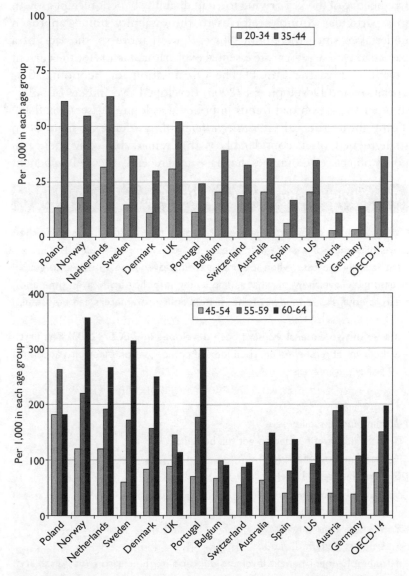

Source: OECD (2003)

is a key problem – and obviously particularly so in those countries belonging to Groups 1 and 3, because potential alternative social benefits for younger workers are not intrinsically of a permanent nature. In these countries in particular, long-term disability benefit dependence needs to be addressed.

Policy trends

Irrespective of the key driving force in disability benefit receipt growth in a particular country, reforms to the disability policy approach undertaken since the mid-1980s and, even more so, the lack of a particular type of reform are essential explanatory factors for the current situation across the OECD. The Organisation for Economic Co-operation and Development (2003) developed two indices of policy in order to assess broad trends in policy development (see Box 9.1). Throughout the OECD, *integration* policy elements have been strengthened, often considerably, with a remarkable convergence in policy objectives. Countries that have until recently focused on benefit

---

Box 9.1: Assessing complex policy trends

With so many different dimensions of policy that matter in assessing the overall stance of a system, it is easy to get swamped in details. This is particularly the case when looking at trends over time. In order to get a reasonable overview of what is happening in policy both over time and across countries, an index of the various policy parameters can be useful.

Indices in two dimensions have been developed in OECD (2003). The first is the level of *compensation*. The index of compensation takes into account 10 policy parameters:

1. coverage;
2. minimum disability level;
3. disability level needed to get full benefit;
4. maximum benefit level;
5. permanence of benefit;
6. medical assessment;
7. vocational assessment;
8. sickness benefit level;
9. sickness benefit duration;
10. unemployment benefit level and duration in comparison with disability benefits.

Each country is ranked on a scale of 0-5 on each of these categories. No attempt is made to assess which of these categories is most important; all have equal rate. A country which has a high total score in the *compensation* dimension is 'generous' in supporting people with disabilities who are not working.

The second dimension is that of *integration*. Again, ten sub-dimensions are taken into account:

1. access to different programmes;
2. consistency of assessment structure;
3. employer responsibility;
4. supported employment programmes;
5. subsidised employment programmes;
6. sheltered employment sector;
7. vocational rehabilitation programmes;
8. timing of rehabilitation;
9. benefit suspension regulations;
10. work incentives.

As with the compensation dimension, each of these sub-dimensions is rated 0-5. A country which has a higher *integration* score is one which has a more active policy in ensuring that people with disabilities can find work.

Details of the points attached to each aspect of policy and the policy stance each country takes can be found in OECD (2003).

payments alone are in the process of implementing a range of employment-related schemes. For instance, hitherto-unknown vocational rehabilitation programmes were introduced in the Netherlands and the UK. Many countries (first in the English-speaking world, but more recently followed by many European countries) have introduced anti discrimination legislation, thereby increasing employers' responsibilities towards people with disabilities. Countries with a more developed integration focus (such as Germany and the Nordic countries) have further strengthened their employment promotion strategy, for instance by streamlining administration and establishing a one-stop-shop philosophy. Countries with gradually maturing public programmes for people with disabilities, such as Korea, Portugal and Spain, have taken other countries' experiences into account and are building their disability policy on a balanced mix of employment-oriented and transfer policies. On average, across 20 countries, OECD (2003) estimated a remarkable ten-point increase on the 50-points integration policy dimension over the 15-year period from 1985 to 2000 (Figure 9.7). The UK ranks 4th in terms of change, raising its position from the 13th to the 8th rank on that dimension.

This activation policy contrasts with a relative lack of reform on the

Figure 9.7: Policy shifts along the two identified policy dimensions (1985-2000)

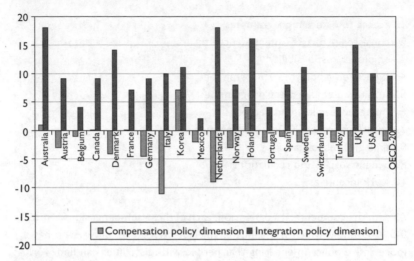

Source: OECD (2003)

compensation policy dimension. While employment-related programmes have seen significant expansion in most OECD countries, benefit programmes have remained virtually unchanged in most cases. Only two countries, Italy (already in the mid-1980s) and the Netherlands (in the mid-1990s) have gone through substantial benefit reforms. In both cases, an extraordinarily high disability benefit receipt level (of around 13% in Italy at that time, and more than 12% in the Netherlands) drove change and reform was broadly characterised by a shift from permanent to temporary benefits, an abolition of own occupation assessment and some sort of reduction in benefit levels. In both cases, effects were quite striking, especially in the case of Italy, which since then fell from the top to an average position in terms of benefit receipt levels. Elsewhere, the general trend has been to reduce the level of compensation, albeit only marginally.

In principle, there is nothing wrong with a policy stance that increases the integration focus of disability policy, without substantially changing the compensation package. In practice, there are dangers in following such an approach. Other benefits (unemployment, social assistance, early retirement) have often become less generous, usually by restricting access rather than by reducing benefit levels. The absence of any such reforms in disability benefit means that it stands out all the more as being the 'dustbin' benefit, to which those who do not wish to work or those who benefit officers despair of activating gravitate. This undermines the more positive, integrationist focus that governments have been trying to follow and which is in the interests of the majority of those on the benefit.

These effects are particularly worrisome in view of the fact that cross-country analysis identified generous disability benefit levels (generosity measured in relation to both previous earnings and levels of competing benefits) and easy access to disability benefits as the key parameters explaining cross-country variation in receipt levels (Figure 9.8). Without making disability benefits less 'attractive' relative to other benefits, better and more effective integration measures will struggle to make much impact.

Policy visions

Correlations such as that given in Figure 9.8 suggest that institutional parameters are central to levels of disability benefit receipt across countries and trends within them: policy matters. In the face of unchanged policy, there is reason to believe that disability benefit receipt

Figure 9.8: 'Generosity' of disability benefits and ease of access are strongly related with disability benefit recipiency levels

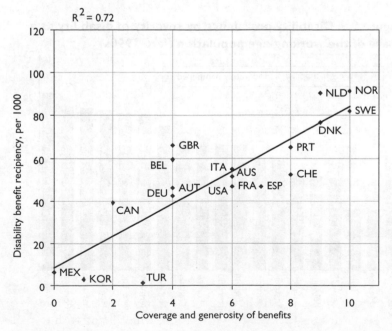

Source: OECD (2003)

will continue to rise over coming years, and that employment rates of people with reduced work capacity will remain low.

First, many countries are still in the process of making other benefit programmes more stringent and several of the reforms already implemented (especially those affecting retirement programmes) will take some years before they attain their full impact. Second, demands at work, especially psychological demands, are likely to increase further. This is reflected in rapidly increasing numbers of people who are granted disability benefits on grounds of mental ill-health, predominantly stress-related diseases. Third, because of demographic ageing, a higher proportion of the population will be in the age groups with greatest risk of disability in the next few decades. Already in the late 1990s, disability prevalence among working-age people across the OECD fluctuated around 14% (as much as 18% in the UK) (see Figure 9.9)[6] with increases over time in many countries.

Finally, in a majority of OECD countries the number of people applying for disability benefits has been increasing more rapidly than the actual inflow onto such benefits. This increase in benefit rejection rates (see OECD, 2003) is also an indicator of future upward pressure on the disability benefit caseload. It has been shown in some countries that rejected disability benefit applicants (and also those removed from the rolls in the course of re-testing of the stock of beneficiaries) are

Figure 9.9: Disability prevalence by severity of disability as a share of the working-age population (late 1990s)

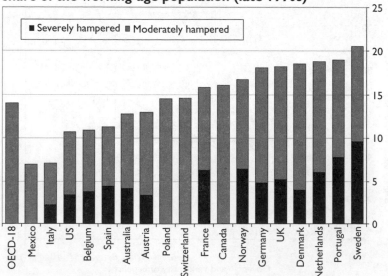

Source: OECD (2003)

highly likely to reapply at a later stage, often without any periods of work in between and with no further change in health status, and that they eventually end up on disability benefits in large numbers.

Reducing disability benefit receipt is only one target for policy, of course. An overly restrictive policy, which denied benefit to those in need, would be an unacceptable outcome. Still, no one should be sanguine about a continued rise in disability benefit receipt that could, if unchecked, undermine public support for an effective compensation package for those in need. High and increasing disability benefit receipt will hold back any significant growth in employment rates of people with reduced work capacity.

As in other areas of social policy, the challenge for the future is to transform the disability benefit scheme from a passive benefit programme into a *flexible labour market programme*. In this context, it will be important to make cash benefits a flexible in-work tool which covers the labour market disadvantage of persons with reduced work capacity, rather than merely providing static and permanent out-of-work income. Work must pay under all circumstances so to raise work incentives. At the same time, active support to find work and to make (or keep) people employable will require a more individualised and tailor-made approach. It will also be necessary to intervene earlier so to keep work motivation high and avoid unnecessary labour market interruption, if not exit. But such an approach can be costly and needs to be monitored vigilantly.

A particularly important and potentially controversial element in such a strategy is the introduction of *mutual obligations*, as have been successfully implemented in other transfer programmes. To make a real difference to the work prospects of people with disabilities, society will sometimes have to accept that it is necessary to put more resources into helping people than it currently does. If it does so, however, it is only fair to expect more from persons with reduced work capacity themselves. This is necessary not only to ensure political support for increased investment in activation measures, but also because such an approach has been shown to change the attitudes of both benefit recipients and those managing the benefit caseload.

There is a strong case for applying active measures on the basis of mutual responsibility for those with disabilities *before* they flow onto benefit, as well as to those in receipt of benefit. One reason for believing this to be a good approach is that, as noted above, outflow in most OECD countries off benefit into employment is virtually non-existent. Several countries apply a 'rehabilitation-before-pension' principle, implying that only in those cases where reintegration efforts have failed should a disability benefit be granted[7]. In combination with a reform of the benefit scheme along the lines outlined earlier in this chapter, such an approach is promising. Even for those who do have recourse to disability benefit, the case for actively pursuing work – as the recipient usually wants – is strong. In combination with individualised, tailor-made activation programmes, a framework of mutual obligations could also be applied to many of the stock of beneficiaries. In this case, recent (and in many cases quite successful) unemployment benefit and welfare or social assistance reform in several countries can provide useful policy blueprints.

Conclusion

There is arguably no other area of social policy where policy has been as ineffective in achieving its goals as disability. Income levels of households in which people with disabilities are present are below those of the rest of the population, though it is true that in many countries they are not significantly lower. However, the major failing of policy is the inability to support work by those with disabilities. There is little doubt that people on disability benefit wish to work. Governments express their view that they would like more people with disabilities to work. The fact that in reality, only 1% of the caseload exits each year to a job is a tragedy for those who never have a chance to fulfil their potential, and to society, with increasing expenditures and loss of potential labour supply being the price of policy failure.

Notes

[1] The views expressed here are those of the authors and do not represent those of the OECD or its member countries.

[2] There are various ways in which these figures can be disputed. In particular, some part of spending on social assistance and on housing benefits goes to people whose incomes are low either because of unemployment or because of some health problem. Perhaps if it were possible to add such expenditures to the totals for unemployment and disability-related spending, the ratio of the latter to the former would fall somewhat, but certainly not by enough to change conclusions on the nature of the relationship. Furthermore, employers and charitable organisations sometimes may have expenditures that in other countries fall on the public purse. We are some way from being able to measure

the total resources which society devotes to meeting the needs, broadly defined, of people with disabilities.

[3] Differences in disability benefit receipt rates are also influenced by differences in the statutory retirement age, which is still below 65 years in several countries (especially for women). Identifiable disabled persons on social assistance schemes are included in Figure 9.2. For further issues regarding cross-country comparability of benefit receipt rates, see OECD (2003).

[4] Data comparability is an issue that has to be kept in mind. Country-specific results in Table 9.1 are estimated from different national population surveys (it is only for EU countries that the same data source could be used), which use somewhat differing definitions of disability and partly also of employment. Added to this are cultural variations in the perception of disability.

[5] United Kingdom numbers in Table 9.1 and Figure 9.5 are based on European Community Household Panel data for the year 1996. Recent Labour Force Survey data show an increase in employment rates by five percentage points in the last five years. Accordingly, employment rates of disabled people are likely to be around OECD average today.

[6] Disability prevalence in Figure 9.9 is self-assessed and defined as a long-term physical or mental health problem, illness or disability that hampers a person in activities of daily living.

[7] However, this general principle is often not applied with the same vigour for older workers with reduced work capacity. People aged 45+ tend to receive vocational training or rehabilitation with much lower likelihood than prime-age workers (see OECD, 2003).

Reference

OECD (Organisation for Economic Co-operation and Development) (2003) *Transforming disability into ability – Policies to promote work and income security for disabled people*, Paris: OECD.

OECD (2004) *Social expenditure database*, Paris: OECD.

TEN

Jobcentre Plus: can specialised personal advisers be justified?

Patricia Thornton

Government has embraced the concept of personal advisers providing individually tailored advice and support to benefit claimants. Recent years have witnessed a move towards such personalised support not just in its flagship New Deals but also in the mandatory 'work-focused interview' regime for new claimants. In the latter, there has been a pronounced shift towards specialist advisers working with claimants of incapacity benefits while there has been no special focus on people with health problems or impairments in the mainstream New Deals. The move towards specialism is contrary to the position of the government's advisory committee for disabled people in employment and training that specialist provision labels people as different and in need of special handling (ACDET, 2001) and in opposition to the principles underpinning the EC's mainstreaming policy.

This chapter examines the research evidence to consider the case for specialist advisers. It draws on the views and experiences reported by incapacity benefits claimants and personal advisers involved in the work-focused interview process and by participants and advisers in the New Deal programmes. Views on process are insufficient evidence from which to reach conclusions on the comparative effectiveness of specialist and mainstream approaches, and thus where evidence is available the outcomes of programmes are taken into account in weighing the arguments.

Jobcentre Plus and deployment of personal advisers

Jobcentre Plus is a central plank of the government's strategy for welfare reform. It provides a single point of delivery for jobs and benefits support for people of working-age. Its formation brought together within the Department for Work and Pensions (DWP) the former Employment Service and the parts of the former Benefits Agency that dealt with social security benefits for people of working-age, both agencies previously having been under the auspices of separate departments. Jobcentre Plus 'Pathfinder' offices were established between October 2001 and January 2002 in 56 sites. The second stage of rollout began in October 2002, and national coverage will be complete by end 2006.

The central delivery feature is the work-focused interview (WFI) that intends that people making fresh claims for working-age benefits should consider work as an option. This, of course, has long been the case for unemployed claimants of Jobseeker's Allowance but in the integrated Jobcentre Plus offices new and repeat claimants of so-called inactive benefits are required to take part in a WFI with a personal adviser as a condition of receiving benefit. The purposes of the interview are to engage people in a discussion about work prospects, experience, skills and barriers to work and how best to tackle them, and to encourage them to take up ongoing help towards work such as through the New Deal programmes or training. Personal advisers may also support job search, liaise with employers, pull in support from other agencies and calculate the financial effects of moving from benefit to employment. It was announced in December 2004 that across the country all new incapacity benefits claimants would be required to attend a WFI from October 2005 (DWP, 2004a).

In addition to having to master both benefits and employment provision in a new system bringing together two cultures, personal advisers have met challenges in dealing with incapacity benefits claimants. Government-sponsored research on the Jobcentre Plus Pathfinders and on 'ONE', which piloted the work-focused approach, found that personal advisers, who typically dealt with several benefit groups, failed to engage with claimants of incapacity benefits. The research evidence is detailed later in the chapter but briefly their difficulties appeared to derive from a lack of confidence in their ability to talk about work with disabled people or people with health problems. The 'solution' has been a move towards personal advisers who specialise in working with incapacity benefits claimants, although there was at first some room for discretion at district level in whether staff were deployed as incapacity benefits specialist personal advisers.

The DWP embraced an unequivocally specialist approach in its Pathways to Work pilots designed for new incapacity benefits claimants. The move towards recruiting and training specialist incapacity benefit advisers was supported by the results of a public consultation on the Green Paper, *Pathways to work* (Secretary of State for Work and Pensions, 2002): nine out of 10 of the 87 organisations and individuals responding agreed that there was a need to develop a set of specialist personal advisers for incapacity benefits clients (Secretary of State for Work and Pensions, 2003). These pilots in seven districts, which began in October 2003 and April 2004, extended the WFI approach. It was made compulsory to attend a series of six monthly work-related interviews with a personal adviser from eight weeks after the benefit claim and to complete an action plan.

Despite the absence of evaluation evidence on the effectiveness of the specialist approach in the Pathways to Work pilots, it was announced in early December 2004, eight months after the second wave of pilots was launched, that the scheme would be extended to a further 14 Jobcentre Plus districts in Great Britain, thus covering "a third of the country" (DWP, 2004a). The existing pilots were to continue and increasingly provide support for longer-term claimants. It also was announced that by 2006 every Jobcentre Plus district would have specialist advisers for people on incapacity benefits.

This rush towards specialist advisers for incapacity benefits claimants is at odds with the mainstreaming approach in the New Deal programmes. Since 1997, a family of New Deal programmes has been rolled out for long-term unemployed benefit recipients, lone parents, people aged 50 plus, and dependent partners of benefit recipients. These New Deals feature a case-management approach with a personal adviser but there is little specialist working with disabled people or people with health problems taking part. The New Deal for Disabled People (see Chapter Three of this volume) is unusual among Jobcentre Plus programmes in that the case management function is carried out entirely by staff working within the contracted job broker organisations, and is not considered in this chapter.

The non-specialist tendency in the New Deals is remarkable given that participants may include recipients of incapacity benefits, in the case of the New Deal for Lone Parents (NDLP), New Deal 50 Plus and New Deal for Partners, and otherwise people who meet the 1995 Disability Discrimination Act (DDA) definition of disability. Almost one in three of those starting the mandatory New Deal 25 Plus for long-term unemployed job seekers between April 2001 and December 2003 were self-defined as DDA disabled. However, up to December 2003, the proportion starting the mandatory New Deal for Young People (NDYP) stood at only 12% (Bivand, 2004). Rates of disabled participants based on self-definitions, which are then entered on administrative records, are not necessarily reliable. The NDLP administrative data at September 2002 showed that only 3.6% of lone parents starting were disabled (Thornton, 2003). Yet, while the findings are not strictly comparable, almost one in four of respondents to a survey of lone parents attending a mandatory series of meeting with a personal adviser said they had a long-standing illness, condition or disability (Coleman et al, 2002). In the New Deal 50 Plus, around one third of participants surveyed had a 'health problem or disability' that affected their ability to work (Atkinson, 2001a). Prevalence of disability in the New Deal for Partners is expected to be very high, given that two-thirds of men and one half of women in workless households have a long-term health problem or disability (Bonjour and Dorsett, 2002).

Work-focused interviews

The ONE pilots

Combining delivery of benefits to people of working-age with work-related advice was tested in the 'ONE' pilots, introduced in 1999. ONE brought together the then Employment Service and Benefits Agency in 12 pilot areas in Great Britain in what was a highly ambitious attempt to refashion work and welfare. The personal adviser model, developed through the New Deal programmes, was at the heart of ONE with an expansion of personalised services to new claimants of inactive benefits (mainly claimants of the three main incapacity benefits and lone parents claiming income support) as well as to unemployed people claiming Jobseeker's Allowance. In April 2000 voluntary participation for applicants for inactive benefits was dropped and they were required to attend a first meeting with a personal adviser as a condition of receiving benefit unless in special circumstances, such as being terminally ill, when the requirement was waived. The ONE pilots were subject to extensive evaluation. The evaluation findings are summarised by Osgood et al (2003) and other reports are referenced here.

The evaluation found that some advisers were not confident about tackling work issues in any depth with people with long-term illnesses, felt trepidation at the prospect of discussing work with some clients on inactive benefits or felt ill-equipped to deal with people with emotional or social problems. There were strong convictions that people on incapacity benefits had been classed unfit for work, and influences on how much advisers discussed work included assumptions that people would need very intensive support on personal and work-related matters (Legard et al, 2002). There was some evidence that personal advisers felt they did not always have the skills to address complex benefit issues or to explore how far people's individual circumstances affected their ability to work. Personal advisers felt they lacked information on specialist community resources to refer people to.

When asked, there was considerable support among incapacity benefits clients in qualitative studies (Osgood et al, 2002) for involving specialist advisers or referral to specialist services, assumed to be more knowledgeable and helpful than personal advisers. However, most people interviewed were previously not aware of these options until they were raised by the interviewer. People who had been referred to a Disability Employment Adviser (a long-standing specialist role) appreciated their knowledge on rights and entitlements and felt this was the right person for the adviser role.

Final results on the labour market impact show that ONE had no discernable effect in increasing employment, and this was true of all three main client groups (Green et al, 2003). There was no effect on incapacity benefits clients in looking for work, nor any evidence of the pilots moving incapacity benefits clients on to Jobseeker's Allowance for unemployed people. Evidence from analysis of administrative benefit records did not suggest that ONE changed the probability of leaving benefit for incapacity benefits recipients (Kirby and Riley, 2003).

In 2002, the House of Commons Work and Pensions Committee report of its enquiry into ONE identified the 'failure of personal advisers to engage with incapacity benefits clients' as a 'major shortcoming' of the pilots (House of Commons Work and Pensions Committee, 2002).

Jobcentre Plus Pathfinders and second stage roll out

Despite the lack of supportive research evidence from ONE, the decision was taken to roll out integrated work advice and benefits administration in the shape of the Jobcentre Plus Pathfinders.

The early evaluations (Lissenburgh and Marsh, 2003) identified problems in serving incapacity benefits claimants similar to those met in ONE. Personal advisers conducting work-focused interviews did not want to cause upset by introducing the topic of work and assumed that incapacity benefits clients were not interested in or able to work. They were particularly anxious about discussing work with people with mental health problems and about asking personal questions about conditions. Only those clients who were thought to be interested in work and more motivated had a work focus to their interview. Otherwise there was little or no probing of barriers to work or clients' relationship with the labour market.

Later small-scale qualitative research with Jobcentre Plus staff that dealt with incapacity benefits claimants, designed to inform the

Pathways to Work pilots, demonstrated that such problems remained (Goldstone and Douglas, 2003). One conclusion from this research was the need for a significant amount of training if personal advisers were to engage effectively with incapacity benefits recipients. Particular difficulties identified by Jobcentre Plus staff in a further study were reluctance to probe into details of their clients' illnesses and their lack of medical knowledge, which they felt made it hard for them to understand how certain illnesses would affect clients (Taylor and Hartfree, 2003).

Although personal advisers saw their role as giving information and signposting people to specialist services, they felt they lacked the knowledge to do so effectively (Lissenburgh and Marsh, 2003; Taylor and Hartfree, 2003). The research by Goldstone and Douglas (2003) found benefits in staff tapping into 'semi-specialist' personal advisers, who dealt with all types of claimant but had additional training or experience in working with disabled people. It found some resistance amongst personal advisers to specialising in working with incapacity benefits claimants.

The views of participants in the Jobcentre Plus WFI regime are found in the report of a representative survey in the second stage of the Jobcentre Plus roll out (Coleman et al, 2004). It is not known whether the adviser was specialist or not. The work-related purpose of the WFI meeting was perceived by incapacity benefits claimants to have been communicated well, work-related topics usually were discussed, and the advice given was considered helpful. On the other hand, only one in five said the advice made them more motivated to find a job and a similar proportion said it had increased their confidence. Reported offers and take up of voluntary follow-up meetings were very limited, and there was little desire for further contact.

There are at the time of writing no published reports on the impact of the WFI regime in terms of movement off benefit or into employment.

Pathways to Work pilots

In the Pathways to Work pilots there was a marked shift towards specialism. Personal advisers were specially recruited and trained to work with claimants who are disabled or have ill-health conditions. Unless exempted because they had the most severe functional limitations or are assessed as least likely to need additional help, new incapacity benefits claimants were required, following the first mandatory interview, to take part in a further five meetings with a personal adviser at roughly monthly intervals. Other features of the pilots were work-focused 'condition management' programmes developed jointly with local NHS providers, a menu of support options to choose from and a 52-week payment of £40 per week on return to work for people with gross earnings of less than £15,000.

An evaluation is under way. The first two published qualitative studies related to the first three pilot areas. In small-scale, early research, staff felt training in interview techniques had helped them to find appropriate ways of raising work and having a supportive role but that they had insufficient understanding of services available to clients (Dickens et al, 2004a). Using the computer-based tool to screen out claimants who would not benefit from the pilot meant putting people into health categories, which challenged personal advisers confidence and medical knowledge (Dickens et al, 2004a). The second study, with more experienced staff, found concerns about working with people with mental health problems including worries about personal responsibility for any negative impacts (Dickens et al, 2004b).

Early evidence of outcomes from the Pathways to Work pilots, drawn from administrative data, indicated that take up of practical services to get back to work, recorded job entries and flows off incapacity benefits were higher in the pilot areas than in non-pilot areas (Hansard, 2004; DWP, 2004b). As yet, it is not known which elements, or interactions of elements, contributed to these outcomes. Given the rapid spread of specialist incapacity benefits personal advisers throughout the country, it seems that evaluations cannot compare outcomes for those who underwent WFIs with specialist advisers compared with those who did not.

New Deal programmes

There are strong indications from research on the New Deal programmes that participants did not see ill-health or disability as the main barrier to employment and that other barriers were more salient. Child-related and financial barriers and lack of skills and confidence were more important barriers to NDLP participants than ill-health or disability (Coleman et al, 2002). While the evaluation reports of the voluntary New Deal 50 Plus refer to the limiting effects that ill-health or impairment could have on the jobs people were able to consider, ageism on the part of employers comes across as the most significant barrier older people face in the labour market (Atkinson et al, 2000; Kodz and Eccles, 2001).

Nevertheless, early findings on the NDLP indicated that participants sometimes saw health conditions and disabilities as limiting the range of job options, and there was a suggestion that specialist help with changing direction to a career that would accommodate their condition would have been useful (Dawson et al, 2000). A survey found little recall of talk about special help or services at mandatory adviser meetings among the one in four who said they had a health problem or disability, and it was unusual to be referred to any specialist scheme (Coleman et al, 2002). It was not reported whether these were seen as gaps in the service or irrelevant to their needs, however.

There is limited research evidence on the attitudes of personal advisers in the New Deal programmes to supporting disabled people and people with ill-health. It is noteworthy that staff in the New Deal 50 Plus were not reported as raising health problems or impairments as a barrier to participation (Atkinson, 2001b). On the other hand, New Deal 25 Plus advisers were reported as feeling unequipped, especially in dealing with people with mental health, alcohol or drugs problems (Joyce and Pettigrew, 2002). Here, Disability Employment Advisers seemed to be widely used, to refer people with physical impairments and mental health problems and as an information source for personal advisers. There is some evidence of New Deal 25 Plus fostering the development of external specialist provision, including for people with mental health problems, but there have been concerns about affordability, and personal advisers' limited understanding of what it entails can impact on the quality of decisions they make on the client's behalf (Wilson, 2002). Qualitative research on lone parent personal adviser meetings found staff identified a need for information on places to refer people with barriers related to health or disability (Thomas and Griffiths, 2002).

Although the New Deal programmes have been evaluated extensively, the impact on disabled people and people with health problems has not always been built into research designs, and findings on service delivery are sometimes fragmented. A common difficulty is that numbers in the research samples are too small to allow for the net impact for those with a health condition or disability to be compared with that for other participants.

Looking at outcomes, in the New Deal 25 Plus, according to DWP analysis of administrative data, disabled participants were only slightly less likely than non-disabled clients to enter paid work (Thornton, 2003). Where a long-term health problem or disability was not work limiting, employment outcomes were not significantly different from those for those who left the programme with no health problem or disability (Bonjour et al, 2001). However, in the NDLP employment outcomes for participants with a work-limiting health problem or disability were found to be poorer than for other young people: they had an increased likelihood of leaving the NDYP with no job to go to (Bryson et al, 2000); and people with mental health problems were less likely to move into employment (Bonjour et al, 2001).

Conclusion

It is clear that DWP is determined to promote specialist advisers for incapacity benefits claimants attending WFIs. However, there is no evidence that specialist advisers lead to better employment outcomes and there is no intention in the Pathways to Work pilots to compare outcomes for those who receive specialist advice with outcomes for those in other areas who do not. There is evidence from the New Deal 25 Plus, where one third of participants are disabled and specialist advisers are not used, that employment outcomes are similar for unemployed disabled and non-disabled people. Of course, other elements of support contribute to employment outcomes alongside advisory input.

The early research found that personal advisers could feel uncomfortable about advising people with ill-health or impairments about employment possibilities, and could rule out broaching the subject. Such difficulties drove the shift in the Pathways to Work pilots to specially recruited and trained advisers. Interestingly, there are no reports of advisers having difficulties working with people with health problems or impairments in the New Deal 50 Plus, where the vast majority of disabled people were on Jobseeker's Allowance and were not marked out as different in the way people on incapacity benefits are. One effective way of changing attitudes might be to increase the proportion of disabled employees within Jobcentre Plus, so that existing staff learn from colleagues who know what it is like to live with a health problem or impairment.

It is hard to understand why government sees the type of benefit received as the common denominator when designing advice and support for return to work. People who have not worked recently, across claimant groups, experience erosion of confidence and social skills and encounter discriminatory barriers. Recognising such commonalities was the reason behind the European Equal programme that replaced employment projects targeted at discrete groups such as disabled people (the HORIZON programme), women and young people.

The main concern for the DWP appears to be the most efficient and effective use of staff resources where there is a link between handling of a benefit claim and work-focused advice. The argument seems to be that it is impossible for a generalist adviser to be sufficiently well informed about medical conditions and their effects, the disability benefits system and the range of external specialist services for disabled people. A model worth exploring, used in one-stop shops in the US system, is that of generalist employment advisers who deal with a range of claimants but are backed by specialists in disability issues behind the scenes. A more radical solution to the self-perpetuating argument that specialist advisers are needed to understand specialist services is to reduce specialist services. There no evidence that specialist services produce better outcomes then generalist provision (Thornton, 2003).

References

ACDET (Advisory Committee for Disabled People in Employment and Training) (2001) *In the mainstream: Recommendations on removing barriers to disabled people's inclusion in mainstream labour market interventions*, London: DWP.

Atkinson, J., Kodz, J., Dewson, S. and Eccles, J. (2000) *Evaluation of New Deal 50 Plus. Qualitative evidence from ES and BA staff: First phase*, Employment Service Report 56, Sheffield: Employment Service.

Atkinson, J. (2001a) *Evaluation of the New Deal 50 Plus: Research with individuals (Wave 2)*, Employment Service Report 92, Sheffield: Employment Service.

Atkinson, J. (2001b) *Evaluation of the New Deal 50 Plus: Summary report*, Employment Service Report 103, Sheffield: Employment Service.

Bivand, P. (2004) 'Securing job outcomes: latest figures', *Working Brief*, no 154, pp 18-21.

Bonjour, D., Dorsett, R., Knight, G., Lissenburgh, S., Mukherjee, A., Payne, J., Range, M., Urwin, P. and White, M. (2001) *New Deal for Young People: National survey of participants: Stage 2*, Employment Service Report 67, Sheffield: Employment Service.

Bonjour, D. and Dorsett, R. (2002) *New Deal for Partners: Characteristics and labour market transitions for eligible couples*, WAE 134, Sheffield: Employment Service.

Bryson, A., Knight, G., and White, M. (2000) *New Deal for Young People: National survey of participants: Stage 1*, Employment Service Report 44, Sheffield: Employment Service.

Coleman, N., Rousseau, N. and Kennedy, L. (2002) *Early findings from lone parent personal adviser meetings: Quantitative survey of clients*, WAE 140, Sheffield: DWP.

Coleman, N., Rousseau, N. and Carpenter, H. (2004) *Jobcentre Plus service delivery survey (Wave 1)*, DWP Research Report 223, Leeds: Corporate Document Service (CDS).

Dawson, T., Dickens, S. and Finer, S. (2000) *New Deal for Lone Parents: Report of qualitative studies with individuals*, Employment Service Report 55, Sheffield: Employment Service.

DWP (Department for Work and Pensions) (2004a) *£220 million expansion of successful scheme helping people on incapacity benefits get back to work*, Press Release, DWP Media Centre, 30 November.

DWP (2004b) *Publication of DWP research report and in-house administrative data analyses: incapacity benefit reforms – Pathways to Work pilots*, Press Release, DWP Media Centre, 2 December.

Dickens, S., Mowlam, A. and Woodfield, K. (2004a) *Incapacity benefit reforms early findings from qualitative research*, W202, Sheffield: DWP.

Dickens, S., Mowlam, A. and Woodfield, K. (2004b) *Incapacity Benefit reforms – The personal adviser role and practices*, W212, Sheffield: DWP.

Goldstone, C. and Douglas, L. (2003) *Pathways to work from incapacity benefits: A pre-pilot exploration of staff and customer attitudes*, W162, Sheffield: DWP.

Green, H., Marsh, A., Connolly, H. and Payne, J. (2003) *The medium-term effects of compulsory participation in ONE. Part one: Survey of clients: Cohort 2, Wave 2*, DWP Research Report 183, Leeds: CDS.

Hansard (2004) HC Deb 18 November 2004 c 1889W.

House of Commons Work and Pensions Committee (2002) *'ONE' Pilots: Lessons for Jobcentre Plus*, HC 426, London: The Stationery Office (TSO).

Joyce, L. and Pettigrew, N. (2002) *Personal advisers in New Deal 25+ and Employment Zones*, WAE 139, Sheffield: DWP.

Kirby, S. and Riley, R. (2003) *Final effects of ONE: The employment effects of full participation in ONE*, DWP Research Report 183 (Part Three), Leeds: CDS.

Kodz, J. and Eccles, J. (2001) *Evaluation of New Deal 50 Plus qualitative evidence from clients: Second phase*, Employment Services Report 70, Sheffield: Employment Service.

Legard, R., Lewis, J., Hiscock, J. and Scott, J. (2002) *Evaluation of the Capability Report: Identifying the work-related capabilities of incapacity benefits claimants*, DWP Research Report 162, Leeds: CDS.

Lissenburgh, S. and Marsh, A. (2003) *Experiencing Jobcentre Plus Pathfinders: Overview of early evaluation evidence*, In-house Report 111, London: DWP.

Osgood, J., Stone V. and Thomas, A. (2002) *Delivering a work-focused service: Views and experiences of clients*, Research Report 167, Leeds: CDS.

Osgood, J., Stone, V., Thomas, A., Dempsey, S., Jones, G. and Solon, R. (2003) *ONE Evaluation: Summary of service delivery findings*, In-house Report 108, London: DWP.

Secretary of State for Work and Pensions (2002) *Pathways to Work: Helping people into employment*, Cm 5690, Norwich: TSO.

Secretary of State for Work and Pensions (2003) *Pathways to Work: Helping people into employment. The government's response and action plan*, Cm 5830, Norwich: TSO.

Taylor, J. and Hartfree, Y. (2003) *Deferrals in Jobcentre Plus: Research into staff understanding and application of deferral guidance for non Jobseeker's Allowance customers*, In-house Report 126, London: DWP.

Thomas, A. and Griffiths, R. (2002) *Early findings from lone parent personal adviser meetings: Qualitative research with clients and case studies on delivery*, WAE 132, Sheffield: DWP.

Thornton, P. (2003) *What works and looking ahead: UK polices and practices facilitating employment of disabled people*, York: Social Policy Research Unit, University of York.

Wilson, R. (2002) *Evaluation of re-engineered New Deal 25 Plus: Case studies*, WAE 111, Sheffield: Employment Service.

ELEVEN

Disability and employment: global and national policy influences in New Zealand, Canada and Australia

Neil Lunt

The study of social policy in the post-war period focused on the activities of nation-states and in particular the development of welfare state institutions. During this time, the range of policy actors: politicians, bureaucrats, pressure groups and voters, all held the belief that domestic intervention could help shape the economic and welfare futures of the population, mitigating any international turbulence that arose. While the 1960s and 1970s witnessed growing interest in comparative and cross-national analysis, the nation-state still remained the basic unit of analysis in these endeavours. During more recent decades however a suite of global changes have lent social policy formation a trans-national character, with recognition that policy problems, policy processes, policy actors, and policy solutions avoid being neatly mapped onto individual nation-states.

Those writing about globalisation fall into one of three broad camps: the hyperglobalists, the sceptics, and the transformationalists (Held et al, 1999). For *hyperglobalists*, global economic and/or technological processes reduce the influence that nation-states previously exerted over domestic policy, and imperatives to maintain a lean and competitive economy constrain domestic government setting and achieving policy goals. Under this perspective, the demands of global capital present a stark future for welfare states with reduced public expenditure and tighter eligibility, while education and training service the supply-side requirements of the economy. So-called *sceptics* deny the magnitude and novelty of global changes, arguing instead that domestic policy remains the route to forging an inclusive society. For Hay and Watson (1999, p 421), globalisation is a 'rhetorical façade' and becomes yoked to a defeatist view that no alternative exists to the homogenous policy measures that are advanced in the name of globalisation. For many sceptics, the organisation and mobilisation of interests within the nation-state and the courage to take alternative policy directions remains the route to securing social justice. For the *transformationalist* view, states retain the possibility of efficacious action, albeit those nation-states must now operate within new boundary conditions.

The field of disability studies – as distinct from the study of disability within the traditional social administration/policy paradigm – has always had a more international and global character. While recognising that the social and economic outcomes experienced by disabled people and particular communities within the broader population are shaped in part by domestic conditions, it has always upheld trans-national considerations within analysis. This includes how processes (variously cultural, economic and political) have served to construct disability and oppress groups across *all* contemporary societies. This shared problematic has been reflected in international solidarity being a defining features of the disability movement (for example, Disabled Persons International), and recognition that disabled people's emancipation is inherently trans-national (for example, the 1981 International Year for Disabled Persons and current attempts to develop a UN Convention on Disability).

Disability and employment is a policy issue of truly global magnitude: an estimated 386 million people of the world's population of working-age are disabled. Unemployment, underemployment, low pay, poverty and lack of vocational training and education are global problems (see ILO, 2003) with a number of potentially converging policy mechanisms and approaches. Global and regional actors with a stake in disability employment policy have emerged, including where national decision making has been ceded to the supranational level (such as the EU). The International Labour Organization (ILO), a specialist agency of the UN, seeks to promote social justice and human and labour rights, including the area of disability policy and vocational rehabilitation. Its *Global employment agenda* (2003) identifies the importance of investing in education and training for disabled people, as well as ensuring basic education, core skills and literacy, and programmes for tackling labour market disadvantage. International Labour Organization Conventions 111 (Discrimination in Respect of Employment and Occupations [1958]) and 159 (Vocational Rehabilitation and Employment [Disabled Persons, 1983]) while non-binding on signatories seek to eliminate discrimination and raise the integration of disabled people within labour markets. The UN is also being pressed to go beyond its existing Convention on Human Rights, and since late 2001 an ad hoc committee has been considering proposals on establishing an international convention on disabled people.

There has also been the emergence of international non-governmental organisations (NGOs) and powerful social movements. Global networks and exchanges increasingly involve governments, think tanks, NGOs, and organisation of disabled people, facilitating the global transfer of ideas and policies. Within disability and employment there is a growing interest in approaches taken at national policy level by overseas governments as well as grass-roots levels. Interest is sometimes fuelled by policy innovations such as the 1990 Americans with Disabilities Act, or from wider political pressures, such as the accession countries of the EU studying the policy approaches of more established member states.

Exploring 'the Commonwealth'

In looking to the experience of other countries, whether mainland Europe or Anglophone countries, it is important to recognise that institutional contexts and policy traditions differ substantially to those of Britain. This said, there is a greater similarity of policy traditions and political and economic culture underpinning the Anglophone bloc of primarily English-speaking nations. These all have an over-arching anti-discrimination law that bounds their disability employment policy (Lunt and Thornton, 1993; Thornton and Lunt, 1997). Putting aside the US, which can dominate comparative discussion, this chapter focuses on some developments within Australia, Canada and New Zealand.

In many ways, the relationship of disabled people to the labour market across all countries is depressingly familiar with historical disadvantage in terms of: labour market activity, unemployment, underemployment, poverty, and rates of pay (Statistics New Zealand, 2001; HRDC, 2000, 2002; ABS, 2004). Economies are also being restructured along similar lines with the constriction of manufacturing and expansion of the services sector. There is also the emergence of part-time and more flexible (or insecure) employment conditions and opportunities, and forms of working arrangements that increasingly include homeworking and teleworking.

In other ways, the political and social landscape of these Commonwealth countries is somewhat unfamiliar: Australia and Canada have a distinction between federal and state levels of policy that complicates outsiders' understanding. While as white settler states, Australia, Canada and New Zealand are all appraising their appropriate relationships with aboriginal and indigenous populations, including the citizenship rights it entails. This includes service provision that is culturally sensitive and devolution of power and resources. Thus, while there are core policy problems and shared concerns for social justice, their socio-historical frameworks and cultural traditions mitigate any simple transference or grafting of policy measures.

Canada, Australia, and New Zealand have anti-discrimination measures in place to tackle employment and this operates as part of a wider commitment to a non-discriminatory and non-disabling society (Australia's 1992 Disability Discrimination Act, Canada's 1985 revision to the Human Rights Act, and New Zealand's 1993 Human Rights Act). Such legislation covers transport, access to goods and services, accommodation, and the labour market. There are differences in whether legislation stands alone or is part of omnibus-type legislation, and whether legislation resulted from grass-roots agitation or was a top-down government initiative.

These countries have not relied solely on legislative redress but have a range of accompanying measures and approaches: incentives, services and persuasion. A comprehensive description of measures across these countries is outside the scope of this chapter.

Canada

Canada was the first country to outlaw disability discrimination at a national level, revising its Human Rights Act in 1985, while the Charter of Rights and Freedoms also prohibits discrimination on the grounds of disability. Since 1986, disability has ostensibly been approached as an issue of citizenship with the focus moving from individuals to a concern with broader social barriers. Responsibility for disability employment policy is divided between the federal/provincial levels in Canada. In legislative terms, for example, the Employment Equity Act (1986) and the Federal Contractors Programme promote employment among federally related contractors, while there are also provincial levels of anti-discrimination legislation.

Services are funded and delivered in a federal and provincial partnership. In 2003, the Social Services Minister approved the Multilateral framework for Labour Market Agreements for People with Disabilities and this replaced Employability Assistance that operated since 1997. The revised Federal Budget that flows to states was increased by Can$30 million and involves a number of agreements signed with states aimed at explicitly enhancing 'employability'. An earlier evaluation of Employability Assistance noted that interventions that work best are individualised, holistic, and emphasise education and in-service training. The study also stresses the importance of highly trained staff, educating employers, and the possibility of voluntary work being used en route to transition (HRDC, 2002).

The Opportunities Fund was introduced in 1997 with its purpose of covering those that may miss out given an emphasis on mainstreamed labour market programmes. The fund assists preparation or skills development, encourages employers to hire, and provides self-employment, and also voluntary opportunities. Within the fund there is a particular focus for Aboriginal Human Resource Agreements. Delivery is decentralised to the regions through Human Resources Center Canada.

Accessibility, portability and an individual focus have been identified as key to the future of disability supports (HRDC, 1998) and there have been a growing number of programmes aimed at providing self-managed or individualised funding where consumers have funding to manage their own supports thereby increasing choice and control.

In the 2003 Budget, the government established the Technical Advisory Committee on Tax Measures for Persons with Disabilities to advise on tax issues that affected the disability community. In addition to a range of wage incentives and job accommodations funds that are available, the most recent budget proposes new tax deductions for disability supports. There is major policy interest in having those not currently in the labour market try a range of work options. An amendment to the federal disability pension allows for benefit reinstatement if a former recipient has ceased working for reasons relating to disability within two years of returning to work. Supported employment options continue to attract significant attention.

Australia

Australian provision for disabled people is the responsibility of both federal (Commonwealth) and state levels. The 1992 Disability Discrimination Act (DDA) covers both levels of government, as well as local government and the private sector, and most States also have their own anti-discrimination legislation.

The DDA has produced some good individual outcomes in terms of individual adjustments being made and providing the opportunity to clarify misconceptions in particular cases. However, if legislation is viewed through a wider lens progress is less encouraging, particularly given the aim is to prevent discrimination occurring rather than simply deal with complaints. Developing standards for reasonable adjustment has been difficult and have remained in draft form since 1998 (HREOC, 2002). A public inquiry into the DDA explored costs and benefits and the effectiveness of legislation. While there were some developments in transport and improved access to premises, it concluded that legislation was 'relatively ineffective in reducing discrimination in employment' and this gave the commission particular cause for concern (Productivity Commission, 2004, pp 37, 52). This lack of progress comes despite employment complaints consistently having been the largest proportion of DDA complaints (53% in 2002/03). Overall employment rates have not improved, while within Commonwealth (public employment) the representation of disabled people fell over the decade following DDA.

Against this background of disappointment, there are also groups that are particularly disadvantaged. People with mental illness or intellectual disabilities are helped less under the legislation than those with physical disabilities. Disabled people in regional areas, as well as those non-English speaking and indigenous populations, continue to be less well served by such legislation. The Act was reasonably effective in improving educational opportunity for tertiary students with intellectual disability, acquired brain injury, multiple chemical sensitivity or chronic fatigue syndrome but less so for those with dual/multiple impairments and those based within institutions.

There are suggestions that more direct strategies are necessary to achieve better outcomes such as an American Job Accommodation Network, along with more positive strategies for employment opportunities. Supported employment is well developed and there are attempts to individualise provision and encourage a range of providers within the market. Disability support services fund a range of training, job search and in-work support of wage subsidies and modifications. The one-stop shop for benefits/employment advice, Centrelink, has specialist Disability Officers with key roles of referral.

Concern at the lack of progress in improving labour market opportunities has led to a public inquiry being enacted in March 2005 by the Human Rights and Equal Opportunity Commission (HREOC) on issues affecting equal opportunity for disabled people in Australia. It will explore the full range of barriers and solutions to employment opportunities in entering, retaining and returning to work for a range of impairment groups – benefits, transport, accessibility of the built environment, social care need, legislation. Although such an inquiry is to be welcomed, its very existence perhaps reflects the frustrating lack of progress in the policy field.

New Zealand

New Zealand's 1993 Human Rights Act outlaws discrimination on a number of grounds including disability and these grounds continue to be the single biggest category of complaint that the Human Rights Commission addresses. Disability policy writ large has undergone a major rethink within New Zealand, resulting in the 2001 Disability Strategy. It introduced 15 objectives, including those covering the delivery of support (education and training), government capacity and development of support; rights of citizenship (specific rights and commitment to a non-disabling society), and inclusion of specific target populations. Implementation of the strategy has become the responsibility of a newly established Office for Disability Issues. Disabled Persons Assembly (DPA) New Zealand supported the introduction of the strategy, perhaps not surprisingly given the document's vision and commitment to the social model of disability. However, more recent criticism has pointed to the huge amount of work necessary, including employment, education and training, to move the strategy to the terrain of policy reality (DPA New Zealand Inc, 2004).

New Zealand has a longstanding commitment to supported employment provision. Following a review of vocational provision a major development has been the *Pathways to Inclusion* commitment, which marks the repeal of the Disabled Persons Employment Promotion Act 1960, and the end of sheltered workshops. A five-year transition period allows the workshop providers to manage the change to the new funding and services environment. In terms of public sector provision, there has been some small growth of the public sector Mainstream programme which provides subsidised opportunities for two years.

A split in eligibility remains between those who have acquired disability as the result of a workplace, sporting or motoring accident or injury (who have access to accident compensation benefits and rehabilitation programmes), and those that have congenital disability or disability resulting from long-term illness. The Ministry of Social Development has stated an intention to develop improved equity and coherence of government-funded services and support for people with disabilities but the distinction of acquired/congenital disability remains.

There has been the development of opportunities for sickness and invalids benefits recipients to enter paid workforce. The Ministry of Social Development has introduced five demonstration projects running for two years (employABLE: *Nga pukenga hei whai mahi*). Four of these projects are offered by community-based groups (on mental illness, mental illness aged under 25, Maori mental illness, Maori chronic physical health). The one scheme run by Work and Income (a government agency) targets new sickness beneficiaries and offers individual case management on a voluntary basis. Its aim is to try and encourage links to be maintained with the labour market, and increase work skills or explore alternative pathways back into work. Concern continues to be expressed that such benefits are used as 'de facto' unemployment schemes and there is an emphasis on 'cutting the tail' of long-term benefit recipients.

Emerging themes

Perhaps the most prevalent theme across countries is their evident lack of progress in improving labour market participation and outcomes for disabled people, and particular disadvantages still exist for groups with learning difficulties and mental health issues. Beyond this starting point, however, it is possible to make some more constructive thematic observations.

Countries are increasingly entering 'review phases' of anti-discrimination measures where questions are asked about the efficacy of such measures in tackling labour market disadvantage. In efforts to ensure more effective legislation, those countries where legislation was a top-down rather than bottom-up initiative (for example, Australia) may be at a disadvantage, as may countries where disability legislation does not stand alone (for example, New Zealand). Arguably, in this review phase a confident and effective domestic lobby can ensure that legislation is fully implemented and given real 'teeth' (as in the experience of Britain and the US).

There is shared recognition that comprehensive statistics and research play a major role in assessing the impact of interventions and informing new policy measures. While New Zealand has been criticised by the ILO for not collecting adequate data regarding the employment of disabled people, the data of Australia and Canada has also been lacking. There is a growing commitment to statistics, monitoring, evaluation and longitudinal research but the impact of particular measures or legislation remains difficult to untangle from the effects of other legislation, services and pensions, and such crosscutting trends as economic restructuring, deinstitutionalisation and technology.

Anti-discrimination legislation does not itself require equality in outcome, which instead is pursued through a range of services and fiscal mechanisms. Legislation does not guarantee a right to training and education. Individuals must be in a position to compete for jobs and meet 'inherent requirements' of particular positions in order to receive protection. All the countries have adopted an explicit supply-side focus and more active labour market initiatives in these countries focus on improving 'employability' and the uniform commitment to reducing the number of long-term benefit recipients. The welfare to work rationale is variously expressed as a wish to achieve fiscal savings, a desire to build economic capital, and a commitment to social rights!

Attempts to 're-wire' the benefit system have also been accompanied by increasing policy attempts to encourage individuals to take risks and try out labour market opportunities without being disadvantaged if such a trial does not work out.

There is a firm commitment across these countries to supported employment as well as to service delivery models that are individually focused and increasingly delivered by grass-roots agencies and niche providers in a contract-driven market. Some consumer-led initiatives are also apparent within this service mosaic. Indigenous populations and minority ethnic groups are also seeking to ensure that delivery involves their cultural principles and paradigms, and increasingly service development is under the control of such communities.

This chapter began by highlighting differences between global and comparative analysis. Adopting an explicit transformationalist perspective, it would appear that there *are* trans-national challenges to devising labour market policy, and clearly poverty and poverty of opportunity remain concerns for disabled people the world over. While some trans-national policy convergence is apparent in the field of disability and employment across western countries, this is a result of domestic political pressures and particular choices being made. The transformationalist view of globalisation offers reason to remain optimistic with effective responses likely to be global, national and local. Inclusive societies and a more just world remain worthy and achievable goals, regardless of hyperglobalist rhetoric to the contrary. Governmental and non-governmental supranational actors will play a key role in identifying policy objectives and lobbying to ensure their realisation. National and local initiatives will continue to matter and to this extent, comparative analysis can pinpoint issues of shared interest, unpack adherence to particular values (for example, 'employability', 'evidence-based', and 'devolution'), and help foster approaches that are effective at eliminating the disadvantage disabled people continue to experience.

References

ABS (Australian Bureau of Statistics) (2004) *Disability, ageing and carers, Australia: Summary of findings*, Canberra: ABS.

DPA (Disabled Persons Assembly) New Zealand Inc (2004) *Disability Strategy: 3rd Progress Report*, Comment of DPA President, Wellington: DPA New Zealand Inc.

Hay, C. and Watson, M. (1999) '"Sceptical" notes on the 1999 Reith Lectures', *Political Quarterly*, vol 70, no 4, pp 418-26.

Held, D., McGrew, A., Goldblatt, D. and Perraton, J. (1999) *Global transformations: Politics, economics and culture*, Cambridge: Polity Press.

HRDC (Human Resources Development Canada) (1998) *In unison: A Canadian approach to disability issues*, Ottawa: HRDC.

HRDC (2000) *In unison 2000: Persons with disabilities in Canada*, Ottawa: HRDC.

HRDC (2002) *Promising practices in employability assistance for people with disabilities (EAPD) funded programs and services evaluation*, Ottawa: HRDC.

HREOC (Human Rights and Equal Opportunities Commission) (2002) '10 years of the DDA: employment forum', Canberra: HREOC.

ILO (International Labour Organization) (2003) *Global employment agenda*, Geneva: ILO.

Kerzner, L. and Baker, D. (1999) *Canadians with Disabilities Act*, Winnipeg, Manitoba: Council of Canadians with Disabilities.

La Forest Review Panel (2000) *Promoting equality: A new vision*, Ottawa: Canadian Human Rights Act Review.

Lunt, N. and Thornton, P. (1993) *Employment policies for disabled people: A review of fifteen countries*, Sheffield: Department of Employment.

New Zealand Disability Strategy (2001) *Making a world of difference*, Wellington: New Zealand Disability Strategy.

Productivity Commission (2004) *Report on the Review of the Disability Discrimination Act, 1992*, Canberra: Productivity Commission.

Statistics New Zealand (2001) *Disability counts*, Wellington: Statistics New Zealand.

Thornton, P. and Lunt, N. (1997) *Employment policies for disabled people: A review of eighteen countries*, York: Social Policy Research Unit.

TWELVE

Disabled people and 'employment' in the majority world: policies and realities

Peter Coleridge

Introduction

Attempts to summarise conditions in 'the majority world' are fraught with great difficulty. Generalisations are dangerous. The difference in the economy and living standards between, say, Malawi and Thailand are enormous. (Malawi has a GNI of $160 per capita, a life expectancy of 37 years, and an infant mortality rate of 113 per 1,000 live births. Thailand has a GNI of $2,190, a life expectancy of 69.2 years, and an infant mortality rate of 24 per 1,000 live births.)

The emphasis in this chapter, therefore, is on broader economic deprivation or poverty rather than specific countries. Clearly employment and unemployment is only one aspect of poverty in the majority world.

Important indicative research has been conducted recently in three African countries (Malawi, Zimbabwe, and Namibia) on the living conditions of disabled people by the Norwegian research institute SINTEF, in conjunction with Southern Africa Federation of the Disabled (SAFOD). Its findings include the following, which apply to all three countries (SINTEF, 2003a, 2003b, 2004):

- mean monthly salaries for disabled people tend to be lower than for the non-disabled;
- those with mental or emotional impairments experienced more barriers to full participation in society than those with other types of disability;
- vocational training and welfare services were reportedly received by a very small percentage of those who needed them;

- emotional support is the most mentioned form of assistance needed;
- economic support was the second most mentioned form of assistance needed;
- within the family, the role of the person with a disability does not appear to be much affected by their disability status;
- schools were found to be accessible to only 20% of the disabled population, and the workplace to 26%;
- activity limitation and participation restriction scores are higher in urban than in rural areas, indicating that complex societies in a sense produce more disability.

Missing from these findings is any mention of unemployment figures. These are almost meaningless in countries where most people work in the informal, unregulated sector of the economy. This, indeed, is the largest difference between the employment situation in industrialised countries and that in poor countries. In Europe and North America, the informal sector scarcely exists except in the shadowy area of barely legal or criminal activity. In very poor countries, however, up to 80% of the work force may earn their living as subsistence farmers, small shopkeepers, barrow peddlers, back-street artisans, repairers, small service providers, and from begging. These means of livelihood are more or less unregulated in the sense that their practitioners do not pay income tax, have no pensions or other benefits, and are outside any minimum wage policies.

Governments have an ambivalent attitude towards this sector. On the one hand, the people in it do not pay taxes and so do not contribute to the national exchequer. But on the other hand, it relieves the government of the burden of finding jobs for millions of people. It is part of a vicious circle: low tax gathering means a cash-strapped government, which then does not have the means to put in place the basis (security, infrastructure, and so on) for private investment in proper economic development. And so, people remain trapped in low-income activities which enable them to survive but not develop. It is probable that the majority of disabled people in developing countries are caught in this poverty trap. This chapter accordingly focuses on the informal sector.

Global policies affecting disabled people in developing countries

A range of international instruments has been formulated over the past two or three decades that directly relates to disabled people. These instruments can be summarised under two main headings: UN conventions which apply to disabled people in both rich and poor countries throughout the world; and policies formulated by the World Bank and International Monetary Fund (IMF) on poverty alleviation, aimed specifically at developing countries. In addition there are guidelines formulated jointly by UN agencies, led by the World Health Organization (WHO), on appropriate approaches to rehabilitation, under the general heading of Community Based Rehabilitation (CBR), which include employment. A list of international initiatives concerning disabled persons from 1955-2002 is presented in Figure 12.1.

United Nations conventions relating specifically to disabled people and employment have been formulated primarily by the ILO (International Labour Organization), whose conventions are binding once ratified. As with all such international instruments, implementation is the responsibility of individual governments, and there are no real sanctions for non-compliance.

The ILO has made a systematic attempt to discover how effective international initiatives have been by examining the impact of laws to

Figure 12.1: International initiatives concerning disabled persons (1955-2002)

- ILO Recommendation concerning Vocational Rehabilitation of the Disabled, 1955
- UN Declaration on the Rights of Mentally Retarded Persons, 1971
- UN Declaration on the Rights of Disabled Persons, 1975
- UN International Year of Disabled Persons, 1981
- The World Programme of Action Concerning Disabled Persons, 1982
- UN Decade of Disabled Persons, 1983-1992
- ILO Convention concerning Vocational Rehabilitation and Employment (Disabled Persons) (no 159) 1983, and Recommendation no 168.
- Council of Europe Coherent Policy for the Rehabilitation of Persons with Disabilities, 1992
- UN Standard Rules, 1993
- The Asian and Pacific Decade of Disabled Persons, 1993-2002 and 2003-12
- Inter-American Convention on the Elimination of All Forms of Discrimination against Persons with Disabilities, 1999
- The African Decade of Disabled Persons 1999-2009
- Proposed UN Convention on the Rights of Persons with Disabilities

Source: ILO (2003)

promote employment and training opportunities for disabled people in certain countries of Asia and the Pacific (Australia, Cambodia, China, Fiji, India, Japan, Mongolia, Sri Lanka, and Thailand) and of East Africa (Ethiopia, Kenya, Mauritius, Seychelles, Sudan, United Republic of Tanzania and Uganda) (ILO, 2003). An important finding of these studies is that international policies on equal opportunities for disabled people are predicated on formal employment, not informal self-employment. Percentage quotas, 'reasonable accommodation', and similar requirements can only be applied in situations where employers can be regulated to some degree. They cannot be applied in the informal sector, but, as stated earlier, this is the only sector open to most disabled people in developing countries.

The Millennium Development Goals and the Poverty Reduction Strategy Paper

There are a number of key global initiatives that set out the terms of the debate about development and poverty. The two most relevant ones are the Millennium Development Goals, formulated by the UN in 2000, and the Poverty Reduction Strategy Paper (PRSP) approach, adopted by the World Bank in 1999.

The Millennium Development Goals aim to:

1. eradicate extreme poverty and hunger;
2. achieve universal primary education;
3. promote gender equality and empower women;
4. reduce child mortality;
5. improve maternal health;
6. combat HIV/AIDS, malaria and other diseases;
7. ensure environmental sustainability;
8. develop a global partnership for development.

These goals need detailed, well-planned, participatory programmes if they are to be achieved, and they cannot be achieved if some people are excluded, including and especially disabled people. While they do not intend to exclude anyone, the reality is that exclusion happens not primarily as a result of prejudice but as a result of ignorance of the reality of certain groups of people, and that is especially true of disabled people.

A major mechanism for reaching these goals is the PRSP approach, a concept launched by the World Bank in 1999 (see www.worldbank.org), and now a feature of the planning processes in many developing countries especially in Africa. This approach is designed to create a process of participatory planning within countries, in contrast to the top-down, externally imposed planning of structural adjustment policies used by the IMF in the 1980s and early 1990s, which are seen to have created as many problems as they tried to solve.

The hallmark of the PRSP approach is indeed participation by *all* stakeholders, including and especially poor people themselves. Participation of the poor is sought at all stages of the PRSP process: formulation, implementation, monitoring, and evaluation. The adoption of the PRSP approach represents a momentous and historic shift in attitudes by the World Bank and IMF towards the true democratisation of development. It is a recognition that top-down, externally imposed ideas do not work, and that if change is to be lasting and sustainable the ordinary people must have their say in what kind of change is required, and how it should be carried out. They should also be actively involved in the process of change.

However, there is a serious problem of ignorance when it comes to disabled people. The World Bank's Sourcebook to the PRSP process does not reflect the huge shifts in thinking about disability that have taken place in the past ten years or so. The book places disabled people, along with children, old people and the chronically sick, in the basket marked "not able to be economically active, in need of special care and welfare". Disabled people, in the eyes of the World Bank Sourcebook, are not participants in development; rather, they are objects of welfare and charity.

Why did the World Bank not get the message? Had it not been listening when it wrote the sourcebook? This book was written in 1998, and fortunately things have changed since then. In the last two years (2002-04), the World Bank has gone through something of a revolution in terms of disability. On the personal initiative of the World Bank President, James Wolferson, it has appointed an extremely able disabled activist as principal adviser, Judy Heumann, and the World Bank has now adopted a policy of mainstreaming disability in all its programmes. However, this was not the case when this sourcebook was written in 1998.

The fact that the World Bank got it so wrong about disability is indicative of a key factor in this discussion: disabled people tend to be trapped in a vicious circle of voicelessness. They were not until very recently listened to in major organisations like the World Bank, so they were missed in its discussions. In the same way, disabled people are not generally included in PRSP discussions, and so disability gets missed out of country poverty reduction strategies.

This is the more astonishing given the enormous amount of development in giving disabled people a voice that has taken place over the past two decades. Organisations like Disabled People's International and Action on Disability and Development, as well as initiatives like the Asia-Pacific Decade of Disabled Persons and the African Decade of Disabled Persons, have greatly strengthened the profile, capacity and credibility of disabled people's organisations (DPOs) in developing countries. Furthermore, international organisations working in rehabilitation such as Rehabilitation International (RI), which 20 years ago was heavily criticised by disabled people for ignoring their voice, have recognised the importance of giving disabled people a platform. At an RI Congress in Oslo in May 2004, most of the speakers were disabled (see www.ri-norway.no).

The formulation currently in progress of a UN Convention on the Rights of Disabled Persons reflects a sea change in the debate about disability globally. This debate can be characterised by the following shifts:

> Policy and programs in favour of persons with disabilities are no longer viewed as a means to rehabilitate and adapt the disabled individual to society, but *to adapt society to the needs of the disabled individual*.

> The concept of *rehabilitation* has given way to the concept of *creating an enabling environment*; the concept of *social assistance* to the one of respect of a society for the *rights of her minorities*.

> More recently, the minority concept has been embedded into the more inclusive one of *social diversity*, of *a society for all*.

> Even though this revolution has occurred in minds and in policies, the profound changes it implies are often not understood. Obsolete concepts like 'sheltered workshops' or 'centres for the handicapped' still enjoy widespread public acceptance. (ILO, 2002; emphasis in original)

In other words, there has been a revolutionary shift in thinking from the individual medical model, in which the disabled person is required to fit in with the norms of an able-bodied society, to the social model, in which society must adapt to the needs and rights of disabled people. However, it takes a long time for such a revolution to have a practical impact on services and opportunities.

The general development debate is now mainly rights-based. It is recognised that poverty is not simply a lack of money or employment; rather, it is a denial of fundamental rights to the decent things of life: health, education, dignity, choice, and opportunity. To be poor means that you are denied these fundamental rights. If everybody had all these rights, there would be no poverty, even though there would still be disparities of wealth. The debate, therefore, is about both rights and the realisation of rights through equal access to services and opportunities.

It is this recognition that has driven the movement behind Community Based Rehabilitation (CBR). Community Based Rehabilitation was first formulated by the WHO as a concept in the late 1970s in an attempt to break away from the institutional approach to rehabilitation in developing countries. It has evolved steadily since then and has been adopted as policy by many governments. The commonly accepted definition of CBR now is that it is a strategy *within community development* for the equalisation of opportunities for people with disabilities. This is the key to its role and its importance in the debate about development, poverty and disability.

I am currently involved in a research project under ILO auspices to find examples of good practice in community-based approaches to skills development and access to work and disabled people's employment activities under CBR programmes. The research to date has covered selected countries in Africa: Uganda, Malawi, Zimbabwe and South Africa. (Asia and the Middle East are still to be done.) However, it is already clear that there are six dominant strategic issues:

- the economic and social context;
- access to education;
- access to training;
- access to capital;
- access to markets;
- access to advice and support.

Disabled people typically suffer from a negative spiral of factors, which drive them into low expectations, low self-esteem, and low achievement (Figure 12.2).

Figure 12.2: Spirals of disabled people's low expectations and esteem

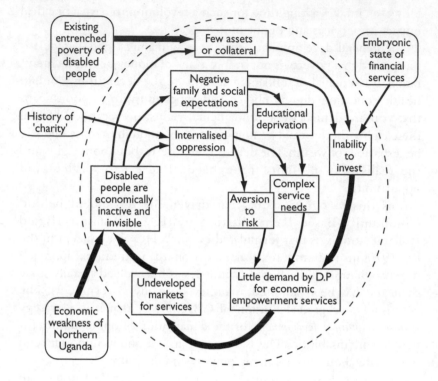

Source: Albu (2004)

The aim of any strategy for the economic empowerment of disabled people must be to break this vicious spiral of factors by focusing on these six strategic issues.

The economic and social context

The strategy must be matched to the context

The range of employment opportunities in any given country depends on the economy of that country. The economy of South Africa is vastly more vibrant than, for example, Malawi, and therefore offers many more opportunities. The strategy must be matched to the context. A failure to understand the local economic context is a principal cause of failure in, for example, vocational training centres.

Formal versus informal sectors

As already emphasised, in many developing countries, especially in Africa, the World Bank estimates that up to 80% of the workforce are engaged in the informal sector. Disabled people will have to compete for work in this sector on the same terms as everyone else. Clearly an approach to employment based on preparation for self-employment in the informal sector will be very different from one based on the idea of job placement in the formal sector. For most CBR programmes in developing countries, the options are strongest in the informal sector.

Rural versus urban

Similarly, there is a major difference in all countries between opportunities in urban and rural areas. Despite the generally vibrant economy of South Africa, Johannesburg offers far more opportunities than a rural area in one of the former homelands. And one of the former homelands in South Africa, where people live in very low-grade housing settlements with little or no access to agricultural land, will present different opportunities from Uganda, where rural families tend to have land that they can farm. If the family is able to farm, then the best option is to strengthen their income from farming by training them, for example, in better livestock production, rather than training the disabled member in a skill such as tailoring. In rural areas, especially, a village of, say, 500 people may have a number of tailors, and training one more will not provide much of an income. Farming provides much better prospects.

For example, a case identified in current ILO research is that of David Luyombo, a disabled veterinary technician in Uganda. He says:

> Traditionally, disabled people, if they are taught anything at all, are taught handicrafts, which have a very limited market in rural areas. It seems to me that the only thing that makes sense in rural areas is farming, and in particular livestock.

David runs a model farm and training centre in Masaka to teach disabled people and their families better animal husbandry.

Focus on the whole family, not just the disabled person

The presence of a disabled person in a family, whether he or she is the main breadwinner or a child, affects the whole family. Families in poor communities usually have survival strategies involving several sources of income. So any employment support activity must take the whole family into account, and if possible involve other members of the family in the training process and access to capital. The idea that the disabled person should be entirely self-sufficient in the sense of not needing any help from others is a non-starter: mutual support and cooperation is the key.

Access to education

Education is the foundation of employment opportunities

Since education in most poor countries suffers from overcrowded classrooms, underpaid teachers, and high dropout rates between primary and secondary school, disabled children have typically been seen as a very low priority for schooling, especially by parents who may be trying to educate half a dozen children and have to make choices. Yet it is here where the change must begin if disabled people are to compete in the job market, whether formal or informal.

The determination of parents that their disabled child should go to school at all costs was the key to the success of a number of those interviewed. This was spectacularly so with David Luyombo (disabled veterinary, Uganda), whose father disowned him when he developed polio as a child, but whose mother insisted he complete secondary schooling.

Access to training

Traditional Vocational Training Courses (VTC) have limited value

To compete in the job market, disabled people need knowledge, awareness, and skills. In the past, vocational training centres teaching such skills as shoe making, tailoring, and metal work were seen as the best way of giving disabled people employable skills, but these are now recognised as having a number of drawbacks. First, they could only offer a limited range of trades, and tended to be inflexible in response to a changing market. Second, it became clear that many of those trained did not get employment, at any rate in the trade they had been trained in. Third, many disabled people did not want to be limited to these fairly menial types of work, but to have opportunities which were intellectually more challenging. Blind people in particular can benefit from employment opportunities that use their brains rather than their hands. It is hard for a blind person to be a skilled craftsmen, but not hard for a blind person to operate a computer with the right software. Fourth, because the graduates often could not find work outside, these vocational training centres tended to become sheltered workshops, disconnected from the real job market.

The realisation now is that alternative forms of training are required, which are more closely attuned to the reality of the market and which offer many more choices than the limited menu of a VTC. Accordingly, two major innovations have come into operation in the past 10 years: apprenticeship training, and entrepreneurial training.

Apprenticeships

In apprenticeship training a disabled person is paired with a skilled person (either disabled or non-disabled) already in successful self-employment, and who provides training on the business site. The main advantage of this type of training is that the apprentice relates to the general public throughout the training period, providing him or her with valuable experience, and sensitising the public to the fact that a disabled person can perform like anyone else. If the training is effective the disabled person will also learn much about entrepreneurial skills as they go along. The possible drawback of the apprenticeship approach is that not all skilled trades people are good trainers, and may simply use the disabled person as free labour.

Entrepreneurial training

In entrepreneurial training, disabled people are taught the skills needed to engage in successful business, whatever technical skill they may or may not have. In the informal sector this is the most important skill required. Entrepreneurial skills include life skills, interpersonal skills, financial skills, management skills, planning skills, and communication skills.

Access to capital

No capital, no self-employment

No amount of training will lead to work in the informal sector unless the trainee has access to start-up capital. Lack of access to capital is the most common reason why trainees from VTCs (whether institution based or apprenticeships) do not enter employment. There are two principal methods for accessing capital: through micro-finance, and through savings.

Micro-finance

Micro-finance is increasingly available to poor people in Asia, as the Grameen Bank model gathers pace. The Grameen Bank pioneered the idea of giving small loans to poor people who have no collateral for regular bank loans. Grameen established the principle of group guaranteed loans in which a group of people come together to receive loans on the condition that they guarantee repayment by each member of the group. This has now become the dominant form of development intervention in Bangladesh. In Africa, too, more and more micro-finance lending bodies are springing up. Generally speaking, however, disabled persons are finding that these bodies will not lend to them because they do not have collateral and because they are seen as a poor risk. In addition, many of these bodies operate a group guaranteed loan scheme, but it is hard for disabled people to be accepted into mixed groups because non-disabled people do not believe they will repay, and it is hard for them to form their own disabled groups because they are often too far apart, especially in rural areas, and may have limited mobility. If micro-credit is not available, the best option for accessing capital is through savings. (Even if micro-credit is an option, savings are still a vital discipline.)

Savings: the traditional merry-go-round system

In poor communities all over the world, a common type of savings is what is called in Kenya the merry-go-round. Here, a group comes together for the sole purpose of saving. Each member puts a fixed sum into a common pot each week or each month, the amount agreed by the group to reflect the realistic possibilities of group members. Each month one person from the group takes a turn in scooping the pot. So, for example, if each member of a group of five puts $3 into the pot each month, every month one person will have $15. This can be used for peak expenditure, such as a school uniform, or for investment in an income generating activity, such as buying extra stock for a shop or materials for a workshop.

A modified version of the merry-go-round

A variation on this system being promoted by, among others, CARE (an international development non-governmental organisation) in various countries is to use the amount scooped from the pot as a loan and not a grant. So the recipient pays it back, at a rate of interest and over a period agreed by the group. In this way, the pot is always growing in size, instead of remaining limited to what is put in each month. Over a period of a year or more a relatively large amount of capital can be saved, which could be used for investment in a piece of machinery or the building of a workshop. Or it could be used as collateral to obtain a larger loan from a micro-credit body.

Savings groups form social capital as well as financial capital

Clearly the main requirement for success in this form of savings is trust between the group members. If someone does not pay in their share, then the whole thing falls apart. However, the main advantage is that it does not rely on outside sources of cash. It also promotes the development of human and social capital, as well as financial capital, because people must be disciplined and they must be strong and cohesive as a group. Most importantly the group members build up a credit record, demonstrating that they are capable of helping themselves and can save, however small an amount. A micro-finance organisation is more likely to look favourably on applicants with this kind of record.

The importance of role models

Additionally, disabled people may be too scattered to form such a group, or not be accepted into a mixed group. This is where role models become very important.

Role models of disabled people succeeding in business are present in many communities. The task of a CBR programme is to find them and make them known, in order to convince both disabled and non-disabled doubters that disabled people are as capable as anybody else, and can be fully contributing members of a mixed group.

Access to markets

Study the market: what can people afford to buy?

A failure to study the market is the second most common reason (after lack of capital) for the failure of small businesses. The first requirement is to understand the nature of the local market. What can people afford to buy? In most poor communities, people are risk averse and will only spend money on what they can afford. In very poor communities, people may be able to afford only food, and that is why so many people in the informal sector in such communities work as petty food traders, selling a small pile of tomatoes or onions. More skilled enterprises such as carpentry may already be saturated. The petty traders have understood that everyone must eat, but people can go without a chair. Repackaging and rebottling into smaller containers (such as cooking oil) is a common way of earning small money because people in poor communities do not have much change in their pockets and cannot afford to buy a large bottle of cooking oil.

Differing attitudes to competition

It is worth noting that poor communities may have a different attitude towards competition than do people in industrialised countries. This is especially true of women. People in poor communities often rely on a supportive social network in order to survive (Ntseame, 2004) The fact that there may be a dozen women all selling tomatoes in the same row in a market is not seen as a disadvantage, but as a supportive network. They may help each other in transporting produce from the wholesaler, and in covering for each other if a child is sick. It is also common to find shoemakers, metal workers, and other such trades all clustered together in the same street in towns and trading centres.

Access to advice and support

Support means knowing that you are not alone

Support is needed at different levels throughout the life of anybody struggling to survive in a harsh world, and obviously disabled people need it especially. At the most minimal level support means knowing that you are not alone in your struggles. At more sophisticated levels it means relationships of creative cooperation with a variety of people and groups who work together to solve individual problems. The most successful entrepreneurs are part of a whole network of community groups of various kinds: savings groups, church groups, a local NGO, perhaps a local council. They are likely to be active promoters of other people's welfare and success as well as their own.

Role models as support

As mentioned earlier in this chapter, one of the most important means of support to a disabled person, who may be stuck in the vicious circle of low expectations, low self-esteem and low ambition, is the use of role models. Community Based Rehabilitation programmes need to seek out good role models and devote resources to exposing them to encourage other disabled people. A good role model, a disabled person who is successful in business, will be far more effective than simple exhortations.

The hallmark of someone who is successful in business (as seen in this research) is that they are outgoing, positive, and concerned about the well being of others as well as themselves. This was often seen in their involvement in the community through membership of groups or committees, their support of disabled children outside their immediate family, and the way they made friends with their customers. In other words, it was those who were most empowered and self-confident as individuals who were most successful in their business. Conversely, those who were depressed, isolated, and full of complaints were the least successful.

References

Albu, M (2004) *Improving business development services with disabled people in North Uganda: Evaluation of an Action Research Project*, Moreton-in-the-Marsh, NUPIDU and APT Enterprise Development.

ILO (International Labour Organization) (2002) *Disability and poverty reduction strategies: A discussion paper*, Geneva: ILO.

ILO (2003) *Employment of people with disabilities: The impact of legislation, Asia and the Pacific. Report of a project consultation*, Report compiled by Barbara Murray, Bangkok: ILO.

Murray, B. (2003) 'Employment of people with disabilities: the impact of legislation: Asia and the Pacific', Report of a project consultation, Bangkok: ILO.

Ntseame, P. (2004) 'Being a female entrepreneur in Botswana: cultures, values and strategies for success', *Gender and Development*, vol 12, no 2. July.

SINTEF (Foundation for Scientific and Industrial Research) (2003a) *Living conditions among people with disabilities in Namibia: A National Representative Sample*, Oslo: SINTEF/University of Namibia.

SINTEF (2003) *Living conditions among people with activity limitations in Zimbabwe*, Oslo: SINTEF/University of Zimbabwe.

SINTEF (2004) *Living conditions among people with activity limitations in Malawi*, Malawi: University of Malawi and the Federation of Disability Organisations of Malawi.

Part Three:
Towards inclusive policy futures

Employment policy and practice: a perspective from the disabled people's movement

David Gibbs

Introduction

This chapter draws on useful insights from organisations of disabled people, their implications for future employment policies and practice. Disabled people have perhaps surprisingly been overlooked in the design, implementation and review of much disability employment policy. I will identify not only evidence of deficits in current policy and practice, but also the roots of these deficits. This chapter will also describe, not only a basis for practical solutions, but also the need for a shift in our understanding of the disability and employment 'problem'. Put another way, I will ask if *social model praxis* might be used to carry out a conversion from a *deficit approach* to disabled people's employment to an *investment approach*, one which can be translated into new more enabling policies for disabled people.

In applying a 'deficit approach', I draw on innovative work that applies for the first time social model ideas to the field of disability and employment in a critical and comprehensive way (Roulstone, 2004). Roulstone's article, presented at one of a series of ESRC seminars organised by the Centre for Disability Studies at the University of Leeds (2003), examines impediments that arise from the view that barriers to disabled people's employment are caused by their personal functional deficits (Martin et al, 1989, p 88). Proposed remedies include user-led research, mainstream living and working, flexible multi-agency support, and the extended use of Direct Payments (including Access to Work funding) in the workplace.

In referring to an 'investment approach', I pick up on ideas from a number of developments in social policy, and add a further assertion: those developments crucially depend for their effectiveness on investment in the resource of disabled people's direct experience. I also think there are good ideas to import from policy studies outside employment issues, from current searching reviews on the role of civil society (the voluntary and community sector), and from 'whole systems' theory.

Policy directions

In Europe, a 'movement towards the rights-based equal opportunities approach to disability' was consolidated as strategy by the mid-1990s (CEC, 1996). The European Union then set a time-frame of six years from November 2000 for measures in member states to ensure that "there shall be no direct or indirect discrimination whatsoever" in employment (European Union, 2000).

In relation to disability, understanding of disability at policy level in particular member states will influence measures adopted. This policy context was the subject of an extensive study at Brunel University (Mabbett, 2002). The study's report and associated papers considered the influence on policy of the social model of disability, that is disability as "a product of the person's social context and environment and its social constructions and beliefs, which lead to discrimination against disabled people" (Mabbett, 2002, p 10). One paper (Mabbett and Bolderson, 2001) closely examined background to the directive and traced the process by which concepts like rights and social inclusion have slowly entered European legislation, where the original emphasis was on economic integration. Despite a change of emphasis to rights, citizenship and social inclusion, however, they caution that "the pure legal principle of non-discrimination is rather 'thin'" (Mabbett and Bolderson, 2001, p 20), and find indications that the Directive "will not necessarily signal a radical shift towards implementation of the social model of disability" (2001, p 27).

Their study equates the social model with rights-based strategy, and sees a close connection with policy on social inclusion. As we move from policy to practice, however, analysis may be clearer if the three are kept distinct. In the UK, the focus of early statements of an emergent disabled people's movement was to define and resist oppression (Hunt, 1966), but the first definitive statements on the social context of disability followed some time later (UPIAS, 1976). The beginnings of a whole-system strategy to apply the social model shortly preceded the founding of the first Centres for Integrated Living (CILs) in the UK in 1985 (Davis, 1990).

Just as the initial fine distinctions separate along a time-scale, they widen too with shifts along the political spectrum. In the UK, as New Labour shifts from a social democratic base into neoliberalism, 'rights' move from a civil to a narrower social setting, and 'social inclusion' from a focus of equality and diversity to one of social deprivation and anti-social behaviour (Levitas, 2001). For disabled people on the threshold of inclusion in their communities, this shift had the effect that they became invisible again.

Policy and practice deficits

The 'drag' on disabled people's inclusion

Employment figures in general are healthier than for many years. The various New Deals have enjoyed undoubted well-documented success. The new Tax Credits have begun to turn social security around, from compensation for exclusion to support with inclusion (see Chapter Seven of this volume). When we look at disabled people's share in these benefits, however, the story is at best mixed (Stafford, 2005). There seems to be some kind of 'drag' in the system that holds us back. I will try to trace the cause of this by stages, up to what I will argue is a fundamental error of thinking.

Experience of administrative obstacles

The Access to Work provisions introduced in 1996 rationalised a range of specific provisions made over the years (like fares to work, technical aids and workplace adaptations) and extended them, most significantly by arrangements for support workers. Support from trained staff to identify appropriate equipment, and so on, and apply for it may be the closest model anywhere in public services to the 'useful technician' hired by an 'average citizen' to supply skills with household maintenance tasks that they do not have themselves. Managers speak confidently of sustained progress with the scheme, and ministers have been satisfied enough to allow budget extensions seldom seen in public services. Official research suggests that the scheme is well received (Thornton, 2005).

And yet, other research with beneficiaries shows a high level of frustration with delays in basic provision, and research with employers shows a low level of awareness of support available to disabled employees and ways to access it. Roulstone et al (2003) summarise the deficits as: narrowness of eligibility requirements, bias towards providing for those already in work, time taken to deliver (with examples of job offers withdrawn because of the delay), lack of disabled people's own perspective on needs, budget-led assessments, and the fragmented nature of provision.

The control system on 'incapacity'

A curious listening impairment throughout public policy has prevented notice of a simple statement that disabled people have been making for over 20 years: *disability and illness are not parts of the same thing*. Why is this not obvious? If you are sick, you stay at home till you are well; if disabled, you face an array of barriers between 'home' and where you want to get to. To recover from illness, you need *less* activity; to overcome disabling barriers, you need *more*. Support needs in those two circumstances could hardly be more different. It seems absurd to expect that one concept, like 'incapacity', could cover both.

'Incapacity' is not overloaded by design, but by default. The original Invalidity Benefit (IVB) began as long-term sick benefit in 1971. When disabled people began to become more economically active, their circumstances fell outside the 1940s settlement of welfare provisions, so medical tests for IVB were stretched to pull them in. This was the first in a procession of add-ons by default: people worn out by heavy work but outside the industrial injury provisions; and then measures of political expediency like convenient 'early retirement' and manipulating unemployment figures. When, as a result, numbers of people on 'incapacity' increased disproportionately, blame was naturally passed to the claimants!

To free the 'missing million' who are excluded from work (Stanley and Regan, 2003), support pathways out would need an administrative flexibility to match these varied routes in. Yet, on the change to Incapacity Benefit in 1995, such helpful case-law principles as had emerged were tossed aside in favour of wholly 'medical' judgements, and a chance to cut the tangle was lost.

It is this tangle that creates the 'drag' I refer to. The medical assessment of incapacity is not a competent basis for supporting movement towards work. Suggested alternatives include dumping segregated categories of public service users altogether (Bolderson and Mabbett, 2001).

Errors in the way need is perceived

If the control system on incapacity is where the deficit really lies, how did it get there? In another paper from the aforementioned seminar series (Gibbs, 2004), an attempt was made to identify underlying barriers in the basic thinking behind 'social care' and related services. They apply equally to sources of the 'drag' on disabled people's inclusion in support towards employment. A distinction was made between three kinds of error; that is, error of categorisation, of prescription, and of relationship.

1. Support need is interpreted in terms of personal deficit. The effect of this is that attention is continually diverted from practical solutions to categorising individuals. Information on measures to support disabled people into employment starts with classification: musculo-skeletal, respiratory, mental, and so on. The 'drag' begins from this basic distraction of attention: the categories needed are of kinds of barriers and kinds of solutions.
2. The perception of personal deficit is gratuitously widened. A process of 'assessment' overrides the primary knowledge source a person's perceptions of their life-course and its obstacles as the basis for decision on support needs. The last time I heard the old mantra, 'They tell me what they want; I tell them what they need', it was uttered by an Employment Service manager.
3. The deficit together with its assumed implications is supposed to define a permanent relationship between a competent provider and a deficient user. A false 'us and them' perception restricts essential communication to a channel in one direction. Any 'user input' is confined within limits set by the one-way management process. These errors themselves make up a closed system: challenge to any of them is taken only as another indicator of deficit.

This argument will seem like an attack on the skills and knowledge base of committed people who are trying to make the best use of training and experience. Therefore, it has to be stressed that the 'errors' I refer to are *systemic*; they are not an inherent part of all individual support relationships. No solution that might be proposed can be made effective without including the perceptions of people who have responsibility to operate the system.

The purpose of this section has been to relocate the concept of 'deficit' where it belongs in the underlying thinking of policy and practice. We can now look at the means by which it can be replaced with something more purposive.

A 'theory' in use for the disabled people's movement

At this time, policy change and implementation have highly centralised control down to quite fine detail set out in 'guidance'. In this environment, it has become pressing to re-examine the role of civil society, and in particular to reaffirm a simple fact: impetus for change comes from two directions, bottom-up as well as top-down. Whenever a group arises in a community in order to confront a social issue, almost in the act of doing so it defines a boundary for itself, affirms some core values, and adopts what might be called a 'theory in use'. In the sector of civil society that has called itself the disabled people's movement, the theory in use has been based on what is usually called the *social model of disability.*

This is also called a social understanding or interpretation, and sometimes referred to as a theory, a philosophy, or even a value system. This overloads it; the social model is a *model.* In the words of Finkelstein, one of the first exponents of a social understanding of disability in the 1970s:

> It is only when we think of a 'model' as a tool, and begin using it to imagine something new that we would like to create, that models become really useful. (Finkelstein, 1996, p 15)

A hard-edged statement of the model would make a core distinction as follows:

> *all* disability is located in environments, communities, administrative structures and cultural attitudes; *all* personal impairment belongs with the diverse wealth of human differences that make up someone's 'personal equation'. (Gibbs, 2002; emphasis added)

Uses of a model begin with the personal insight it brings. Without anything else, change is triggered by the recognition that barriers to a personal life-course are not in someone's body but in their environment. The owners of the model are all those who have come to this recognition. To pass from imagining change to creating change, the model then has to link with a practical framework. For our organisations this was a construct called the 'seven needs'. The needs set out were:

1. information;
2. peer support;
3. housing;
4. technical aids;
5. personal assistance;
6. transport;
7. environmental access.

This is not simply a list, because it follows a logical sequence, each step relating to all those preceding. In fact, the construct is a simple kind of *whole system*. By its use, ways are opened up to inclusive non-segregated solutions to other needs, like access to training, earned income, active leisure, participation in community and political life.

Social model praxis

The long game

For 20 years, the social model has been applied by organisations of disabled people to develop pilot alternatives to dependency-creating services. Examples of these show how grassroots solutions arose which since have begun to enter policy development. The crucial points to make about this process are, first, that it has proved to be quite long; and second, that its inception is likely to be wholly outside the notice of policy makers. A full generation may elapse before the development process enters a strategic stage of public service recognition.

Examples should relate first to the primary needs as set out above, since effective support into employment often will depend on solutions to those needs.

Housing adaptations

To promote barrier-free housing and home adaptations, organisations of disabled people applied a social understanding of disability to produce detailed design proposals (Lewis, 1992). This perspective from direct experience complemented the 'Lifetime Homes' concept developed about the same time (Rowe, 1990) and adopted by the Joseph Rowntree Foundation with input from housing experts. Currently these issues are active again because of a need to find solutions to serious deficits in the way Disabled Facilities Grants are provided for home adaptations. Strong arguments are now being brought into the review process that support a 'whole-system invest-to-save' strategy (Heywood, 2003) in which much of the early thinking is incorporated.

Technical aids provision

Local planning structures in the 1980s allowed Derbyshire Centre for Integrated Living (DCIL) to have effective input to joint Health and Local Authority strategy for services to disabled people. Through a joint working party on provision of home equipment, this led to a pilot project that demonstrated the conversion from a deficit approach requiring elaborate assessments to a simple distribution system (JAPWP, 1988). The evidence of that successful pilot has continued to be used in national policy review forums. Review included examples of how 'health and social care' could create inappropriate specialisation, wasteful practice, and added disability (Mandelstam, 1996). Government guidance eventually adopted the principles of integrated and simplified provision that had been demonstrated in practice (DH, 2001).

Measuring disablement

In 1989-90, a Disability Benefits Consortium of disability organisations sought to influence the government's review of social security for disabled people. Drawing on experience supporting claims and appeals, DCIL, representing the British Council of Disabled People, took an illustration from data in the Surveys of Disability in Great Britain (Martin et al, 1989). In the survey, 31% of disabled people had earnings from employment compared with 69% of the general population. This average figure went down with increased grade of disability in the ten grades used for the survey, but even at Grade 1, only 48% had earnings, a differential equivalent to a 30% employment disability. To relate this figure to functional deficit, the survey's grades could be very roughly mapped across to the 'loss of faculty' scale used in the Industrial Injuries Scheme at the time. Based on welfare rights experience with the scheme, Grade 1 would never score above the lowest category for loss of faculty, set at 0-8%. A loss of faculty equivalent to the observed 30% disadvantage would be in category five or six (equivalent to a below-knee amputation). It was a rough and ready comparison, but left little doubt that only a small part of actual employment disadvantage could be related to any measured personal functional deficit. The greater deficit, then, lay elsewhere.

I argued earlier in this chapter that its location is the system of social security control based on *incapacity*. New proposals to remove 'categories' and link personal support to measures for social change (Bolderson and Mabbett, 2000) are taking up the case that was being made by disabled people themselves 10 years earlier.

Implementing an investment approach

The argument here is that an emergent process with its inception in direct experience is an invariable precursor of any useful social change. In a 'deficit' approach, where perception of support need is displaced into labelling and measuring attributes of individuals, the process is simply not engaged. An 'investment' approach, on the other hand, would accept a public service role at several stages:

- encouraging the process of inception without in any way seeking to manage it;
- supporting or participating in the trials and applications by which models are 'cashed out';
- supplying the skills and organisation to extend successful applications into general use.

With the best of intentions, this entire process soon may be colonised within a centrally controlled hierarchy. A much-extended role is being constructed for the voluntary and community sector as auxiliary service providers. The distinctive contributions of peer support and self-help are easily lost in this process, as managers seek high volume delivery with easily monitored 'standards'. There are clear arguments, based on the effective use of public resources, against diverting the sector from its primary role (CENTRIS, 2003). If this argument is correct, the position is more serious than that: the diversion would sever public administration from a primary source of knowledge production and innovation.

Towards an investment approach in employment services

Origin and purpose

At what point after the modest beginning described earlier does an initiative 'light up' as an agent of change? Is it when it gains some measure of official recognition, or when it begins to *change lives*? A goal of this chapter is to identify the primary source of knowledge needed for social change as the lived and shared experience of people who go through the process of re-defining, re-valuing and re-interpreting their social relationship.

Accessing this knowledge source is problematic in the present policy context. Both the sourcing of knowledge and the setting of purpose have become highly reductive processes that actively distance themselves from their human framework. Each needs to go through the kind of 'conversion' I have described, and possible approaches to this are suggested below.

Knowledge and evidence

The point about sourcing knowledge above is not opposed to 'evidence-based practice' as such; rather, it questions the boundaries of what constitutes 'evidence'. At times contention on this issue has seemed to leave irreconcilable positions, which might be set out as:

- it is not evidence unless it achieves an objective detachment;
- it is not evidence unless it remains attached to human contexts, goals and consequences.

Either position can command passion. The first still dominates to a degree that strongly affects what research is funded, published, and heard in the development of public policy.

A means of conversion lies in use of whole systems theory, especially in the underlying principle that *only an interaction can generate knowledge* (Midgley, 2000, p 76). It follows that if the object of knowledge, for instance a group of people using a service, is not an *actor*, then the knowledge about it is deficient. Public health solutions, for example, may fail if they look for an average gain without knowing about the range of public responses that will influence take-up. Social relationships that lack this 'structural coupling' are characterised as "impaired human social systems: they have lost their vigour and have depersonalised their components" (Maturana and Varela, 1998, p 199). I do not venture to enquire how general this condition might be; it is certainly the condition of disabled people in relation to support structures designated for them.

Targets

Managers all through public services are charged to implement programmes of modernisation driven by working to targets. Now, targets in the business marketplace are about the production of goods.

Public services, as well as organisations in civil society, are about people. Targets applied to people treat them as commodities, hence as objects, which is the key permission for a whole raft of practices ranging from relic welfare paternalism to wholesale infringement of human rights.

A reaction against the dominance of number targets has begun, with a dawning recognition that "when we measure life, we reduce it" (Boyle, 2001). Other means are needed to monitor the progress of individuals towards life-course goals, of labour forces towards a profile reflecting the population, and of communities towards inclusion. Principles that might be set out to safeguard against the depersonalising effects of measurement are:

• that no target can be said to exist until evidence is provided by feedback from the people concerned;
• that in the long term, the only acceptable targets for people are ones they have set for themselves and monitor for themselves.

There are many ways to attach value other than by numerical measurement. Work by the Social Policy Research Unit at York University has sought practical ways to focus on the *outcomes* of services (Qureshi, 2001). In parallel with this emphasis, 'user organisations' have asserted their own views of standards through projects like 'Shaping Our Lives' (SOL, 2003). The emphasis so far is on primary 'social care' services, within the consumerist boundaries set by policy and research funding. A further stage of conversion, opening up options to move on from 'social care', would require that outcomes are set independently of what services already exist, and become the basis for service design and administration.

The effect of this conversion on support into work is that measures of progress are not limited to attainment of target numbers or to means of support specified in advance. It is also necessary to identify those aspects of support to which people attach particular *value*. These will be about experience of the support pathway, workplace relationships, and advancement opportunities, as well as simply being in a job. The challenge is to find measures appropriate to a range of value criteria within the whole environment.

Employment support as a 'professional allied to the community'

To the extent that both 'social care' services and employment services intended for disabled people still rely on diagnostic categories, assessment, and professional prescription, they remain attached to a background (not far distant) of segregated institutions and workshops. They have not achieved a final conversion of their thinking to supporting full inclusion in accessible workplaces and communities.

To set a course for that conversion, two vulnerable processes need serious investment:

1. Something has to be pulling from the community end as well as something pushing from the policy end.
2. The social model must be used to imagine how a support profession working directly to a disabled people's mandate might operate.

Finkelstein (1999) has introduced the concept of a 'profession allied to the community', in contrast to 'professions allied to medicine'. Within the disabled people's movement and its organisations are many pilot services and projects that are highly innovative in their theory and practice. To the extent that they develop new competences, have an independent training framework in the discipline of disability equality training, and adopt ways to monitor outcomes, these have begun to 'professionalise'. Fragmented at present, these projects have the potential to network and conjoin, perhaps within a regional framework of public administration. In doing that, they will have the basis of a true profession allied to the community.

This profession will be constructed around practice consisting of targeted intervention at points during a life course where someone encounters disabling barriers that their own resources cannot overcome. Its outcome will be a barrier-free transition that strengthens an individual's resources simultaneously. By focusing on barriers, support becomes developmental rather than palliative; it influences whole systems as well as individual progress; and it invests both in individuals and in the community that gains their active contribution.

References

Bolderson, H. and Mabbett, D. (2001) 'Non-discriminating social policy? Policy scenarios for meeting needs without categorisation', in J. Clasen (ed) *What future for social policy?*, The Hague: Kluwer Law International, pp 199-210.

Boyle, D. (2001) 'You can count me out', *The Observer*, 14 January.

CEC (Commission of the European Communities) (1996) *A new European Community disability strategy: Commission on Equality of Opportunity for People with Disabilities*, Brussels: CEC.

CENTRIS (Centre for Research and Innovation in Social Policy and Practice) (2003) *Unravelling the maze – A survey of civil society in the UK*, Newcastle: CENTRIS.

Davis, K. (1990) *A social barriers model of disability: Theory into practice (the emergence of the 'seven needs')*, Derbyshire Coalition of Disabled People, (www.leeds.ac.uk/disability-archiveuk/index.html).

DH (Department of Health) (2001) *Guide to implementing community equipment services*, London: DH.

European Union (2000) The 'General Equal Treatment Directive', Directive 2000/78/EC, articles 1,18.

Finkelstein, V. (1996) 'Modelling disability', (www.leeds.ac.uk/disability-archiveuk/index.html).

Finkelstein, V. (1999) 'Professions allied to the community (PACs), I, II', (www.leeds.ac.uk/disability-archiveuk/index.html).

Gibbs, D. (2002) 'The social model in practice', *Coalition: The magazine of the Greater Manchester Coalition of Disabled People*, September, p 26.

Gibbs, D. (2004) 'Social model services – an oxymoron?', in C. Barnes and G. Mercer (eds) *Disability policy and practice: Applying the social model of disability*, Leeds: The Disability Press, p 144.

Heywood, F. (2003) 'The effectiveness of housing adaptations', Paper presented to the 'Adaptations: Taking a long-term view' conference, York, 29 September.

Hunt, P. (1966) 'A critical condition', in P. Hunt (ed) *Stigma: The experience of disability*, London: Geoffrey Chapman, (www.leeds.ac.uk/disability-archiveuk/index.html).

JAPWP (Joint Aids Provision Working Party) (1988) *Report of the Joint Aids Provision Working Party*, Derby: Derbyshire County Council.

Levitas, R. (2001) 'Government more concerned with conformity than poverty', *Society Guardian*, 23 March.

Lewis, B. (1992) *Access for life: A case for adaptable, accessible homes in a barrier-free environment*, Derby: Derbyshire Coalition of Disabled People.

Mabbett, D. (2002) *Definitions of disability in Europe: A comparative analysis. Final Report*, London: Brunel University.

Mabbett, D. and Bolderson, H. (2001) 'A significant step forward? EU social policy and the development of a rights-based strategy for disabled people', Paper presented to the Annual Social Policy Assocation Conference, Queen's University Belfast, 24-26 July.

Mandelstam, M. (1996) *Going to market: Equipment and products for disabled and older people – An overview*, London: The Disabled Living Centres Council.

Martin, J., White, A. and Meltzer, H. (1989) *Disabled adults: Services, transport and employment*, Office of Population Censuses and Surveys (OPCS) Surveys of Disability in Great Britain, London: HMSO.

Maturana, H. and Varela, F. (1998) *The tree of knowledge: The biological roots of human understanding*, London: Shambhala.

Midgley, G. (2000) *Systemic intervention: Philosophy, methodology, and practice*, London: Kluwer/Plenum.

Qureshi, H. (ed) (2001) *Outcomes in social care practice*, York: Social Policy Research Unit, University of York.

Roulstone, A., Gradwell, L., Price, J. and Child, L. (2003) *Thriving and surviving at work: Disabled people's employment strategies*, Bristol: The Policy Press.

Roulstone, A. (2004) 'Employing the social model: What are the implications of the social model of disability for UK employment policy', in C. Barnes and G. Mercer (eds) *Disability, policy and practice: Applying the social model of disability*, Leeds: The Disability Press.

Rowe, A. (1990) *Lifetime homes: Flexible housing for successive generations*, London: Helen Hamlyn Foundation.

SOL (Shaping Our Lives) (2003) *Shaping our lives – From outset to outcome. What people think of the social care services they use*, York: SOL and Joseph Rowntree Foundation.

Stafford, B. (2005) 'New Deal for Disabled People: What's new about New Deal?', Chapter 3, present volume.

Stanley, K. and Regan, S. (2003) *The missing million: Supporting disabled people into work*, London: IPPR.

Thornton, P. (2005) 'Jobcentre Plus: can specialised personal advisers be justified?', Chapter 9, present volume.

UPIAS (Union of the Physically Impaired against Segregation) (1976) *Fundamental principles of disability*, London: UPIAS and the Disability Alliance, (www.leeds.ac.uk/disability- archiveuk/index.html).

FOURTEEN

Changing minds: opening up employment options for people with mental health problems

Jenny Secker and Bob Grove

Introduction

Historically, if people with enduring mental health problems have been seen as capable of work at all, this has been framed as 'therapy' to be undertaken in sheltered, socially excluded settings. Real work in real workplaces has been seen as something to be put off until recovery, in the clinical sense of the disappearance or control of 'symptoms', is complete, in effect indefinitely for many people. This chapter starts by examining that historical context, contrasting it with the research evidence regarding the work aspirations of people with enduring mental health problems and their potential to become valued employees. The authors argue that what is required to enable people to fulfill their potential is a shift from a clinical model of recovery from mental ill-health towards a model more akin to a social model of disability.

To support that argument, the results of a study exploring approaches to employment support for this group are presented. In conclusion, the chapter looks at the progress being made in developing appropriate supported employment in the UK and at the challenges ahead.

The historical legacy – a waste of potential

The use of 'constructive occupation' has been part of mental healthcare since the development of the mental hospitals. For the most part, however, it has been assumed that the best people can hope for is low-grade, low-paid work within institutional or protected settings. Yet where more ambitious schemes have been tried, 'patients' have often risen to the challenge, causing some psychiatrists to question their assumptions. This thread of questioning and experimentation re-emerged several times during the 20th century, but in the end has always been overwhelmed by clinical pessimism and a presumption that people must be 'cured' before they can work.

In the 1950s and 1960s, British psychiatry led the way in vocational rehabilitation through pioneers such as Rudolf Freudenberg, Douglas Bennett and Donald Early, and they in turn derived many of their ideas from earlier work in Germany. Freudenberg was himself German by birth and was influenced by the work of Dr Herman Simon, Director of the psychiatric hospital at Gütersloh in in Western Germany. Simon's own crucial experience had occurred much earlier, in 1905 at nearby Warstein, when he had taken over a new asylum in a very derelict and unfinished condition. He recruited the patients to finish off the works and noted that there were significant improvements in the condition of many of these people, notably the most disturbed (Burleigh, 1964).

For Simon, the most important ingredient in this process was that the work was *real*. It was essential and had an obvious and urgent purpose, which was shared by the staff and the patients, who were valued as workers. To produce such a situation under ordinary asylum conditions, run by its own staff, not depending on any contributions from the patients, was more difficult.

While Superintendent of Netherne Hospital in Surrey, England, Freudenberg developed rehabilitative schemes that emphasised the importance of work. Local employers set up satellite workshops in the hospital and every attempt was made to ensure that all patients did some paid work every day. By 1967, 100 out of 122 hospitals surveyed had some form of industrial therapy provision (Wansborough and Miles, 1968).

The classic studies of Wing and Brown (1970) found that at Netherne there were many fewer cases of severe schizophrenia, compared with less 'active' hospitals. The so-called 'natural history' of schizophrenia, with its decline into inactivity and 'negativism', thus proved to be highly dependent on the opportunities provided for meaningful activities and the most malignant element was 'the amount of time doing nothing', a rediscovery of Simon's experience 50 years previously.

However, the success of these industrial therapy schemes was limited. There may have been benefits in terms of reduction of symptoms and stability, but they did not lead to many people returning to open employment, and they were not adaptable to changing industrial conditions. When mass unemployment hit in the 1980s, all hope that people would move on into open employment vanished and the myth that people with serious or long-term conditions could not compete in the modern labour market reasserted itself. Even when the major mental hospitals closed it was not unusual for the industrial therapy unit to remain open for patients living in the community to return to each day. Lip service was paid to rehabilitation but when preparation for returning to real life takes two or more years it becomes a way of life in its own right. Of course, both staff and patients adapted to this way of life and one might assume that most people with mental health problems have settled for alternatives to employment.

The reality is quite different. It is clear from surveys carried out in the UK over the past few years that the great majority of people with enduring mental health problems, as many as 90% in some studies, aspire to a real job with real wages (Bates, 1996; Rinaldi and Hill, 2000; Secker et al, 2001). So the assumption that people do not want to work is plainly unfounded. But are they able to work? Early research in the US focused on the question of which mental health service users might be able to find and keep a job, but found little evidence that individual demographic, clinical or social characteristics made any difference (Anthony, 1994). What did appear to make a difference was the individual's motivation and the sort of support they received in pursuing and achieving their ambitions. Given the right support, it became clear that anyone with the motivation to work could succeed in finding and keeping a job (Bond, 1998).

In the US, the model of employment support developed on the basis of this body of research is known as Individual Placement and Support (IPS) and a Cochrane review of the evidence for the efficacy of the approach has now demonstrated beyond doubt that it works (Crowther et al, 2001). In the UK, however, although the 1990s saw the establishment of a growing number of supported employment projects, mainly in the voluntary sector, little research had been undertaken and it was unclear what approaches were being used and how well these worked. The study described in the following section was designed to find answers to those questions.

Finding and keeping a job: a study of employment support in the UK

Since the aim of the study was to explore experiences of employment support from the perspectives of those involved, semi-structured interviews were used to carry out the research. Five projects offering employment support to people who had experienced mental health problems agreed to help with the study and with their assistance 17 clients were recruited to take part. All 17 clients gave permission for their employment project worker and workplace manager to be interviewed and a total of 51 interviews were carried out.

Analysis of the interview data led to the construction of a framework encompassing a continuum of approaches to the provision of employment support, with two projects, described here as Projects A and D, at the extremes of the continuum. Because these two projects were so different, it was important to understand why this was and what the implications might be in terms of outcomes for their clients. A total of seven cases were studied from the two projects, four from Project A and three from Project D. Of the seven clients concerned, five had been able to retain their job for 12 months or longer while two, both from Project A, had experienced the breakdown of their job within a matter of weeks. The following sections describe the different approaches to employment support at the two projects, draw out the reasons for that difference and consider the relative strengths and limitations of the two approaches.

Approaches to employment support

At Project A, a two-tier approach to assessment and job preparation was in place, reflecting the traditional expectation that to embark on paid employment clients should have recovered from their mental health problems, or at least be more or less symptom free, if necessary with the aid of medication. When new clients were referred to the project, an initial interview was carried out to assess whether the client had recovered sufficiently to move straight to job finding or whether job preparation was required as part of a process of convalescence.

When a client was assessed as sufficiently recovered, further assessment or job preparation was seen as unnecessary and the client's mental health problems were not seen as having implications for work. Instead the focus was on how readily they would fit into and function in the world of work. The assistance provided for these clients consisted of an invitation to attend a job club, held on one morning each week, where information about vacancies was made available. Although help with the application process was provided if required, project workers did not see it as part of their role to explore clients' career options with them in any detail or assist them in pursuing their goals.

When new clients were thought to require job preparation, the emphasis was on using this period of 'convalescence' to bring their skills up to scratch through a structured training course and to develop the stamina required to cope with work through an unpaid work placement. Although it was hoped in some cases that an unpaid placement might lead to paid work, as with clients who were assessed as ready for work on referral, project workers did not see it as their role to help with this:

> "We don't find patient employment, we let them find their own. The idea is they find employment, we support them in every way possible, they're getting the confidence, getting stamina back and getting a job is a bonus as we see it. But the patient has to find it themselves." (Project A worker)

Equally, in identifying placements workers did not seek to pursue clients' individual career goals. Instead, the project relied on an established pool of employers, allocating placements on the basis of what was available coupled with an assessment of whether clients would fit in at that workplace. Once a potential placement had been identified an interview was arranged and a project worker would accompany the client to the interview. However, it was regarded as the responsibility of the client to let the employer know of any needs they might have. In effect, the project worker's role was seen as that of an 'introducer', as one workplace manager put it, and identifying and resolving any potential problems was not part of the process of negotiating a placement. What was important, from the project workers' point of view, was that the employer should feel confident that their own needs would be met, in terms of the client's capacity to do the work required.

Once an unpaid placement had been set up for a client, the system for providing support consisted of visits to the placement every two weeks, with a formal review after six weeks. From the workers' accounts, the two-weekly visits were fairly informal, involving a brief discussion with the client followed by a separate meeting with the manager. As at the stage when placements were being set up, the focus remained on how well the client was doing the job required by the employer. Because the visits involved separate discussions with the client and manager, there was no opportunity for clients to discuss their needs with managers, or for managers to provide feedback to clients. Here again, then, the focus appeared to be more on the client's performance in the job than on their needs.

When unpaid placements did lead to paid work, contact with the project was minimal and workers had no contact with clients' workplaces unless they were requested to do so by clients. The arrangement for clients was that they should drop into the job club or contact the project for an appointment during job club hours if they wanted to discuss any concerns, and contact outside these hours was discouraged. As the following project worker indicated, the provision of follow-up support in paid work was antithetical to the project's equation of readiness to work with recovery from illness:

> "It's not fair to clients to be in contact. If they're working they've left their illness behind them … they don't want us going in and visiting and talking to the employer."

A first indication of the different approach taken at Project D was an assumption that all clients would need a period of assessment and job preparation. The three clients interviewed from the project all described a thorough process of assessment and preparation before starting work and workers at Project D did not describe other cases where clients had moved straight into work. In contrast, all four clients from Project A had obtained paid work within two months or less.

The assumption that clients would need a period of assessment and preparation stemmed from a view that construed mental health problems not as an illness from which people needed to recover in the clinical sense before working, but as an intrinsic aspect of a client's life experience that had implications for work. In accordance with this view, workers at Project D made extensive use of individual interviews, not to assess clients' ability to fit into the world of work but to understand, and enable the client to understand, the career options and type of workplace that might best suit them. In this context, clients' mental health problems were not the sole focus of assessment, but were viewed as one of a range of potentially relevant issues, alongside other aspects of their life experience.

As at Project A, the job preparation activities offered at Project D included a structured training course, together with practical assistance and a job club. In addition to these activities, however, the one-to-one work undertaken with clients was used to enable them to address any problems and barriers to work as these were identified. Although job preparation was therefore intensive at Project D, this was seen only as a step along the way, to be built on once clients were in work. At this project, the emphasis in job finding was on negotiating work trials for clients in the explicit expectation that, if the trial were successful, paid work would result. In keeping with the focus of assessment and job preparation on their particular needs, clients were not expected to fit in with what was available. Where an appropriate placement was not available, efforts would be made to find a suitable employer specifically for that individual.

This attention to clients' needs was also evident in the way in which work trials were negotiated with employers. At Project D, it was standard practice for workers to accompany clients to interviews. The primary purpose of these initial meetings with employers was seen as ensuring that the client's needs would be met and support for the client in achieving this was seen as essential. At this project, then, clients were not expected to make their way into work independently. On the other hand, nor was the negotiation of a placement seen as purely a matter for the worker. Instead the emphasis was on interdependence and shared responsibility. However, employers' needs were also recognised, not only in terms of the client's ability to do the job but in terms of the manager's own support needs. As one worker described the process:

> "I always talk to the client first about what they want me to talk to the employer about. What's our strategy, what are we going to say you need. So I go in expecting that the person I'm providing can do the job. I know they can otherwise I wouldn't be putting them forward, and I say that. And I say that I'm expecting them to be treated like a normal employee, but there are certain things, you know, the reasonable adjustments, but we get those out of the way at the start – this is what their needs are.... But I think what persuades them is by saying that I will come and I will do whatever you want, whenever you want, I will be there."

At Project D, workers also saw providing ongoing support to clients as a central role, both during their work trial and once they were in paid work. As with work experience placements at Project A, the support provided consisted of informal contact combined with more formal reviews. Here again, however, the emphasis was not so much on how well the client was meeting the employer's needs per se, as on enabling the client to address any problems and develop into the job. To this end, the reviews themselves were very different from those at Project A, in that a structured process was used to enable the client and their manager to provide feedback to each other. Before each review, both the client and manager were asked to complete an assessment form. These forms were returned to the project worker before the review and were then used as the starting point for discussion. Once each party had provided feedback to the other, the worker would summarise what had been said and, where it seemed necessary, encourage the client and manager to set goals for extending the client's skills and experience. At the end of each review the question of whether further reviews were needed was raised and a date agreed for the next review if required. Thus both the frequency of subsequent reviews and the length of time over which the worker would remain involved were a matter for ongoing negotiation.

Explaining the difference

In essence, the two approaches to employment support at Projects A and D were underpinned by contrasting models of the nature of recovery from mental health problems. At Project A, the approach was clearly underpinned by a clinical model within which clients referred to the project were seen as needing to move from being ill to being more or less well again before getting a job. From this perspective, the primary purpose of employment support was one of enabling clients at the 'convalescent' stage, those who were not yet sufficiently well, to become ready for work. Once clients were perceived to be ready for work, they were treated as autonomous, independent adults who could be expected to fit into and function in the workplace like anyone else.

At Project D, clients were not expected to have put their problems behind them before starting work. From the perspective of workers at this project, clients' mental health problems were seen as potentially having ongoing implications for work and they were not expected to be able to quickly fit into a job unaided. Rather, the approach was based on an assumption of interdependency and initial vulnerability. In turn, clients' recovery and entry into work was seen in terms of an ongoing, incremental process involving adaptation and adjustment in the interaction between the individual and the work environment, a process in which they would inevitably require support, at least for some time.

This second model has considerable resonance with the social model of disability and with a related reconceptualisation of recovery that is gaining ground in the field of mental health. In this context, recovery is viewed as establishing a satisfying and meaningful life with an impairment, rather than waiting to be without it, although complete recovery in the clinical sense is not seen as beyond hope (Deegan, 1994). In turn, the process of recovery involves the reintroduction of the individual into a socially accepting and acceptable environment.

Strengths and limitations

In the IPS model based on research in the US, emphasis is placed on rapid job finding with minimal prevocational job preparation (Drake et al, 1996). From this perspective, a strength of the approach at Project A was the speed with which some clients were able to move into paid work. However, the success of this approach in the US also depends on features lacking within the approach at Project A, including attention to clients' individual preferences, continuous assessment and ongoing support.

In the two cases from Project A where clients were able to retain their jobs, a lengthier process of assessment and preparation was arguably unnecessary, but in the other two cases there were indications that the process was insufficiently thorough. In one case, the client explained that his expectations of employment support had included not only assistance with preparing for and finding a job, but also with understanding the implications for employment of his mental health problems. However, this help had not been forthcoming and the client experienced a recurrence of his mental health problems within a matter of weeks and lost his job. The second client also began to experience problems soon after starting work and she too lost her job. In this case the client had been encouraged to return to her previous job with an agency providing care for older people with little assessment of her needs. Her own account suggests that a more detailed assessment would have indicated alternative career options:

> "I didn't want to do elderly care because I found this very stressful and if you are a sufferer from depression it's not necessarily helpful.... I was desperate for permanent work.... I wanted something permanent with a regular income."

A further limitation of the approach at Project A stemmed from the view of clients assessed as ready to look for work as independent, autonomous adults who required no further help. The accounts of clients from Project A suggest that when they were left to raise their needs themselves they were unlikely to do so, while the project's similar 'hands-off' approach to clients once they were in paid work was also a clear limitation when problems arose. As one worker himself commented, in the absence of follow-up support the opportunity to help clients resolve problems and keep their job was lost.

In many ways, the approach at Project D avoided these limitations.

As has been seen, the job-finding process at Project D was based on a detailed assessment of clients' skills and needs coupled with careful consideration of the extent to which a job would match these. Equally, follow-up support was negotiated with both clients and managers as a matter of course. An indication of the strength of this approach was that all three clients from the project had been able to retain their jobs for a considerable period of time. Although it might be thought that the intensity of the approach would be unwelcome to some clients and workplace managers, this was not the case with any of the people we interviewed, and some of the managers involved with Project A would clearly have welcomed more intensive support.

The answer to the question the study set out to address, then, was that a wide range of approaches were being taken in the UK to providing employment support, some underpinned by traditional, clinical ideas about recovery and readiness to work and others by a social model of recovery akin to the social model of disability. It was clear from the accounts people gave us of their experiences of the two approaches that those underpinned by a social model hold far greater promise for the development of supported employment in the UK.

Progress to date and the challenges ahead

The best evidence available shows that most people who want to, even those with severe and/or recurring conditions, can do paid competitive work if they are provided with the right kind of support. It is also clear that some organisations in the UK are already providing such services and achieving successful outcomes. However, the legacy of the illness model is still very much with us and even where people are trying to raise hopes and expectations they are sometimes subverted by quite inappropriate but very powerful and deeply embedded assumptions. One of the most pernicious of these is the assumption that recovery is synonymous with being permanently symptom free and that being permanently symptom free is a precondition for obtaining open employment. Even where this assumption is not explicit it can all too easily creep into the messages that people receive, damaging self-belief and destroying hope. Those in this study who were expected to make it without support once they were apparently well enough to do so were in fact doomed to painful failure, with all its attendant feelings of disappointment and remorse at having let themselves and others down *again*.

The argument of this chapter is therefore that a social model of recovery is a necessary underpinning to services that support people with mental health problems into paid work. Such a model makes no presumptions about present or future 'wellness', but rather concentrates on the support and adjustments people need (and are entitled to) to achieve their ambitions and perform at their best. The authors believe strongly that this approach also fits well with the evidence on what works to get people into paid employment. The challenge for mental health services is to overturn years of conditioning that concentrates on problems and symptoms and to recognise that the best medicine of all is hope of a better life.

Acknowledgements

The research data we draw on to support our argument was previously published in *Disability and Society*, vol 17, no 4, pp 403-18 as an article entitled 'Recovering from illness or recovering your life? Implications of clinical versus social models of recovery from mental illness for employment support services'. We are grateful to the publishers (www.tandf.co.uk/journals/carfax/09687599.html) for permission to use some of the same material here. The research was supported by the Economic and Social Research Council, Award No RO22250144.

References

Anthony, W.A. (1994) 'Characteristics of people with psychiatric disabilities that are predictive of entry into the rehabilitation process and successful employment outcomes', *Psychosocial Rehabilitation Journal*, vol 17, no 3, pp 3-14.

Bates, P. (1996) 'Stuff as dreams are made on', *Health Service Journal*, vol 4, no 33, p 1.

Bond, G.R. (1998) 'Principles of the individual placement and support model: empirical support', *Psychiatric Rehabilitation Journal*, vol 22, no 1, pp 11-23.

Burleigh, M. (1964) *Death and deliverance: 'Euthanasia' in Germany 1900-1945*, Cambridge: Cambridge University Press.

Crowther, R.E., Marshall, M., Bond, G.R. and Huxley, P. (2001) 'Helping people with severe mental illness to obtain work: systematic review', *British Medical Journal*, vol 332, no 7280, pp 204-7.

Deegan, P. (1994) 'The lived experience of rehabilitation', in L. Spaniol and M. Koehler (eds) *The experience of recovery*, Boston, MA: Boston Center for Psychiatric Rehabilitation.

Drake, R.E., Becker, D.R., Biesanz, J.C., Wyzik, P.F. and Turrey, W.C. (1996) 'Day treatment versus supported employment for persons with severe mental illness: a replication study', *Psychiatric Services*, vol 47, no 10, pp 1125-7.

Rinaldi, M. and Hill, R.G. (2000) *Insufficient concern*, London: Merton Mind.

Secker, J., Grove, B. and Seebohm, P. (2001) 'Challenging barriers to employment, training and education for mental health service users: the service user's perspective', *Journal of Mental Health*, vol 10, no 4, pp 395-404.

Wansborough, S.W. and Miles, A. (1968) *Industrial rehabilitation in psychiatric hospitals*, London: King Edward's Hospital Fund.

Wing, J.K. and Brown, G.W. (1970) *Institutionalism and schizophrenia: A comparative study of three hospitals 1960-1968*, Cambridge: Cambridge University Press.

FIFTEEN

Enabling futures for people with learning difficulties? Exploring employment realities behind the policy rhetoric

Dan Goodley and Ghashem Norouzi

Introduction

In this chapter, we contemplate the current nature of employment for people with learning difficulties and aim to envisage an enabling future. We critically consider some of the contemporary employment policies and programmes in Britain, make reference to a recent study of work experiences of people with learning difficulties and unpack the discourses and philosophies that underpin some of the interventions of professionals and policy makers.

First, we outline what we mean when we use the term 'learning difficulties'. Second, we explore how employment is considered in the 2001 White Paper, *Valuing people*. Third, we critically examine the impact of supported employment and its relationship with normalisation. Fourth, we analyse the concept of 'real jobs' and the service culture in which many people with learning difficulties are confined. Fifth, we assess the involvement of disabled professionals and organisations of disabled people in the employment of people with learning difficulties. This is an important point of consideration if the political and policy landscape of disability and employment is to be dictated by disabled people and their organisations. We end with a number of questions to further debate.

Learning difficulties: a social phenomenon

> What should concern us is the mystifying fact that so many
> social scientists ... do not regard mental retardation as a

social and cultural phenomenon. I say mystifying, because nothing in the probabilistic world of social scientific reality is more certain than the assertion that mental retardation is a socio-cultural problem through and through. (Dingham, 1968, p 76)

The term 'learning difficulties' describes people who have been labelled at some point in their lives as requiring specialist 'mental handicap/ learning disability services' (Walmsley, 1993). We opt for this term, instead of other synonyms such as 'mental handicap', 'mental impairment', 'developmental disabilities' or 'learning disabilities', because it is the term preferred by many in the self-advocacy movement (Goodley, 2000). As one member of the British movement puts it:

If you put 'people with learning difficulties' then they know that people want to learn and to be taught how to do things. (Quoted in Sutcliffe and Simons, 1993, p 23)

Understanding what we mean by 'learning difficulties' is crucial to our analysis, primarily because people who have been assigned this label face particular employment barriers. The 1999 Labour Force Survey reported that some 'impairment groups' are associated with relatively high employment rates, such as diabetes and hearing impairment, while other groups have much lower employment rates such as those with the labels of mental health problems and learning difficulties. Indeed, around two thirds of those with learning difficulties are out of work and on state benefits. In addition, according to the Equal Opportunities Review study (1996), people with learning difficulties had the highest unemployment rate of all people with impairments (37%). In attempting to understand what we mean by 'learning difficulties', we might be tempted to consider the ways in which 'impairment of mind' has been assessed to reveal identifiable organic, neurological or genetic origins. Yet, for us, learning difficulties is best understood as an artefact of disabling society; a construction that says a lot about the values and preoccupations of our society (Goodley, 2001). As social researchers and allies to the self-advocacy movement, our stance on the origins of learning difficulties is captured well by the following expert commentary:

I may need help in some things, but I'm not retarded. I can take care of myself .... Everyone needs help. Some people need more. Even the ones in the outside – the normal people, have marriage counsellors and other people to help them. (Martin Levine, Canadian self-advocate, quoted in Friedman–Lambert, 1987, p 15)

Clearly, the phenomenon of labour will have a difficult relationship with individuals whose humanity has been assessed in terms of social (in)competence, (mal)adaptive functioning and (low) intelligence. Such perceived individual deficits lie uneasily with the expected 'abilities' necessary for meaningful work (Goodley, 2001). Therefore, following the social model of disability (Oliver, 1990), our position is not to understand barriers as a function of an individual's impairment but to consider the social origins of those disabling barriers. We are therefore interested in the ways in which employment, as an element of society, demands particular skills and abilities that inevitably exclude certain sections of society from paid work. Crucially, we also look to society for remedies. People with and without learning difficulties are interdependent. Some require more relational links than others. While someone might have complex needs or 'severe learning difficulties', it is best to think of these as support requirements rather than individual failings. We now turn to some of those issues that are of importance to people with learning difficulties at the start of the 21st century.

Work: valuing people?

The meaning of work is complicated. Smits (2004) argues that the world of work is experiencing transformational change: frequent skill updates are required to maintain employment in many fields, flexible careers are required for survival as new endeavours emerge and old forms of work disappear, while virtually everyone is now part of the competitive global workforce. This take on labour in late modernity/capitalism raises particularly important issues for people with the label of learning difficulties. Supporting people simply to obtain paid work and contribute to their communities has wider connections with the ways in which society values people with learning difficulties. The 2001 White Paper, *Valuing people: A new strategy for learning disability for the 21st century* (DH, 2001), outlines the government's objective of enabling more people with 'learning disabilities' to participate in all forms of employment, wherever possible in paid work, and to make a valued contribution to the world of work. Such a stance is not unique, building as it does on well-established literature about the individual and socioeconomic advantages of employment (Hyde, 1996; Burchardt, 2000; Pannell and Simons, 2000). It is, however, a clearly articulated strategy for policy and practice in relation to the life chances of people with learning difficulties post the 1995 Disability Discrimination Act (DDA), and following the agitations of the International Disabled People's Movement. It is important to keep in mind a number of overlapping key concerns of *Valuing people*, which include the promotion of legal and civil rights, independence, choice and inclusion. In relation to work, a number of key ideas are promoted in the White Paper:

- changes to incapacity benefit so that individuals are not put off trying to work;
- changes to therapeutic earnings (see later in this chapter);
- chance to claim Disability Living Allowance while working;
- personal advisers and job brokers to help individuals make decisions about work.

These policies raise real concerns about the nature of work being promoted, adopted or denied. More generally, it remains to be seen whether or not employers and work cultures are open to changing their practices, in ways that include people with learning difficulties as valued employees. Wilson (2003) envisages good practices at work where employees, working alongside job coaches, proactively support their colleagues with learning difficulties. This is not without problems, of course, as some employees may feel resentment at taking on the responsibilities of support normally reserved for specialist workers and key workers. The White Paper draws on an implicit philosophy of building up elements of good practice in relation to the cumulative inclusion of people with learning difficulties at work. Here, the issue of supported employment is significant and not without dilemmas.

Supported employment and normalisation

Valuing people outlines the government's commitment to supported employment, which has traditionally been the main route to employment for people with learning difficulties. The government's Supported Employment Programme (SEP) is operated by the Employment Service. Over 22,000 disabled people are employed at a cost of over £155 million, including over 10,000 people employed by the organisation Remploy and over 12,000 people by the SEP run by local authorities and voluntary bodies. Forty per cent of those people on the SEP have the label of 'learning disabilities' (DH, 2001). In April 2001, the programme was renamed WORKSTEP, with the explicit aim of supporting disabled people particularly those who have barriers to finding and keeping work (DWP, 2003; DWP and DH, 2004). Pallisera et al (2003) suggest that supported work programmes should provide people with the necessary support, both within the workplace and outside it, for them to be able to carry out their work in an ordinary environment of the community. O'Bryan et al (2000) pinpoint the following three elements to supported employment:

- A person is hired and paid by a real employer.
- The job done meets the person's requirements and the employer's required standard.
- The person and the employer receive just enough help from a support organisation to ensure success.

Too often the supported work context provides the safest and most protective environment for people with learning difficulties, with the associated exclusion from more risky community-based work contexts. A study of social firms by Secker et al (2003) highlights further the problems of supported employment. Social firms originated in psychiatric rehabilitation but now exist as potentially transformative places for the employment of people with learning difficulties: particularly in a context where local authorities are being urged to modernise day services. Secker et al report the views of service users who failed to complain about not receiving wages because they found the work 'easy'. It could be argued, therefore, that the blurring of service user and employee not only threatens to institutionalise but also suppress the development (and dissent) of people with learning difficulties.

In a key analysis, Wilson (2003) notes how the philosophies of normalisation (and its associated framework of social role valorisation) continue to underpin the provision of supported employment. Normalisation, particularly in the US, emphasises the involvement of individuals with learning difficulties in the normal activities of everyday life (including the workplace). While such ideas have helped to challenge the segregation of disabled people from mainstream work, the emphasis is on producing as 'normal' a worker as possible and reducing 'devalued behaviours' in the workplace (Wilson, 2003, p 103). The emphasis is on the individual to change rather than the culture of the work place, the views of employers or the expectations of supported employment services. The focus is on the independence and individual development of the worker who, with appropriate training, should be able get on in work. Yet, the extent to which the culture changes in terms of becoming an inclusive or diverse workplace remains to be seen. Indeed, a current concern of the Disability Rights Commission (DRC) is the extent to which key agencies, including Job Centre Plus, fail to take a proactive role in promoting awareness among employers of the DDA and of good practice in recruiting and retaining disabled people as 'able' employees (DRC, 2004). That said, clearly supported employment contrasts often markedly and more positively with the traditional day centre.

Bass and Drewett (1996) note that supported employment was found to provide engaging and rewarding activities for people of all levels of ability, with most supported employees saying they found their work activities stimulating and enjoyable. This contrasted with their day services where people said they had much less to do, were often bored and where higher levels of disengagement were measured (see also Simons, 1998; Beyer et al, 1999, 2004). O'Bryan (2004) has outlined the following guidelines for people with learning difficulties and their families, in ensuring engaged supported employment practices:

- good information about what job and support options are currently available in their area;
- the expectation of all professionals that most people will wish to have a career and that it is possible;
- job coaches and other champions who will find out each person's ideal job and develop job and career opportunities from which to choose;
- job coaches and other champions who will work with government people, such as New Deal job brokers and benefit advisers, to successfully support people into the work they want;
- good information about White Paper developments and Partnership Board decisions which will affect people's job and career opportunities.

The ubiquitous aim of reconstructing day services continues to have very widespread impact upon the employment experiences of people with learning difficulties.

Service culture, therapeutic earnings and real jobs

There is a clear tension between plans to support people with learning difficulties into employment and the government's commitment to reconfiguring day services for people with learning difficulties. *Valuing people* outlines plans to bring together education, employment and care issues through the work of 'Learning Disability Partnership Boards'. Interestingly, the White Paper identifies the public sector as a key context for employment opportunities for people with learning difficulties. While central and local government and the NHS form some of the largest employment groups in the nation, we remain concerned about these aims to deploy people with learning difficulties, in different ways, in the existing service culture. So, for example, an individual moves from being a service user of an adult training centre to being one of the centre's cleaners. Their employment experiences remain located in the normalising service industry. This view of the welfare state as paternalistic and self-perpetuating is hardly new. Marxist critiques identify capitalism's exclusion of a whole section of the proletariat from the production process (Russell, 2002). Exclusion from the mainstream ensures inclusion in welfare. By keeping people with learning difficulties in the context of the public sector, key health and social care jobs are developed and maintained.

Olsen (2003) argues that such specially adapted work is ambiguous. It is usually labelled as the kind of work offered by the welfare state and at the same time usually lacks a significant aspect of what is recognised as ordinary work. There is a fine line between day centre worker and sheltered worker. It should be noted that sheltered employment is not without stigma, as an informant in Olsen's (2003) study points out: working in a sheltered workshop is something one might hide from more social included peers. Hyvärinen et al (2002) compare and contrast sheltered work, sheltered integrated work and supported employment. They suggest that the first two are essentially about personal care while the latter is about employment. The danger with service-based work is that it is difficult for professional and service users to step out of the ingrained roles in which personal care often overrides employment.

The White Paper recognises the ways in which the interaction between social security benefit rules and employment can result in disincentives to work for some people with learning difficulties (DH, 2001). From April 2001, the earnings disregard in income-related benefits rose from £15 to £20. The existence of the Disability Living Allowance (DLA) provides further support for people in work. However, the extent to which people with learning difficulties and their families negotiate DLA with wages remains unclear. Indeed, the increase to £20 for therapeutic earnings may well hinder rather than support more people accessing full-time paid work. Russell (2002) argues that the disability benefit system serves as a socially legitimised means by which employers can avoid hiring or retaining non-standard workers and 'morally' shift the cost of supporting the 'deserving disabled' onto poverty-based government programmes. Similarly, but more specifically, factories in China 'employ' disabled people on very low wages to stay at home because the tax advantages exceed the wages involved (Pierini et al, 2001).

The tendency for 'compulsory unemployment' is crucial to an analysis of the employment of people with learning difficulties: large numbers of people are left jobless in part because mainstream economists believe that a threshold of unemployment is necessary to avoid inflation (Russell, 2002). Similar consequences can be obtained, paradoxically, by enlarging the active reserve army of labour: this is good for business because it disciplines labour, keeps wages and inflation low (Russell, 2002). Such occurrences explain Roulstone's (2002) refusal to accept the assertion that employment integration is necessarily good for disabled people. However, what is the current state of affairs for people with learning difficulties, are there real jobs out there? Some interesting findings emerge from a recent study of the employment experiences of people with learning difficulties that surveyed the employment statistics of 200 people so labelled in work. While 50% of the respondents were in paid work, half of these received the minimum wage or less; 65% worked full time and 75% worked in non-segregated workplaces (Norouzi, 2005: forthcoming). Clearly, this demonstrates some evidence of more mainstreamed work, though the figures remind us that people with learning difficulties are hardly breaking down barriers to promotion, career and personal development.

Disabled professionals' interventions: organisations of disabled people

At a time when potentially more and more people with learning difficulties are being prepared for work, the role of professional employment advisers and officers appears to be crucial. Job coaches continue to play a huge role in accessing work locations (Wilson, 2003). WORKSTEP and employment services attempt to promote work experience over a set period of time (DH, 2001). The reconfiguration of services allows opportunities for joined up working between day services and employment teams (Olsen, 2003).

What about the involvement of organisations of disabled people in promoting and recognising the confidence and skills of disabled people? This is an important question if the political and policy landscape of disability and employment is to be dictated by disabled people and their organisations. Indeed, historical analyses of the self-advocacy movement have pinpointed the early involvement of organisations of disabled people in working alongside comrades with learning difficulties to promote self-empowerment. These coalitions of self-advocacy groups bring together disabled activists, established counter-politics of disability and campaigning activities in order to promote self-advocacy among the membership (People First of Washington State and University of Oregon, 1984; Dybwad and Bersani, 1996; Goodley, 2000). The role of organisations of disabled people would appear to be a significant part of envisaging an enabling work future for people with learning difficulties.

A research project that has recently started, entitled 'Jobs not Charity', brings together the University of Sheffield with two organisations of disabled people: Breakthrough UK Ltd (BUK) and Greater Manchester Coalition of Disabled People (GMCDP). The aims of the research are to explore the good practices of these organisations in terms of how they impact on the employment experiences of disabled people (www.shef.ac.uk/jobsnotcharity). Both organisations boast strong representation of disabled people (100% membership for GMCDP; over 50% of the employment team of BUK) and both are involved in different ways in supporting the employment experiences of disabled people. How these organisations work alongside other disabled people, including people who have been assigned the label of learning difficulties, remains to be seen at this early stage of the research. Yet, preliminary discussions raise interesting questions and considerations for the focus of this chapter:

- To what extent do disabled professionals, including employment officers, job coaches and advocates enhance the support of other disabled people?
- How do professionals and organisations implement a social model of disability in practice?
- In what ways can disabled professionals and their organisations change the culture of workplaces and support the disabled employee (a key issue for the DRC, 2004)?
- How do organisations of disabled people ensure that disabled people thrive and survive at work? (Roulstone et al, 2003)

Olsen (2003) suggests that 'real work' is something that includes a certain amount of toil. In Olsen's analysis of six life stories, the social role and identity of being professional in one's job, of competence, of being valued clearly emerge. Moreover, Olsen identifies a number of ways in which people with learning difficulties talk of work as a sign of nobility, self-empowerment, being useful, a pleasant environment and an important pastime. Our overriding concern is that meanings about work can only be truly embraced and developed into realities when the social model of disability underpins policy and practice. It is crucial, therefore, not to divorce the implications of government legislation, guidance and policy from the potentially emancipatory practices of organisations of disabled people.

Conclusions

In order to continue the debate about the employment of people with learning difficulties, we would like to end with two questions. First, what is the meaning of work in the knowledge society? While we have limited evidence to suggest that more people with learning difficulties are working in non-segregated settings, sometimes with a wage, the fact that so many continue to be excluded, not paid and ignored by many major employers raises questions about the meaning of work in the 21st century. The issue here is not simply one of tackling the benefits system and promoting work opportunities. In a society increasingly caught up in the generation of knowledge and the provision of educational experiences, the differentiation of people in terms of knowledge-ownership is augmented. People labelled as having learning difficulties will increasingly experience marginalisation from these knowledge developments. Therefore, it is paramount that the meaning of work, and how to make work meaningful, is addressed in social policy debates. It is crucial that knowledge is viewed as multi-faceted; as a product of relationships; as potentially emancipatory and as a process to which all citizens can contribute. We must ensure, therefore, that the place of people with learning difficulties in this developing knowledge society remains at the fore of disability studies thinking about employment and the labour market.

Second, how do ideology and employment interact? We should remain critical about New Labour ideologies: blurring libertarian and social democratic ideologies, that promote rights with responsibility discourse. The rights of people, who have been marginalised from mainstream education, culture and communities, continue to be denied. Therefore, being thrown into work with its accompanying responsibilities raises real concerns about the impact of these ideologies on the life opportunities of people with learning difficulties. Recent interventions by organisations of disabled people in promoting work opportunities have been closely linked to the politicisation and conscious-raising aims of these organisations. Hence organisations like

BUK and People First have supported disabled people with previous experiences of segregation not only to pursue work opportunities but also to become active knowledge agents about their rights, legislation and perceived responsibilities. The input of organisations of disabled people appears to be a crucial development. Therefore, no debate about work and disabled people can take place without the involvement of organisations of disabled people, including representative organisations of people with learning difficulties. 'Nothing about us, without us' remains a fitting slogan to embrace during wider considerations of the meaning of work in a rapidly changing world.

References

Bass, M. and Drewett, R. (1996) 'Supported employment for people with learning disabilities', *Plain Facts*, issue 5, York: Joseph Rowntree Foundation.

Beyer, S., Kilsby, M. and Shearn, J. (1999) 'The organisation and outcomes of supported employment in Britain', *Journal of Vocational Rehabilitation*, vol 12, no 3, pp 137-46.

Beyer, S., Grove, B., Schneider, J., Simons, K., Williams, V. Heyman, A., Swift, P. and Krijnen-Kemp, E. (2004) *Working lives: The role of day centres in supporting people with learning disabilities into employment*, DWP and DH Research Report 203, Leeds: Corporate Document Services (CDS).

Burchardt, T. (2000) *Enduring economic exclusion: Disabled people, income and work*, York: Joseph Rowntree Foundation and York Publishing Services Ltd.

Dingham, H.F. (1968) 'A plea for social research in mental retardation', *Journal of Mental Deficiency*, vol 73, no 1, pp 2-4.

DH (Department of Health) (2001) *Valuing people: A new strategy for learning disability for the 21st century*, London: DH.

DRC (Disability Rights Commission) (2004) *Disability Rights Commission response to the Department for Work and Pensions consultation document 'Pathways to work'*, (www.drc-b.org/publicationsandreports/campaigndetails.asp?sectikon=emp&id=204).

DWP (Department for Work and Pensions) (2001) *New Deal for Disabled People: National survey of incapacity benefits claimants*, DWP Research Report 160, London: DWP.

DWP (2003) *The net costs and individual benefits of the supported employment programme*, Leeds: DWP.

DWP and DH (Department for Work and Pensions and Department of Health) (2004) *Working lives: The role of day centres in supporting people with learning disabilities into employment*, DWP Research Report 203, Leeds: DWP.

Dybwad, G. and Bersani, H. (eds) (1996) *New voices: Self-advocacy by people with disabilities*, Cambridge (MA): Brookline Books.

Equal Opportunities Review (1996) Vol 7, Dublin: National Rehabilitation Board.

Friedman-Lambert, P (1987) 'How would you like it?', *Entourage*, vol 2, no 2, pp 15-17.

Goodley, D. (2000) *Self-advocacy in the lives of people with learning difficulties*, Buckingham: Open University Press.

Goodley, D. (2001) '"Learning difficulties", the social model of disability and impairment: challenging epistemologies', *Disability and Society*, vol 16, no 2, pp 207-31.

Hyde, M. (1996) 'Fifty years of failure: employment services for disabled people in the UK', *Work Employment, and Society*, vol 10, pp 683-700.

Hyvärinen, M., Vesala, H.T., and Seppälä, M. (2002) *Sheltered workshops today*, FAAMR Research Report 35, Helsinki: Finnish Association on Mental Retardation.

Labour Force Survey (LFS) (1999) *Disability statistics*, February 2000, (www.disability.gov.uk/dissum99.html).

Norouzi, G. (2005: forthcoming) *Employment opportunities for adults with the label of learning difficulties*, PhD Thesis, Sheffield: University of Sheffield.

O'Bryan, A., Simons, K., Beyer, S. and Grove, B. (2000) *A framework for supported employment*, York: York Publishing Services.

O'Bryan, A. (2004) 'Person centred planning and supported employment', (www.valuingpeople.gov.uk/documents/PCPEmploy.doc).

Oliver, M. (1990) *The politics of disablement*, London: Macmillan.

Olsen, T. (2003) 'Nobility or stigma? Intellectually disabled people's stories about work', Paper presented to the NNDR Annual Research Conference, Jyvaskyla, Finland, 18-20 September.

Pannell, J. and Simons, K. (2000) *Paid work and housing: A comparative guide to the impact of employment on housing and support for people with learning disabilities*, Brighton and York: Pavilion and Joseph Rowntree Foundation.

Pallisera, M., Vila, M. and Valls, J. (2003) 'The current situation of supported employment in Spain: analysis and perspectives based on the perception of professionals', *Disability and Society*, vol 18, no 6, pp 797-810.

People First of Washington State and University of Oregon (1984) *Speaking up and speaking out. A report on the First International Self-advocacy Leadership Conference*, July, Tacoma (WA).

Pierini, J., Pearson, V. and Wong, Yu-Cheung (2001) 'Glorious work: employment of adults with a learning disability in Guangzhou from the perspective of their parents', *Disability and Society*, vol 16, no 2, pp 255-72.

Roulstone, A. (2002) 'Disabling pasts, enabling futures? How does the changing nature of capitalism impact on the disabled worker and job seeker?', *Disability and Society*, vol 17, no 6, pp 627-42.

Roulstone, A., Gradwell, L., Price, J. and Child, L. (2003) *Surviving and thriving at work: Disabled people's employment strategies*, York: Joseph Rowntree Foundation.

Russell, M. (2002) 'What disability civil rights cannot do: employment and political economy', *Disability and Society*, vol 17, no 2, pp 117-35.

Secker, J., Dass, S. and Grove, B. (2003) 'Developing social firms in the UK: a contribution to identifying good practice', *Disability and Society*, vol 18, no 5, pp 659-74.

Simons, K. (1998) *Home, work and inclusion: The social policy implications of supported living and employment for people with learning disabilities*, York: Joseph Rowntree Foundation, York Publishing Services Ltd.

Smits, S.J. (2004) 'Disability and employment in the USA: the quest for best practices', *Disability and Society*, vol 19, no 6, pp 647-62.

Sutcliffe, J. and Simons, K. (1993) *Self advocacy and adults with learning difficulties: Contexts and debates*, Leicester: National Institute of Adult Continuing Education.

Walmsley, J. (1993) 'Explaining', in D. Shakespeare, P. Atkinson and S. French (eds) *Reflecting on research practice: Issues in health and social welfare*, Buckingham: Open University Press.

Wilson, A. (2003) '"Real jobs", "learning difficulties" and supported employment', *Disability and Society*, vol 18, no 2, pp 99-116.

SIXTEEN

Barriers to labour market participation: the experience of Deaf and hard of hearing people

Jennifer Harris and Patricia Thornton

Introduction

The labour-market situation of Deaf[1], deafened and hard of hearing people has never been robustly and systematically researched in the UK. There are beliefs that these groups can be poorly served by public careers and employment services, can be restricted by service providers' and employers' assumptions about suitable work, may take jobs below their abilities, may earn less than hearing people and see restricted opportunities for job mobility and career progression. In sum, it is believed that Deaf and hard of hearing people face multiple and cumulative disadvantages in accessing worthwhile jobs and pursuing careers.

This chapter reviews the research evidence in support of these beliefs about social exclusion from and within the labour market[2]. Research taking deafness and employment as the sole or main focus is extremely rare in the UK, however, and some supporting evidence is drawn from research in the US.

Labour market participation

Deaf and hard of hearing people are not a homogeneous group. The great majority of hard of hearing people develop a hearing loss with increasing age and are likely to use residual hearing, amplification and lip-reading within everyday interactions. An estimated 128,000 people in the UK under the age of 65 became 'deafened' as adults as a result of an accident or disease and often rely on lip-reading and text communication (RNID, 2000a). It is thought that around 50,000 to 70,000 deaf people use British Sign Language (BSL) (RNID, 2000b), mostly people who were born deaf or became deaf in early childhood, and they generally identify with Deaf culture that they claim is both generated and promulgated through the use of BSL (Padden, 1980; Harris, 1995).

It is apparent that people who have been deaf from birth or early childhood, adults who become deafened and those who acquire partial hearing loss face barriers in the labour market which relate to differing communication requirements and the point at which hearing impairment occurs within the life course. A few studies have focused on the employment experiences of some groups, notably young people and Deaf people. However, large-scale surveys, notably the Labour Force Survey (LFS), unhelpfully mask the differences in communication requirements and histories of hearing impairment by using the catchall category 'difficulty in hearing'.

The LFS is the main national source of data on labour market participation. Its accuracy is questionable because respondents are asked if they have any long-term 'health problems or disabilities'; only those who reply in the affirmative are asked to identify their problems from a list. It is thus possible that deaf or hard of hearing people who do not see themselves as having a health problem or disability are excluded. Many people who identify with Deaf culture do not consider that they are disabled, although may accept the label to gain social concessions (Harris, 1995; Padden and Humphries, 1988; Dye et al, 2001), and it is possible that people with partial hearing loss who have not received medical attention do not consider it to be a health problem. Furthermore, the standard analyses of the LFS data are based on the 'main' condition as defined by the respondent, under-representing people with partial hearing loss who consider another health problem or 'disability' to be their main condition.

As a result of these deficits, the LFS greatly underestimates the working-age deaf and hard of hearing population. Based on the spring 2002 LFS, there is an estimated number of 127,000 people of working-age in Great Britain whose main condition is 'difficulty in hearing' (DRC, 2002). This estimate is in stark contrast to the RNID estimate of over 2.25 million deaf and hard of hearing men and women of working-age in Great Britain (RNID, 2000a), which is based on the standard epidemiological source (Davis, 1995).

Bearing in mind its shortcomings, analyses of the LFS have estimated the economic activity rate of people with 'difficulty in hearing' variously at ten and fifteen points below that of the general population (Twomey, 2001; Sly et al, 1999).

Difficulty in finding employment

Research has tended to focus on issues of under-employment – limits on occupational choice, jobs below one's potential, and limits to promotion – more than on barriers to obtaining employment.

In 1999, RNID carried out a postal survey of Typetalk subscribers achieving a 12% response rate (Bradshaw, 2002). The report is based on responses from over 1,000 people of working-age, the majority describing themselves as 'profoundly or severely deaf'. It is hard to draw meaningful conclusions given the unrepresentative nature of the sample and the low response rate. However, it is worth noting that despite having higher levels of qualification, the respondents' employment rate was well below that of the general population. Of particular interest is the strength of agreement to statements that deafness and hearing loss had prevented them from getting a job (70% of those answering the question) and that seeking work was a struggle because hearing people did not understand their communication requirements (68%).

Early research in the US indicated that economically active deaf people had more difficulty than hearing people in finding jobs. Although labour force participation rates for deaf people and their qualification levels were approximate to those of the general population, deaf workers had consistently higher unemployment rates than the general population (Barnartt and Christiansen, 1985). According to a summary by Boone and Long (1988), deaf women suffered 50% more unemployment than women in general and pre-vocationally deaf people had great difficulty in obtaining employment.

Recent UK research on the demographics of the Deaf Community (Dye et al, 2000) indicates that Deaf people may be more likely to be employed than hearing people, but this finding is unreliable given deficiencies in the quota sampling method used. Nevertheless, the authors conclude that it is likely that Deaf people do not have problems finding a job; rather it is likely that they have problems in finding the right job for their skills.

Concentration in less skilled jobs

Two UK studies among Deaf people in the 1980s, reported by Kyle et al (1989), found that Deaf people tended to be concentrated in unskilled and semi-skilled jobs and relatively few were in positions with managerial or supervisory responsibility. In a 1981 study of all members of the Deaf community living in the Avon area (Kyle and Allsop,

1982), among the 200 of working-age just under half were in unskilled or semi-skilled jobs, and in a national study of over 200 deaf and partially-hearing people aged 21-25 the proportion was over six in ten (Kyle and Pullen, 1985).

North American research in the 1980s demonstrated that deaf workers were concentrated in blue-collar occupations, jobs characterised by low job security and little opportunity for advancement beyond entry level, and deaf women were much more disadvantaged than deaf men, typically choosing less skilled employment (Barnartt and Christiansen, 1985; Boone and Long, 1988).

A study in the late 1990s interviewed 236 Deaf people aged 18-75 throughout the UK on a range of topics (Dye et al, 2000). This study indicated a shift away from traditional manual trades but still under-representation of Deaf people in management and professional jobs.

In the 1980s, Kyle et al (1989) argued that part of the explanation for concentration in unskilled and semi-skilled jobs was the very low levels of qualifications and literacy among deaf school leavers, a problem in other developed countries as evidenced by a European Commission study (Jones and Pullen, 1990). Research from the US around the same time found that although the qualifications of deaf people were approximate to those of hearing people, pre-vocationally deaf people had lower levels of educational attainment than the general population (Barnartt and Christiansen, 1985; Boone and Long, 1988). Barnartt (2004) found that by 1991 educational differences related to hearing status for both sexes had largely disappeared, but women regardless of hearing status and hearing men became overwhelmingly likely to be white collar workers, which was not true of deaf men.

In the UK more recently, Dye et al (2000) found Deaf people in their 20s were less likely to have a higher educational qualification than their hearing peers although nearly three-quarters of Deaf people aged 18-29 carried on into further or higher education.

Analysis of the LFS found the proportion of people whose main health problem or 'disability' was 'difficulty in hearing' with no educational qualifications to be higher than in the general population, and employed people with 'difficulty in hearing' more likely than hearing people to be in semi-skilled or unskilled jobs (RNID, 2000a).

Thwarted ambitions and jobs below abilities

The EC study of Deaf people's employment, mentioned earlier in this chapter, was carried out in 11 countries, including the UK (Jones and Pullen, 1990). It found evidence of occupational segregation in most countries, with clustering in certain trades. The findings were based on interviews with 217 Deaf people and group discussions, with respondents recruited through national Deaf Associations. The study reported thwarted ambition, with Deaf people rarely having the opportunity to follow the occupation of their choice, and the authors commented that jobs rarely reflected people's evident abilities.

As Kyle et al (1989) point out, part of the difficulty stems from hearing people's attitudes. They demonstrated empirically that hearing people were much less likely than deaf people to think that deaf people could do certain specified jobs. They cite evidence from the early 1980s (De Caro et al, 1982) that hearing people's stereotypes prevented them from giving appropriate advice even when deaf people held appropriate qualifications. Assumptions on the part of schools, colleges and careers services about the types of jobs deaf people can do are well documented in other research of the period (Sainsbury, 1986; Bannerman et al, 1989). In the early 1990s, Harris (1995) interviewed 22 Deaf people in employment. The fact that half were in manual jobs was found to be related to the types of advice given when choosing a career, effectively limiting options to a few narrow trades.

Underemployment and limits to promotion

Underemployment emerged as a key issue in an enquiry into the employment of deaf people in 1987 (RNID, 1987). Information was gathered via non-representative surveys: one of which was mainly of people deaf from birth or early childhood, recruited through intermediaries and personal contacts; and the other of members of a national association of deafened people. Respondents felt their jobs were boring, routine and unchallenging. A common experience was feeling stuck in the job, unable to gain promotion with abilities unrecognised. Social isolation and stress at work were widely reported.

Limits to promotion are a key theme in the literature. In one early UK study, 63% of a sample of over 200 deaf people thought promotion impossible, compared with 16% of a control group of hearing people (Kyle and Allsop, 1987, cited in Kyle et al, 1989). The EC study (Jones and Pullen, 1990) found Deaf people's promotion inhibited by 'communication problems'. A strong perception that promotion is less likely among deaf people was found more recently in the RNID 1999 postal survey of Typetalk users (Bradshaw, 2002). Here, three in four of those who answered the question agreed to the statement that opportunities for promotion were less than hearing colleagues'.

There is rather little evidence of the employment experiences of people who become hearing impaired in adulthood. Kyle et al (1989), reviewing their own work, comment on the likelihood of early retirement and curtailment of career prospects, and a tendency for hard of hearing workers to accept positions they would not have taken before impairment.

Limited earnings and quality of working life

There is no sound information on relative earnings of deaf, hard of hearing and hearing workers but some pointers from two studies. Respondents in the RNID survey cited (Bradshaw, 2002) had lower earnings from full-time work despite having higher qualification levels than the general population. Dye et al (2002) found the salary difference between Deaf people in manual/unskilled and professional occupations to be less than would be expected, but Deaf non-manual and professional workers were found to earn little more than the national average for all workers.

There has been very little research into the quality of working life. A 1980s study of 123 people aged 20-60 who acquired hearing loss in adult life (Jones et al, 1987) highlighted lowered expectations of the quality of life at work and anxiety that the job or social relationships might be jeopardised if the extent of hearing loss was uncovered.

Employers' assumptions and limited career options

Occupational limitations and underemployment are often attributed to employers' assumptions about deaf people's abilities. A small qualitative study for Derby City Council (Edwards et al, 2000) found Deaf people insisted that they had been discriminated against in seeking employment specifically because they were deaf, and they believed that prospective employers were ignorant about their capabilities and potential. The main issue was underemployment. Participants believed that employers and colleagues made unjustifiable assumptions and did not consider making adjustments to remove barriers. Deaf people said that as a result they settled for jobs below their capabilities or even made a deliberate choice to move to a lesser status job to escape stress and risk to mental health. The report recommended guidance and information to challenge employers' and statutory agencies' assumptions about abilities.

In a qualitative study of the employment experiences of Deaf people, Harris (1995) suggested that employers work within set assumptions of what is, or is not, appropriate work for Deaf people to undertake.

Surveys of employers' attitudes, within the framework of recruitment and retention of disabled people, provide some corroboration. A 1994 survey for the Department of Employment (Dench et al, 1996) conducted telephone interviews with 1,250 employing organisations with more than ten employees. Only one in five respondents believed it would be possible to employ someone with 'difficulty in hearing' in *every* job in their organisation, and one in seven said it would be impossible to employ someone with difficulty in hearing in *any* job. The main perceived barrier related to the unsuitable nature of the work, mainly because hearing was deemed essential but also because of safety implications.

Dench et al (1996) commented on the disadvantages stemming from the increasing importance of customer service and emphasis placed on verbal/audio communication skills. An earlier government-funded survey of the employment of disabled people (Morrell, 1990) had shown that employers prioritised 'the ability to speak clearly and quickly' and 'good hearing'. In the most recent government-funded research with employers about employing disabled people (Roberts et al, 2004), staff interviewed in case studies suggested that people with a severe hearing impairment would struggle in a communication role and felt that this significantly restricted employment options.

In a survey of disabled people's labour-market participation carried out for the (then) Department for Education and Employment (DfEE) (Meager et al, 1998), one in four people of working-age 'with difficulty in hearing' said they had experienced discrimination in the labour market for related reasons. The findings point to the need for adaptations to overcome employment barriers. Among the disabled people surveyed, by far the highest proportion of those requiring adaptations to the working environment was people with 'difficulty in hearing' (one in four).

Access to employment services

There is a dearth of robust evidence on the effectiveness of many of the interventions that can assist deaf and hard of hearing people into and in employment. While there are some specialised services, mainly run by voluntary sector organisations, many government services available to deaf and hard of hearing people are designed for disabled people or unemployed people in general. The Jobcentre Plus Access to Work programme is exceptional among government services in including provision for deaf people in the form of assistance with communicator support at interview and on the job.

There is considerable anecdotal evidence that deaf and hard of hearing people face barriers to service provision and believe services are insufficiently tailored to their requirements. Only a few studies have examined issues of access to any public services by deaf and hard of hearing people, and generally hard of hearing people's service requirements are poorly understood (Harris and Bamford, 2001).

A report of a consultation meeting convened for the (then) DfEE to identify barriers facing disabled people in government services (Grass Roots Group Plc, 2001) elicited the views of Deaf and deafened people on employment and training. The group emphasised unmet communication requirements in accessing services – an issue that has emerged in other studies (RNID, 1987; Bradshaw, 2002; Edwards et al, 2000). The DfEE consultation also found that deaf and hard of hearing people experience difficulties in accessing uncoordinated agencies with widely different standards. These points are supported by Harris and Bamford's (2001) study of deaf and hard of hearing people's access to services which found both groups face problems in employment situations in accessing assisting devices and dealing with the bureaucracy surrounding the divisions between social and health services.

There are some indications that deaf and hard of hearing people are not well represented among users of government initiatives. The evaluation of the New Deal for Disabled People Personal Adviser pilot, for eligible people in receipt of incapacity benefits, found only 2% of participants surveyed cited 'difficulty with hearing or speech' as their main impairment (Loumidis et al, 2001).

There are also limited research findings on the appropriateness of services. A large-scale representative survey of users' views of Access to Work (Thornton et al, 2001) found users with a hearing impairment most likely to say that Access to Work did not meet their requirements and most likely to question its usefulness.

Conclusion

Deaf, deafened and hard of hearing people face considerable barriers to full labour market participation. While in the UK there is a lack of robust research evidence concerning their labour market participation, evidence pieced together reveals lower employment and higher underemployment than hearing people and a concentration in less skilled jobs. It appears that they tend to take jobs below their qualification levels and abilities, earn less than hearing people and face restricted opportunities for job mobility and career progression. These disadvantages can be compounded by poor advice on careers thought suitable for deaf and hard of hearing people, discriminatory attitudes on the part of employers and problems in accessing employment services. The picture that emerges is one of social exclusion and thwarted ambitions.

In the light of the severity of these issues and their evident entrenched nature, there is quite a considerable way to go before it could be claimed that deaf and hard of hearing people experience equal access to employment.

Notes

[1] 'Deaf' with an upper case 'D' denotes people who consider themselves to belong to a cultural and linguistic minority group which uses sign language as its first or preferred language. In reporting research we replicate the authors' terms.

[2] This chapter draws on work commissioned by RNID and carried out by the authors.

References

Bannerman, C., Miller, J. and Montgomery, G. (1989) *Deaf workers are good workers:An enquiry into options and realities about the Deaf workforce*, Scottish Workshop Publications.

Barnartt, S.N. and Christiansen, J.B. (1985) 'The socioeconomic status of deaf workers: a minority group approach', *Social Science Journal*, no 22, pp 19-32.

Barnartt S.N. (2004) *American Deaf women's inequality: Is deafness or femaleness to blame?*, (www.lancs.ac.uk/fss/apsocsci/events/dsaconf2004/abstracts/barnartt.htm).

Boone, S. and Long, G. (1988) *Enhancing the employability of deaf people: Model interventions*, Springfield (IL): Charles Thomas.

Bradshaw, W. (2002) *The employment situation and experiences of deaf and hard of hearing people*, London: RNID.

De Caro, J., Evans, L. and Dowaliby, F. (1982) 'Advising deaf youth to train for various occupations', *British Journal of Educational Psychology*, no 52, pp 220-7.

Davis, A. (1995) *Hearing loss in adults*, London: Whurr.

Dench, S., Meager, N. and Morris, S. (1996) *The recruitment and retention of people with disabilities*, Brighton: Institute for Employment Studies.

DRC (Disability Rights Commission) (2002) *Disability briefing: October 2002*, Research and Evaluation Unit, London: DRC.

Dye, M., Kyle, J. with Allsop, L., Denmark, C., Drury, A. and Ladd, P. (2000) *Deaf people in the community: Demographics of the Deaf community in the UK*, Bristol: Deaf Studies Trust.

Dye, M., Kyle, J. with Allsop, L., Drury, A. and Richter, J. (2001) *Deaf people in the community: Health and disability*, Bristol: Deaf Studies Trust.

Edwards, J., Young, A.M., Gibbs, D. and Maelzer, J. (2000) *Disabled and Deaf people's access to employment in the City of Derby*, Derby: Derby City Council.

Grass Roots Group Plc (2001) *Workshop of disabled people to identify barriers to government services, equipment, housing, the built environment*, London: DfEE.

Harris, J. (1995) *The cultural meaning of deafness: Language, identity and power relations*, Aldershot: Avebury.

Harris, J. and Bamford, C. (2001) 'The uphill struggle: services for Deaf and hard of hearing people; issues of equality, participation and access', *Disability & Society*, vol 16, no 7, pp 969-79.

Jones, L., Kyle, J. and Wood, P. (1987) *Words apart: Losing your hearing as an adult*, London: Tavistock Publications.

Jones, L. and Pullen, G. (1990) *Inside we are all equal: A social policy survey of deaf people in the European Community*, London: European Community Regional Secretariat of the World Federation of the Deaf.

Kyle, J. and Allsop, L. (1982) *Deaf people and the community*, Bristol: School of Education, University of Bristol.

Kyle, J. and Pullen, G. (1985) *Deaf people and the community*, Bristol: School of Education, University of Bristol.

Kyle, J., Thomas, C. and Pullen, G. (1989) *Assessing deaf people for employment and rehabilitation*, Project Report, Bristol: Centre for Deaf Studies, University of Bristol.

Loumidis, J., Stafford, B., Youngs, R., Green, A., Arthur, S., Legard, R., Lessof, C., Lewis, J., Walker, R., Corden, A., Thornton, P. and Sainsbury, R. (2001) *Evaluation of the New Deal for Disabled People personal adviser service pilot*, DSS Research Report 144, Leeds: Corporate Document Services (CDS).

Meager, N., Bates, P., Dench, S., Honey, S. and Williams, M. (1998) *Employment of disabled people: Assessing the extent of participation*, Research Report RR69, London: DfEE.

Morrell, J. (1990) *The employment of people with disabilities: Research into the policies and practices of employers*, Research Paper 77, London: Employment Department.

Padden, C. (1980) 'The deaf community & the culture of deaf people', in C. Baker and R. Battison (1980) (eds) *Sign language and the Deaf community; Essays in honour of William Stokoe*, US, National Association of the Deaf, pp 90–100.

Padden, C. and Humphries, T. (1988) *Deaf in America: Voices from a culture*, Harvard: Harvard University Press.

RNID (Royal National Institute for the Deaf) (1987) *Communication works: An RNID inquiry into the employment of deaf people*, London: RNID.

RNID (2000a) *Factsheet: Statistics on deafness*, London: RNID.

RNID (2000b) *Factsheet: Training as sign language interpreter*, (www.rnid.organisation.uk).

Roberts, S., Heaver, C., Hill, K., Rennison, J., Stafford, B., Howat, N., Kelly, G., Krishnan, S., Tapp, P. and Thomas, A. (2004) *Disability in the workplace: Employers' and service providers' responses to the Disability Discrimination Act in 2003 and preparation for 2004 changes*, DWP Research Report 202, Leeds: CDS.

Sainsbury, S. (1986) *Deaf words: A study of integration, segregation and disability*, London: Hutchinson.

Sly, F., Thair, T. and Risdon, A. (1999) 'Disability and the labour market: results from the winter 1998/9 LFS', *Labour Market Trends*, September, pp 455–65.

Thornton, P., Hirst, M., Arksey, H. and Tremlett, N. (2001) *Users' views of access to work*, Employment Service Report 72, Sheffield: Employment Service.

Twomey, B. (2001) 'Disability and the labour market: results from the summer 2000 LFS', *Labour Market Trends*, May, pp 241–51.

SEVENTEEN

Work matters: visual impairment, disabling barriers and employment options

Philippa Simkiss

Introduction

As the 500th Jobcentre Plus office opens in Middlesbrough and the UK government talks about 'full employment in every region' (DWP, 2003), this chapter draws attention to the high proportion of blind and partially sighted people who are not in work. It highlights the issues facing blind and partially sighted job seekers, examines critically the interventions that have been designed to help them into work, and suggests solutions and recommendations to policy makers and employers alike about how best to redress the current situation.

The Royal National Institute of the Blind (RNIB) is the leading voluntary sector organisation supporting people with sight loss in the UK. It became the organisation 'of' a few years ago with a growing membership of over 12,000 blind and partially sighted people. The membership votes for assembly and board members and these groups set strategy. Blind and partially sighted people are at the heart of the policy-making process. *Work matters* (RNIB, 2004) is an example of our employment campaigning work. The key element of this campaign was a network of blind and partially sighted spokespeople across the UK who demonstrated how they succeed in a range of jobs.

As a result of the RNIB Work Matters campaign and the Beyond the Stereotypes report (Simkiss and Baker, 2004) a number of parliamentary questions have been tabled on key disability employment programmes which impact people with visual impairments. For example, attention has been paid to the Access to Work budget, rehabilitation programmes for blind and partially sighted people, disability leave legislation and employment rights of blind and partially sighted people. The campaign culminated with Work Matters fringe events at the Trades Union Congress (TUC) and Labour Party Conferences at which Brendan Barber, Director General of the TUC, promoted the report, David Blunkett, the then Home Secretary, lent his support, and Digby Jones, Director of the CBI said, "We need regulation in this area".

The RNIB's policy and campaigning is based upon consultation with blind and partially sighted people through the governance structure, membership, research and service delivery. In 2003/04, RNIB regional and national employment staff in England alone supported 842 blind and partially sighted people to gain or retain employment through direct placement activity and indirect activity such as Access to Work assessments and vocational guidance. We provided training to 462 employers to implement accessible recruitment and retention practices. We also provided 2,446 people with free employment advice and advocacy support.

Blind and partially sighted people and the labour market

In 2003, RNIB research showed that only 27% of blind and partially sighted people of working-age in the UK were in employment (Bruce and Baker, 2003). This figure has not changed significantly since similar research was published in 1991 (Bruce, McKennell and Walker, 1991) when 25% of blind and partially sighted people were in paid employment. This is not only below the employment rate of the non-disabled population of the UK, which in spring 2002 stood at 80.7%, but is also significantly below that for the general disabled population, which, at the same time, was 47.6% (ONS, 2002). Obviously, blind and partially sighted people are at a serious disadvantage in the labour market.

This disadvantage can be explained, in part, by the fact that recent government research (Roberts et al, 2004) shows that nine out of ten employers believe that employing a person with impaired vision would be either difficult or impossible. Despite the best efforts of blind and partially sighted people to find work, it would seem that measures such as the introduction of the Disability Discrimination Act 1995 (DDA) and a number of government schemes designed specifically to assist disabled people into employment have largely failed.

Continued barriers to obtaining and retaining paid employment

Legislation

Despite the DDA, employment rates for blind and partially sighted people have not improved over the last ten years. One reason for this is lack of awareness of the legislation. Recent government research (Roberts et al, 2004) found that more than one in three employers (37%) were unaware of Part Two of the DDA (employment provisions) or of any other legislation relating to disabled people and employment. Furthermore, only 3% of employers with less than 15 employees were aware that after October 2004 the DDA would apply to their businesses.

Although the DDA does assist disabled people on an individual level, and provides them with financial compensation when they are discriminated against, legislation does little to persuade employers that blind and partially sighted people can work on an even footing with non-disabled people (Roberts et al, 2004) and systematic discrimination persists. For example, a quick scan of the local press will reveal job advertisements in which an applicant is required to hold a driving licence with no indication of the provision of alternative transport through reasonable adjustments.

Government initiatives

Jobcentre Plus is the government agency responsible for providing employment-related services to all disabled people of working-age, often through Disability Employment Advisers (DEAs). These advisers act as referring agents to specific employment-related programmes aimed at disabled job seekers, and subcontract their delivery to service providers. Through the subcontracting regime, DEAs have diminishing contact with reasonable adjustments and the practical solutions that can enable disabled people in the workplace. In addition, the management of DEAs has been transferred from Disability Service Teams to local Jobcentre staff and DEAs have taken on broader responsibilities. It is possible that DEA knowledge of the particular needs of people with specific impairments and the interventions that can make a positive difference is being diluted by structural changes in Jobcentre Plus.

There are other instances where mainstreaming support for job seekers has not helped blind and partially sighted people. Jobpoints in Jobcentre Plus Pathfinder offices are not accessible to those who cannot read the screen. An official response from Jobcentre Plus following a report (Loebl, 2002) on the poor accessibility of Jobpoints in Pathfinder offices, was that anyone who cannot use the kiosks will get personal one-to-one attention from a member of staff using their computer. We have yet to test this out with 'mystery shopping'.

In addition, the Jobcentre Plus 'Search for a Job' website is not fully accessible to those who use speech access. We have recently sent a report, complied by a tester who is registered blind, to Jobcentre Plus pointing out specific difficulties in navigating the website and finding any jobs to apply for when using JAWS speech software (Smith, 2004).

There is a range of literature about the government's welfare-to-work programme, and other contributors to this book evaluate the current welfare-to-work programme in some depth. Here, then, I will simply raise some observations based on work with blind and partially sighted people. One problem associated with the various schemes is that many of the contractors who bid to run the programmes fail to take into account the costs of equipment that some blind and partially sighted people need. For example, RNIB has a Work Preparation contract for certain areas of Scotland, and the proposal for the contract was designed with equipment costs in mind. Sadly, almost all of the other contractors in Scotland have gained their contracts by submitting low-cost bids which cannot provide the funds for this equipment. As a result, blind and partially sighted people are effectively excluded from participation. It is clear that if welfare-to-work programmes are to succeed for blind and partially sighted people, their needs should be incorporated fully into awarded contracts.

The New Deal for Disabled People programme (NDDP) works on the basis of independent agencies acting as job brokers. The RNIB has experience of providing such a service in the South West of England. Research published by the Department for Work and Pensions (DWP) (Ashworth et al, 2003) shows that 2% of participants in NDDP state that "difficulty seeing" is their main disability, so we know that blind and partially sighted people are not getting jobs in large numbers through this programme. Marketing of the programme needs to be directed towards blind and partially sighted people; staff need to be trained to support people with sight loss to overcome the specific barriers they face in finding employment. These barriers often take the form of inaccessible information and equipment; training that providers offer should meet the needs of blind and partially sighted people.

Workstep is a scheme aimed at disabled people who have more complex needs, and aims to encourage people into supported employment within the regular labour market. The number of blind and partially sighted people taking part in the WORKSTEP programme in 1999 was 609 – less than 3% of the total number of WORKSTEP participants. Once more, blind and partially sighted people are not gaining access in large numbers, and the evidence suggests that WORKSTEP programmes are designed to assist those disabled people who are perceived as being closest to the labour market (Corden and Thornton, 2003). There is also evidence that blind and partially sighted people are missing out on similar intermediate labour market initiatives. Arksey et al (2002, p 20) reported that "people with mental health problems were considerably over represented in transitional employment [and] intermediate labour market schemes", but people with a visual impairment were not represented at all. Supported employment providers need to proactively consider how to include more blind and partially sighted people in their provision.

Specialist knowledge is vital if blind and partially sighted people are to be assisted successfully into employment. Support in areas linked to employment (such as access to information, mobility, use of assisting technologies and specialised rehabilitation and training services) should be central to any programme which intends to help blind and partially sighted people. If blind and partially sighted people are to achieve greater inclusion in welfare-to-work programmes, the government must ensure that services are sensitive to their needs by developing contractual agreements with organisations committed to impairment sensitive provision.

Challenges and solutions

The attitudes and awareness of employers and service providers

A recent DWP report (Roberts et al, 2004) shows that, in a survey of 2,000 employers, a massive 92% said that they thought it would be either "difficult" or "impossible" to employ someone with impaired vision. Indeed, people with impaired vision, according to this research, are perceived the most difficult to employ of a wide range of disabled people. In fact, blind and partially sighted people succeed in a wide variety of jobs. Bruce and Baker (2003) asked blind and partially sighted workers about the jobs they were doing, and the range was extensive. This study included people working as a care assistant, a futures trader, a PR consultant, a sheet metal worker, a script reader, a child physiotherapist, solicitors, a stonemason, a test rig operator and a security guard. Many employers who have experience of employing disabled people feel that they are no different to other employees and provided as good a service as their peers (Roberts et al, 2004). Like the rest of the workforce, blind and partially sighted staff can be set targets and employers can expect them to deliver as the best person for the job. In RNIB's *Work matters* DVD (2004), blind and partially sighted people and their employers talk frankly about the work that they do. Here are just two examples:

> Brian was just the best person for the job. (Manager of a day centre and employer of Brian Fitzpatrick. a partially sighted Day Centre Officer)

> When we interviewed Kate, she was the best person for the job at the time irrespective of her disability. (Elaine Russell, employer of Kate Howard, a Community Support officer who is blind)

With the right support, blind and partially sighted people can achieve success in work but for every person working successfully, there are three more who are not (Bruce and Baker, 2003). If nine out of ten employers believe that it would be difficult or impossible to employ a blind or partially sighted person, it is no surprise to find that people who experience constant rejection and discrimination eventually become disillusioned about their chances of ever finding work. Kelly Muggeridge is 36 years old and was born without sight. Her story is told in *Seeing beyond the stereotypes* (Simkiss and Baker, 2004). She says:

> Employers are not giving people with visual impairment a chance. When they think about equal opportunities employers don't include blind people.

While employers claim that it is their practice to employ the best person for the job, it would seem that too few believe that this person could be blind or partially sighted. The UK government could do more to raise awareness among employers by publicising the range of jobs that blind and partially sighted people do successfully.

Inaccessible recruitment and selection

Inaccessible information is a significant barrier to blind and partially sighted job seekers, and recruitment procedures can sometimes work against them (Bruce and Baker, 2001). Employers need to assess their recruitment processes to ensure that blind and partially sighted people are given the same opportunities as their sighted peers. Often job advertisements in newspapers appear in small print which blind and partially sighted people cannot read (Bruce and Baker, 2001). The RNIB itself has a policy that its advertisements are printed in 14 point, and we ask that all employers adopt a similar practice.

The use of the Internet by blind and partially sighted job seekers is increasing, especially by those who can use speech or magnification software to surf the net. However, many sites do not comply with current European standards on accessibility, and searching these sites can be difficult and time consuming (DRC, 2004). Employers should check that the websites to which they post job advertisements are accessible.

In late 2003, RNIB contacted 56 medium- and large-sized employers across the UK to see how they would respond to requests for application packs and forms in a variety of different formats. These requests were made in response to advertisements placed in local newspapers, and the results show that there is very little awareness of the information needs of blind and partially sighted job seekers, even when there has been a specific request for information in a particular format. Only two of these employers managed to send out all the information in the format requested. Some employers had managed to provide information in the appropriate-sized text, but had neglected to do the same for the application form, whereas others had ignored the request altogether. Four of these employers actually sent the information so that it arrived after the closing date had passed (Simkiss and Baker, 2004).

Under the DDA, employers must provide application forms, company information or letters in an appropriate accessible format. Roberts et al (2004) found that although 42% of employers stated that it would be easy for them to provide application forms in alternative formats, findings from their case studies suggest that companies have not given a great deal of consideration to the potential adjustments that should be made to assist disabled people through the application process. The authors report that managers in many businesses would welcome guidance on best practice in recruitment.

RNIB calls on employers to:

- assess their recruitment processes to ensure that blind and partially sighted people are given the same opportunities as others;

- make their job advertisements accessible to all, and provide all relevant information in the appropriate format. (Information and application forms should be based on clear text guidelines, have clear and legible fonts and good contrast between text and background);
- listen carefully to what blind and partially sighted people need, and provide exactly what is asked for and at the same time as for fully sighted applicants.

Job retention policies

People who develop sight loss often give up their work because they believe difficulties that have arisen cannot be overcome. This is also true of those whose condition worsens. A process of 'disability leave' may be necessary to allow these people time away from work to adjust and learn new working methods and for the employer to make the adaptations needed to enable the employee to resume work.

Disability Leave (DL) is a scheme to enable newly disabled people or people whose impairment deteriorates to retain their employment. It does not simply refer to a 'leave' entitlement; rather a whole process of assessment, advice seeking, and retraining, with leave being just one element of what is available to newly disabled employees. Organisations can ensure that they retain experienced staff by implementing an effective DL policy that includes assessment, retraining and adaptation for employees who become disabled through illness or accident, and those who experience deterioration in an existing condition (RNIB, 1993).

The Royal National Institute of the Blind wants DL to become as well known as maternity leave. We are campaigning for government to provide a financial incentive to employers to apply DL by establishing a fund for the assessment, rehabilitation and retraining of people on DL and funding for the loan of equipment as required on return to work. The Irish government introduced such a fund in 2002, called the Employee Retention Grant Scheme (RNIB, 2002). Funding is available to support the retention of any existing employee, at all levels and occupations within a private sector company, who acquires a disability (occupational or otherwise) that impacts on their current ability to do the job.

The costs of adjustments

Employers worry about the financial costs of employing blind and partially sighted people (Roberts et al, 2004) while remaining largely ignorant of schemes such as Access to Work (Edwards, 2004; Goldstone and Meager, 2002). The latter can provide practical and financial support for adaptation of premises and equipment, special aids, support workers and travel to and from work. At the current time, the government has no targets for increasing awareness of this scheme (Baroness Hollis of Heigham, 2003), but it is vital that such a target is introduced. A practical way to promote the scheme is for a prompt about Access to Work to be introduced on Jobcentre Plus client interview schedules so that when disabled people are first interviewed they are advised of its existence.

Access to Work does have some limitations, not least its budget (£44 million for 2003/04), which is always fully spent. If the scheme were to be promoted more fully, then this budget would have to be increased to meet a rise in demand. In any case it seems reasonable to anticipate that demand on Access to Work will rise as a result of the extension of the DDA to small employers in October 2004. The government must ensure that the budget for Access to Work keeps pace with demand, and that the scheme is extended to cover people on work placement and volunteers (Disability Employment Coalition, 2004).

Intermediate labour markets

Evidence that many employment service providers focus on disabled people who can be made 'job ready' in a reasonably short time has already been cited (Corden and Thornton, 2003). Neither this approach nor anti-discrimination legislation has had a significant impact on unemployment levels of disabled people. The challenge to support those who are furthest from the labour market into gainful employment remains:

> Innovative approaches for the future will need to learn from some of the cutting edge work in Intermediate Labour Markets which provide pathways to work through community-based activity.

So said David Blunkett, UK Secretary of State for Education and Employment, in 2000. Mr Blunkett, for one, is confident in the role played by community enterprise in leading people who are furthest from the labour market towards gainful employment. The Employment Continuum report (RNIB, 2002) highlights the activities of local entrepreneurs and social enterprises that are finding a link between unemployment and sustainable work for disabled people through the adoption of diverse funding streams. It demonstrates that the creation of jobs by promoting social enterprise and an employment continuum in the intermediate labour market can provide sustained employment for disabled people who are often excluded from more traditional employment provision.

To implement good practice in social enterprise it is important to consider both the supply and demand sides of the employment equation. Commercial trading, capital start up, partnership, on-going financial support, the added value of work, assessment of workers, rehabilitation and training, progression, ongoing support and provision of optimum solutions for engagement with the labour market are all important. Government could help by creating the economic and social environment that enables the development of new initiatives and sustains existing opportunities. This includes bringing together the specialists who can support disabled people, entrepreneurs with the ability to trade in the commercial sector and financial subsidy in the form of benefits, tax credits, training grants and capital start up grants to ensure viability. Reforming the benefit system or providing grants to small businesses will not have a significant impact on the high level of unemployment of blind and partially sighted people unless there is also a significant expansion of employment continuum opportunities.

Conclusion: key points of policy and practice

People with sight loss succeed in a wide range of jobs but most employers are not aware of this. The DDA (1995) has not had a significant impact on the employment levels of disabled people (Social Trends, 2004) and it has achieved very little in encouraging employers to perceive disability, particularly blindness or partial sight, positively. Without properly funded and resourced schemes that encourage employers to take on blind and partially sighted workers, such as AtW, the DDA will act only as a compensatory measure for instances of discrimination rather than a positive force for change.

Employers continue to discriminate against blind and partially sighted applicants at every stage of the recruitment process. Job advertisements that are too small or indistinct to read, application forms and information packs that are inaccessible, and which arrive late, and interview practice that fails to provide reasonable adjustments for candidates are common.

Many of the programmes that have been designed to assist disabled people into work are failing blind and partially sighted people. Here are some practical policy initiatives that the government could introduce to alleviate this situation:

- Contractual arrangements for specialist input to ensure delivery of impairment sensitive provision within existing programmes.
- Increasing the budget for the Access to Work scheme and advertising all elements, especially those that are not related to equipment.
- Ensuring that rehabilitation and training programmes are adequately funded so that they meet the needs of blind and partially sighted people.
- Introducing legislation to support DL to give people who develop a disability time away from work to adjust and learn new working methods.
- Promoting the development of supported employment opportunities and intermediate labour market solutions.
- There are also practical implications for employers' human resources policies and practices. These need to:
  ‣ make job adverts and selection procedures accessible for all;
  ‣ guarantee an interview for all disabled applicants who meet the essential criteria for the job;
  ‣ use the resources available in the Access to Work scheme;
  ‣ develop a comprehensive equality policy that includes DL and ensure that all staff understand the policy and deliver it.

Finally for statutory service providers the implications are to:

- ensure that services are fully accessible to blind and partially sighted people by providing impairment sensitive support in mainstream and specialist programmes;
- ensure that staff are fully trained to support people with sight loss to overcome the specific barriers they face in finding employment, such as inaccessible information and equipment;
- ensure that Jobcentre Plus considers how it can meet the needs of blind and partially sighted people in all Jobcentres.

References

Arksey, H., Thornton, P. and Williams, J. (2002) *Mapping employment focussed services for people with disabilities*, DWP Report 93, London: DWP and Social Policy Research Unit, University of York.

Ashworth, K., Hartfree, Y., Kazimirski, A., Legge, K., Pires, C., Reges de Bearnan, S., Shaw, A. and Stafford, B. (2003) *New Deal for Disabled People national extension: First wave of the first cohort of the survey of registrants*, DWP Report 180, London: DWP and Centre for Research in Social Policy, National Centre for Social Research.

Baroness Hollis of Heigham in Response to a Parliamentary Question, 25 February 2003 [HL1611].

Bruce, I. and Baker, M. (2001) *Access to written information: The views of 1,000 people with sight problems*, London: RNIB.

Bruce, I. and Baker, M. (2003) *Employment and unemployment among people with sight problems in the UK*, London: RNIB.

Bruce, I., McKennell, A. and Walker, E. (1991) *Blind and partially sighted adults in Britain: The RNIB survey*, London: HMSO.

Corden, A. and Thornton, P. (2003) *Results based funded supported employment: Avoiding disincentives to serving people with greatest need*, DWP Report W160 , Sheffield: DWP and Social Policy Research Unit, University of York.

Disability Employment Coalition (2004) *Access to work for disabled people*, London: RNIB.

DRC (Disability Rights Commission) (2004) *The web: Access and inclusion for disabled people, A formal investigation conducted by the Disability Rights Commission*, London: The Stationery Office.

DWP (Department of Work and Pensions) (2003) *Full employment in every region*, (www.w2w.org.uk; www.dwp.gov.uk).

Edwards, A. (2004) *The views of blind and partially sighted users of Access to Work*, London: RNIB

Goldstone, C. and Meager, N. (2002) *Barriers to employment for disabled people*, DWP Report 95, London: DWP and NOP Consumer and the Institute for Employment Studies.

Loebl, R. (2002) *JobCentre Plus Pathfinder Office: Report on technology for service users*, Internal RNIB document.

ONS (Office for National Statistics) (2002) *Labour Force Survey*, London: ONS.

ONS (2004) *Labour Force Survey*, London: ONS

RNIB (Royal National Institute of the Blind) (1993) *Disability leave: A guide for employers*, London: RNIB.

RNIB (2002) *Constructing an employment continuum: Creating jobs by promoting social enterprise*, London: RNIB.

RNIB (2004) *Work matters*, (DVD), London: RNIB

Roberts, S., Heaver, C., Hill, K., Rennison, J., Stafford, B., Howat, N., Kelly, G., Krishnan, S., Tapp, P. and Thomas, A. (2004) *Disability in the workplace: Employers' and service providers' responses to the Disability Discrimination Act in 2003 and preparation for 2004 changes*, DWP Report 202, London: DWP.

Simkiss, P. and Baker, M. (2004) *Beyond the stereotypes: Blind and partially sighted people and work*, London: RNIB.

Smith, D. (2004) *Jobcentre Plus website accessibility for Jaws users*, Internal RNIB document, London: RNIB.

Social Trends (2004) London: The Stationery Office.

EIGHTEEN

Disabled people and employment: the potential impact of European policy

Hannah Morgan

Introduction

The European project, currently realised in the European Union (EU), has it foundations in the economic and inherently capitalist imperatives of the initial European Economic Community (EEC) established by the Treaty of Rome in 1957. The primary focus of the embryonic community was on facilitating economic integration, with wider social issues considered only insofar as they were deemed necessary to achieve the functioning of the common market. Thus, it is in this context that an employment-based disability policy emerged.

In the 50 years since its inception, the rationale of this project has evolved both in scope and scale to a state that would be almost unrecognisable to its founders. The EU could now be viewed as being primarily concerned with constructing what Castells (1998, p 333) describes as a 'project identity' whereby its democratic deficit and lack of popular mandate is addressed by the development of a "blueprint of social values and institutional goals that appeal to a majority of citizens without excluding anyone in principle".

This chapter will discuss the shifting paradigms that have emerged in European debates about employment, social policy and disability during this most recent period of identity and consensus building. Furthermore, it will suggest that the aims and objectives of these often overlapping areas of policy are characterised by tensions between competing and perhaps increasingly divergent, drivers in this process of identity production. The replacement of the concept of citizen–worker (and the parasitic rights of dependent family members) with a more inclusive notion of citizenship based on nationality provides for the first time the opportunity for a comprehensive rights-based disability paradigm (Morgan, 2004; Morgan and Stalford, 2005). The aim here, therefore, will be to discuss the development of this paradigm and to offer pointers to its future development.

Background and context

Disabled people make up a significant percentage, about 10% (CEC, 2003), of the current EU population, a proportion likely to increase over time. However, the experience of disabled citizens of the EU has been characterised by an absence of their collective concerns and aspirations from agenda setting and decision making processes resulting in the marginalisation of issues relating to disability from the mainstream of EU policy and legislation. This led to the charge that disabled people became in effect 'invisible citizens' (EDF, 1995) without adequate protection in law or provision through policy.

The publication in 1993 of the United Nations Standard Rules of Equalisation of Opportunities for Persons with Disabilities (UN, 1993) gave international recognition to a rights-based approach to disability and provided the impetus for a more social model orientated EU disability strategy. The intervening period, marked annually by a European Day of Disabled People and, with much fanfare, in 2003 by the European Year of Disabled People (EYDP), has seen a clear attempt by the institutions of the EU to re-orientate their disability policy and to respond to charges and claims levelled against them by disabled people and their allies.

Organisations of and for disabled people are choosing to mobilise to an unprecedented extent at an EU and pan-European level, evidenced by establishment of organisations such as the European Network on Independent Living (ENIL) in 1989, the European branch of Disabled People International (DPI-Europe) in 1992 and in 1996, the creation of the European Disability Forum (EDF) to provide an:

> independent voice in the political debate at European Union level which is truly representative of the whole spectrum of disabled people and parents of disabled people unable to represent themselves. (EDF, nd)

In addition, wider networks of local, regional, national and supra-national disability groups have begun organising collectively to articulate their concerns about the status of disabled citizens, for example via the recent Tenerife Declaration produced by the first European Congress on Independent Living (ECIL, 2003), the

Strasbourg Freedom Drive (ENIL, 2003) and European Parliament of Disabled People held in November 2003 as part of the EYDP (EPDP, 2003). The broad agenda that emerges is one concerned with issues of rights, non-discrimination, independent living and the mainstreaming of disability, encapsulated in a focus on the degree to which disabled people can actively apply and develop their EU citizenship (Morgan and Stalford, 2004).

The emerging European Union disability policy

The development of a European disability policy can be broadly divided into three phases mirroring to some extent the more general development of the social dimension of the Union. First, a period of 'benign neglect' (Mosley, 1995) from the founding treaty in 1958 until the early 1980s. This was followed by a more focused attempt by the EC to 'creep softly' towards to the establishment of a Disability Strategy in 1996, and finally the adoption of a more radical rights-based approach in the mid-1990s. The aim here is not to provide a comprehensive overview of the development of EU policy in relation to disability (for a more detailed review of the development of disability policy, see Geyer, 2000a; Mabbett and Bolderson 2001), but rather to point to key influences and trends, particularly the relationship between disability policy and the wider concerns of employment policy.

Benign neglect, 1958-81

Very little attention was paid to the needs and concerns of disabled people during the early years of the EEC. Indeed, EEC disability policy during this period can be described as 'virtually non-existent' (Geyer, 2000a, p 187). The Treaties of Paris and Rome were silent on the subject of disability and the majority of disabled people. Those who did not gain entitlement to the worker's rights established by the treaties were only indirectly the concern of the EEC and the beneficiaries of the creation of the common market (Geyer, 2000a; Hantrais, 2000). Thus, disabled people were left out of the master plan (Waddington, 1999, p 139).

For much of this period, broader 'social policy' concerns remained subordinated to economic ones and concentrated at the member state level.

As a result, social and disability policy, such as it was, was subsumed within a broader employment policy concerned predominantly with the free movement of labour, health and safety and other measures designed to complement economic integration.

Creeping softly, 1981-96

The impetus for developing the 'social dimension' of the EEC came from a concern in the 1980s that "the European project would be seen as benefiting big business, bankers and politicians, while ignoring the needs of workers and citizens" (Kleinman, 2002, p 86). To this end, Jacques Delors, as President of the EC, proposed the "creation of a European social area" as a pre-requisite of economic integration (1986, cited in Neilsen and Szyszczak, 1991, p 32). However, as Article 5 establishes, the institutions of the EEC may only act within the competences assigned to them by the treaties (for fuller discussion relating to EC competence and disability, see Waddington, 1997). In addition, there remained substantial resistance in the Council and at member state level to the development of a fully-fledged EC social policy separate from the concerns of economic integration, illustrated by the UK's opt-out from the 1989 Social Charter. Despite these restrictions, the EC made substantial progress in developing a range of social policy initiatives during this period via a process known as 'competence creep', which utilises 'soft-law' measures such as non-binding (less controversial and often aspirational) resolutions, communications and guidelines to facilitate action in areas not explicitly mentioned in treaties and to build "new constituencies of support" for EU action (Wendon, 1996, p 8, cited in Mabbett and Bolderson, 2001, p 15).

A key element in this process in relation to disability was the creation of two successive Community Action Plans: Helios I (1988-91) and Helios II (1993-6). The central aim of the Helios programmes was to 'promote the social integration and independent lifestyle' of disabled people and as such represented a shift in community thinking about disability away from a somewhat blinkered focus on employment and labour market participation and a gradual reorientation of policy objectives towards wider areas of concern. Indeed, Hurst (2004, p 300) asserts that before 1993 the European institutions viewed disability solely as "an issue of rehabilitation and social care and provision".

The process of pan-EEC exchange fostered by the programmes precipitated a growing awareness among disability (and other) organisations of the potential of EU Treaty law (Quinn, 1999, p 304) that was shared by the EC's recognition that:

people with disabilities undoubtedly face a wide range of obstacles which prevent them from achieving full economic and social integration. There is therefore a need to build the fundamental right to equal opportunities into Union policies. (CEC, 1993a)

Consequently, the EC proposed:

at the next opportunity to revise the Treaties, serious consideration must be given to the introduction of a specific reference to combating discrimination on the grounds ... of disability. (CEC, 1993b)

A rights-based strategy, 1996-present

Considerable attention has been paid to the reorientation of EC thinking in line with a rights or social model based approach to disability (see Quinn, 1999; Waddington 1997, 1999). The EC itself points to the 1996 Council Resolution, *Equality of opportunities for people with disabilities* (CEC, 1996), as an endorsement of an approach concerned with barriers and participation at the highest levels of the European project. The resolution encouraged member states to 'empower' disabled people's participation, to remove barriers to this participation and to open up 'various spheres of society', although the focus remained on participation in employment. The culmination of this "sea change in attitude" (Quinn, 1999, p 310) was the inclusion of disability in the anti-discrimination clause of the Treaty of European Union (1997). The adoption of Article 13 EC was highly symbolic, for the first time disabled people were explicitly recognised at the heart of the European project. However, the treaty does not confer additional rights for disabled citizens. The granting of new competencies to the EEC is not a guarantee of action, but rather leave to act should the EEC choose (EDF, 1998, p 23). Moreover, action requires the unanimous approval of (the more circumspect) Council. Furthermore, the potential impact of action is constrained by the continued exclusion of areas of paramount importance in tackling disablement such as education and housing from EEC competence. Nonetheless, the changes to the treaty do have a significant practical impact. It provides a legal basis which EEC institutions can utilise for new legislation and action to ensure better account is taken of the needs of disabled people across the whole community programme.

Mainstreaming disability

Mainstreaming, particularly around equalities issues, is now common practice at both the member state and European level. In essence it is the consideration of the needs of a particular group at all stages of policy and decision making processes and complements rather than replaces specific action targeting designated groups. Mainstreaming also involves assessing whether a policy or action will have a different impact on different groups. The process of mainstreaming in social policy was adopted at the European level first in relation to gender and race and latterly to older people and disability (Geyer, 2000b). More recently, it has been extended to the areas of human rights (CEC, 2002) and children's rights. In the context of disability policy, the EC described it thus:

> Mainstreaming requires well-informed policy-making and wide participation in the policy making process to ensure that disabled people, and their diverse needs and experiences, are at the heart of policy-making each time it has an impact, directly or indirectly, on their lives. (CEC 2003, p 6)

An example is the EC's recent work to encourage member states to consider disability within each of the ten Employment Guidelines of the European Employment Strategy, rather than simply addressing issues of disability as part of the guideline on disadvantaged groups (Social Dialogue.net, 2004). The shift towards mainstreaming disability is viewed by the EC as a central plank of a rights-based response to disability, which it signalled in the 1993 Green Paper on social policy:

> special facilities, institutions and legal rights are obviously necessary, but they should not be an obstacle or an alternative to the principle of mainstreaming, that is to say, acceptance of people as full members of society. (CEC, 1993b, p 48)

This was formally adopted in the 1996 Council Resolution, *Equality of opportunity for people with disabilities* (CEC, 1996). In his analysis of mainstreaming in three areas of EU social policy, Geyer (2000b) rates the success of this strategy as 'partial' (in comparison to 'successful' in relation to gender and failure in the field of older people). Geyer points to the treaty provision for gender equality and the strength of the women's lobby as the key factors in ensuring gender has been effectively mainstreamed in EU policy. Thus, the lack of a formal and forceful legal base that empowers EC action remains a significant barrier. The increasing political impetus around disability issues is countered by 'mainstreaming competition' and 'overload' as well as concern about the resource implications of such a policy.

As suggested earlier in this chapter, the requirement for unanimous agreement by the Council of Ministers, permission for action is a considerable constraint on the development of disability policy leading the EC to utilise 'soft law' as a method of consensus and momentum building. This practice of 'competence creep' can be viewed as a key element of project identity creation whereby 'social values and institutional goals' are constructed through an incremental process of consensus building. This aspect of the European project has been termed 'Europeanization' and can be summarised thus:

> the concept of Europeanization refers to a set of processes through which the EU political, social and economic dynamics become part of the logic of domestic discourse, identities, political structures and public policies. (Radaelli, 2000, p 4)

The 'Europeanization' of disability policy paradigms?

The exact extent of EU influence on approaches and responses to disability in the member states is hard to pinpoint for a number of reasons. First, the EU has drawn extensively on supranational, national and sub-national discussions and debates in the development of its disability strategy, making it difficult to establish which direction influence is flowing in. The EU was clearly inspired and given a certain degree of legitimacy by the development on universal instruments such as UN Standard Rules and the European Declaration on Human Rights to which most member states are signatories. Furthermore, the trend from welfare-based rehabilitation orientated policies towards an approach grounded in rights is an international one embraced in responses based in constitutional, civil and criminal law (Waddington, 2001). Indeed Waddington (2001, p 162) suggests that, far from leading this trend, Europe, whether the EU or its member states, "is lagging behind other parts of the world", such as North America and Australia, and has developed its rights-based disability policy "more or less simultaneously" with many other countries and regions.

Second, the EU is essentially collectivist and consensual in its nature, what Bulmer and Radaelli (2004) term 'governance by negotiation';

whereby the institutional structure of the EEC means that policy is usually the result of a process of negotiation between the different EU institutions, member state governments, social partners and other interest groups. In addition, commitment to the 'subsidiarity principle', where decision making and action takes place at the lowest effective level, remains strong. Furthermore, the emphasis in EC guidance tends to be on securing specific outcomes or harmonising approaches rather than stipulating particular policy tools or methods.

Third, as Hvinden (2003) suggests, there are a number of other factors that influence the development of similar policy across member states. He points to the common challenges faced by European governments such as globalisation and changing demographics, and the emergence of epistemic communities among experts and policy makers. Finally, he notes the impact of the development of an increasingly vocal and coordinated disability movement bringing considerable pressure to bear on both member states and the institutions of the EU. However, despite these influences, there remains "much cross-national divergence in the objectives and instruments of disability policy of Western European countries" (Hvinden, 2003, p 610). This reflects a broader trend across social policy, in which "similar concerns and approaches by EU countries do not necessarily translate into similar decisions and outputs by member states" (Moreno and Palier, 2004, p 4).

Equal citizens: an emerging EU policy paradigm?

Citizenship of the EU was formally established by the 1992 Treaty of Maastricht which granted the status to all nationals of the member states (Article 17 ex 8 EC). The EC Treaty provided a set of modest political rights (such as the right to vote and be a candidate in municipal and European elections) and more significantly "the right to move and reside freely within the territory of the member states" (Article 18 EC). This opens up access to a range of welfare and employment related rights for those who migrate within the EU. There is symbiotic relationship between European citizenship and the free movement provisions with the result that citizenship is only really meaningful in the context of intra-union migration.

The (disabling) barriers to mobility that exist for many Europeans have the potential to make this status a 'hollow concept'. Moreover, even if an individual wishes to migrate they must satisfy certain criteria to qualify under the provisions and obtain access to the panoply of social rights available in another member state which can be summarised as follows: You must be an EU national *and* either economically active (that is, a worker) or, economically self-sufficient (that is, not dependent on welfare benefits). Certain family members such as spouse, child or parent, enjoy these rights parasitically (based on their 'dependency' on the worker).

The limitations inherent in these criteria are well documented in relation to their disproportionate marginalisation of women and children (Scheiwe, 1994; Lundström, 1996; Moebius and Szyszczak, 1998; McGlynn, 2000; Ackers and Stalford, 2004), same-sex and cohabiting couples (Stychin, 2000; Wintemute and Andenaes, 2001) and third country nationals (Peers, 1996). More recently, attention has been paid to the deficiencies of the free movement provisions in respect of disabled people (Waddington and van dei Mei, 1999; Morgan 2004; Morgan and Stalford, 2005). While it has been suggested that "Community law does not (intentionally) seek to deny this right to people with disabilities" (Waddington and van der Mei, 1999, p 8), in practice a range of factors limit the accessibility of EU citizenship for disabled people. These include the interpretation of concepts such as 'worker' and 'dependent family member' (which is explored in detail in Morgan and Stalford, 2005), disparity between social security systems and welfare provisions in different member states, the current restrictions on exporting benefits as well as a variety of non-legal barriers in fields such as transport, employment and housing.

Two key limitations further inhibit the utility of EU citizenship for disabled people. First, the rights that arise through free movement are based on an ethos of non-discrimination, which only provides access to those rights and entitlements available to nationals in the member state to which they migrate. Additional social rights are not created nor are the inequalities inherent in national policies and laws affecting disabled people addressed. Second, and more fundamentally, is the narrow interpretation of contribution embodied in the treaty (Morgan and Stalford, 2005). The development of the European project as primarily an economic one has resulted in the evolution of a citizenship and social policy centred around citizen-worker, someone who contributes via the paid labour market thereby excluding those who contribute by non-economic means such as the provision of informal care (Ackers, 1998; Ackers and Dwyer, 2002; Ackers and Stalford, 2004) or voluntary or community based activity (Barnes, 2004).

The development of a more coherent rights-based approach to EU citizenship could address the deficiencies of a free-movement based conception of citizenship. Indeed, particularly in the context of disability, citizenship is not just about securing access to social entitlement, a broader, rights-based approach to citizenship incorporates more ideological notions of participation, inclusion and equality (Barton, 1993) while acknowledging individuals' contributions as everyday social actors (Cockburn, 1998).

Conclusion

The continued development of a European social model based upon shared 'social values and institutional goals', but achieved through a variety of policy, legislative and legal mechanisms should consolidate the hegemony of a rights-based approach to disability within the EU. It appears likely that further extension of the European project will be centred on a process of formalising the status of its citizens illustrated by the commitment to a European Constitution that includes the Charter of Fundamental Rights initially published in 2000 (CEC, 2000). This broader rights-based approach to citizenship is a significant means by which to extend EU nationals' rights beyond the economic imperative of the free movement provisions to a more inclusive and positive declaration of their specific needs and values.

As well as seeking to promote the substance of tangible entitlement, a rights-based model of citizenship provides an important platform not only for promoting individual autonomy and agency, but also for exposing and crediting disabled people's contribution to society through their formal and informal, direct and indirect participation in the labour market.

References

Ackers, L. (1998) *Shifting spaces: Women, citizenship and migration in the European Community*, Bristol: The Policy Press.

Ackers, L. and Dwyer, P. (2002) *Senior citizenship? Retirement migration and welfare in the European Union*, Bristol: The Policy Press.

Ackers, L. and Stalford, H. (2004) *A community for children? Children, citizenship and internal migration in the European Union*, Aldershot: Ashgate.

Barnes, C. (2004) *'Work' is a four letter word? Disability, work and welfare*, Paper presented to the 'Working futures?' seminar, University of Sunderland, 3-5 December 2003.

Barton, L. (1993) 'The struggle for citizenship: the case of disabled people', *Disability & Society*, vol 8, no 3, pp 236-48.

Bulmer, S.J. and Radaelli, C.M. (2004) *The Europeanisation of national policies*, Belfast: Queens' papers on Europeanisation 2004/1.

Castells, M. (1998) *End of millennium*, Maldon and London: Blackwell Publishers.

CEC (Commission of the European Communities) (1993a) *First report on citizenship of the Union*, COM(93) 702, Brussels: EC.

CEC (1993b) *Green Paper on European Social Policy – Options for the Union*, COM(93) 551, Brussels: EC.

CEC (1996) *Resolution of the council and of the representatives of the governments of the member states meeting within the council of 20 December 1996 on equality of opportunity for people with disabilities*, Brussels: EC.

CEC (2002) *European Union Annual Report on Human Rights – 2002*, (europa.eu.int/scadplus/leg/en/lvb/r10108.htm).

CEC (2003) *Equal opportunities for people with disabilities: A European action plan*, (Communication from the Commission to the Council, the European Parliament, the Economic and Social Committee and the Committee of the Regions), COM (2003) 650 final, Brussels: EC.

Cockburn, T. (1998) 'Children and citizenship in Britain', *Childhood*, vol 5, no 1, pp 99–117.

ECIL (European Congress on Independent Living) (2003) *Tenerife Declaration: Promote independent living – End discrimination against disabled people*, Tenerife: ECIL.

EDF (European Disability Forum) (n.d.) Introduction to the European Disability Forum, (www.edffeph.org/en/about/intro/intro.htm).

EDF (1995) *Disabled people's status in the European Union treaties – Invisible citizens*, Brussels: EDF.

EDF (1998) *Guide to the Amsterdam Treaty*, Brussels: EDF.

ENIL (European Network on Independent Living) (2003) *Strasbourg freedom drive 2003*, (Leaflet) Dublin: ENIL.

EPDP (European Parliament of Disabled People) (2003) *Manifesto from the European Parliament of Disabled People to the European Parliament (and all prospective election candidates) regarding the 2004 European Parliamentary elections*, Brussels: EDF, (www.edffeph.org/EPDP2003/documents/AMENDED/20final/20Manifesto/0EN.pdf).

Geyer. R.R. (2000a) *Exploring European social policy*, Cambridge: Polity Press.

Geyer, R. (200b) 'Can mainstreaming save EU social policy? The cases of gender, disability and elderly policy', *Current Politics and Economics of Europe*, vol 10, no 2.

Hantrais, L. (2000) *Social policy in the European Union*, (2nd edn), Basingstoke: Macmillan.

Hurst, R. (2004) 'Legislation and human rights', in J. Swain, S.French, C. Barnes and C. Thomas (eds) *Disabling barriers – Enabling environments*, (2nd edn), London: Sage Publications.

Hvinden, B. (2003) 'The uncertain convergence of disability policies in Western Europe', *Social Policy and Administration*, vol 37, no 6, pp 609-24.

Kleinman, M. (2002) *A European welfare state – European Union social policy in context*, Hampshire: Palgrave.

Lundström, K. (1996) 'Family life and the freedom of movement of workers in the European Union', *International Journal of Law, Policy and the Family*, vol 10, pp 250-80.

Mabbett, D. and Bolderson, H. (2001) *A significant step forward? EU social policy and the development of a rights-based strategy for disabled people*, Paper presented to the Annual Social Policy Association Conference, Queen's University Belfast, 24-26 July.

McGIynn, C. (2000) 'A family law for the European Union?', in J. Shaw (ed) *Social law and policy in an evolving European Union*, Oxford: Hart.

Moebius, I. and Szyszczak, E. (1998) 'Of raising pigs and children', *Yearbook of European Law*, vol 18, pp 125-56.

Moreno, L. and Palier, B. (2004) *The Europeanization of welfare: Paradigm shifts and social policy reforms*, Paper given at the ESPAnet Conference, St. Anthony's College, Oxford, 9-11 September.

Morgan, H. (2004) *What a difference a decade makes? Disability Policy in the EU 1993-2003*, paper given at the Socio-Legal Studies Association Annual Conference, University of Glasgow, 6-8 April.

Morgan, H. and Stalford, H. (2005) 'Disabled people and the European Union: equal citizens?', in C. Barnes and G. Mercer (eds) *The social model, Europe and the majority world*, Leeds: The Disability Press.

Mosley, H. (1995) 'The "social dumping" threat of European integration: a critique', in B. Unger and F. Van Waarden (eds) *Convergence or diversity – Internationalization and economic policy response*, Avebury, Aldershot, pp 182-99.

Neilsen, R. and Szyszczak, E. (1991) *The social dimension of the European community*, Denmark: Handelshojskolens Forlag Nyt Nordisk Forlag Arnold Busck.

Peers, S. (1996) 'Towards equality: actual and potential rights of third country nationals in the European Union', *Common Market Law Review*, vol 33, pp 7-50.

Quinn, G. (1999) 'The human rights of people with disabilities under EU law', in P. Alston, M. Bustelo and J. Heenan (eds) *The EU and human rights*, Oxford, The Oxford University Press, pp 281-326.

Radaelli, C. (2000) *Wither Europeanization? Concept stretching and substantive change*, paper presented at the PSA Annual Conference, London, 10-13 April, (www.psa.ac.uk/cps/2000/Radaelli%20Claude.pdf).

Scheiwe, K. (1994) 'EC law's unequal treatment of the family: the case law of the European Court of Justice on rules prohibiting discrimination on the grounds of sex and nationality', *Social and Legal Studies*, vol 3, pp 243-65.

Social Dialogue.net (2004) 'Discussion paper on disability mainstreaming in the European Employment Strategy', (www.socialdialogue.net/docs/si_index/7.EN_Mainstreaming_in_Employment.pdf).

Stychin, C. (2000) 'Consumption, capitalism and the citizen: sexuality and equality rights discourse in the European Union', in J. Shaw (ed) *Social policy in an evolving European Union*, London: Hart, pp 259-77.

UN (United Nations) (1993) *Standard rules on the equalisation of opportunities for people with disabilities*, New York: UN Resolution 48/96.

Waddington, L. (1997) 'The European Community and disability discrimination: time to address the deficit of powers', *Disability and Society*, vol 12, no 3, pp 465-79.

Waddington, L. (1999) 'The European Community's response to disability', in M. Jones and L.A. Basser Marks (eds) *Disability diversability and legal change*, The Hague: Kluwer Law, pp 139-52.

Waddington, L. (2001) 'Evolving disability policies: from social welfare to human rights: an international trend from a European perspective', *Netherlands Quarterly of Human Rights*, vol 19, no 2, pp 141-65.

Waddington, L. and van der Mei, A. (1999) *Free movement of disabled people in the European Union: An examination of relevant Community provisions and a discussion of the barriers to free movement*, Brussels: European Disability Forum.

Wintemute, R. and Andenaes, M. (eds) (2001) *Legal recognition of same-sex partnerships: A study of national, European and international law*, Oxford: Hart.

NINETEEN

Missing pieces: the voluntary and community sector's potential for inclusive employment

Lorraine Gradwell

The voluntary and community sector (VCS) contains over 162,000 registered charities as well as a large number of unregistered not-for-profit organisations, associations, self-help groups and community groups. The sector includes small community-based organisations with no paid staff through to large charities with thousands of paid staff and multi-million pound incomes. Drake (1996) chronicles the development of the charitable sector, from its roots in the wake of the industrial revolution through to the modern day. He outlines how the sector has adapted according to social changes, successfully transforming itself from having principally a shelter and alms-giving function to being a modern day major service provider, typically in response to government funded contracts.

The VCS is much larger than might generally be thought. For example the sector in 2002 had:

- a total income of £20.8 billion and an operating expenditure of £20.4 billion;
- assets totalling £70.1 billion;
- a workforce comprising 569,000 paid employees;
- a contribution of £7.2 billion to UK Gross Domestic Product (GDP) (NCVO, 2004).

Despite the particular challenges and difficulties the sector might face, we will see that it clearly has much potential to improve the employment prospects of disabled people both by being an inclusive employer and by offering volunteering activities as a pathway to developing work related skills. There are also direct opportunities to promote inclusive employment through a range of service delivery activities, such as delivering Jobcentre Plus programmes or running a Direct Payments scheme.

In this chapter, I will focus mainly on the voluntary and community sector (VCS) who work in the field of 'disability', and especially those organisations providing employment related services. Looking at the activities of the larger VCS organisations, I will consider how helpful they are in promoting the employment of disabled people, particularly in the light of the 'targeting' of this sector by the government to deliver a variety of employment support programmes for disabled people. Finally, examining the experience of organisations run by disabled people themselves over the last 20 years, as well as the track record of the 'disability charities', I will be asking why valuable lessons about employing disabled people are apparently being ignored by policy makers and practitioners alike.

Defining 'disability'

Defining 'disabled people' is problematic, with disabled people themselves not always agreeing on definitions, and the government and other regulatory bodies having a wide range of 'official' and often contradictory operating definitions of disability (Burchardt, in Millar, 2003). At the heart of the confusion lies the Disability Discrimination Act (DDA) (1995), which carries the definition that organisations, including employers and service providers are legally obliged to work to and comply with. The DDA says that a person is disabled:

> if he (sic) has a physical or mental impairment which has a
> substantial and long-term adverse effect on his ability to
> carry out normal day-to-day activities. (DDA 1995, Part 1)

For strategic and policy purposes, Breakthrough UK Ltd, the voluntary-sector organisation that I manage, which provides training and employment support to disabled people, has adopted the following definitions of 'impairment' and 'disability' in order to provide a framework for the development of services and activities:

> *Impairment* is certain individual appearance(s) or certain
> functional limitations of the mind, body or senses.

> *Disability* is the disadvantage or restriction of activity caused
> by a society which takes little or no account of people

who have impairments, and thus excludes them from mainstream activity.

These definitions are based on the social model of disability, which originated with the Union of Physically Impaired Against Segregation (UPIAS, 1976) and which was subsequently developed by Mike Oliver (Oliver, 1983). Very briefly, the social model is a tool with which to explain and explore the exclusion and discrimination that people with impairments experience. It illustrates how barriers are generally externally imposed (for example, steps), rather than being intrinsic to a feature or characteristic of the individual (for example, being a wheelchair user). Disabled people's organisations have for the last 20 years been refining and developing this analysis and approach. Basing our services on the social model of disability leads Breakthrough UK Ltd to a practice of not only supporting the individual disabled person to achieve their goals, but also of supporting them to tackle the imposed barriers which are preventing them from being independent.

The voluntary and community sector (VCS)

To try to describe the range of VCS and/or charitable organisations is also problematic. As stated earlier the sector includes small, community-based organisations with no paid staff through to large charities with thousands of paid staff and multi million pound incomes. The sector makes a distinctive social and economic contribution to our society, addressing a range of issues from supported housing to donkey sanctuaries and from wholefood coops to door-to-door transport agencies.

In terms of their relationship to disability, most charities have developed individualised medical or welfare approaches to disability:

> Since traditional charities conceive of disability as being the consequence of individual impairments, it follows that for them, change (rehabilitation, adaptation or cure) must also be located within the individual. The general acceptance of this analysis, which also perceives disability as being problematic, legitimises intervention in the form of ameliorative, palliative and consolatory activity. (Drake, 1996, p 151)

As well as being a complex mix of organisations and activities, the VCS is a rapidly growing sector. In terms of employment growth,

85,000 jobs were created in the voluntary sector in the five years between 1997 and 2002. Moreover, the estimated number of volunteers is three million, the equivalent of 1.5 million full-time workers, while 61% of volunteer-involving organisations have disabled volunteers (VSNTO, 2004). Their potential then, as employers, for providing inclusive employment to disabled people is obviously a great opportunity.

Challenges and difficulties

The very real challenges and difficulties of the VCS can revolve around planning and funding matters, especially for smaller organisations which often have to respond to a seemingly perpetual call for innovation. At the same time, they have to deal with the short term-ism that results from year-on-year funding, with little provision made for core costs such as management. Increasingly, VCS organisations are called upon to be more 'business like' and, like their private-sector counterparts, the smaller organisations, including those run by disabled people themselves, feel there is an uneven playing field in which they find themselves in unequal competition with large, multi-million pound charities. As the government moves increasingly closer to a 'contract culture', the 'market' inevitably favours the larger, well-established charities which have economies of scale and increasingly adopt a business-like approach to tendering for services. The sector thus becomes more and more competitive, chasing ever more lucrative contracts and adopting more 'aggressive' fundraising strategies. As Drake (1996) points out:

> Helping 'those less fortunate' is a valued activity, the roots of which go deep in British culture. The traditional voluntary agencies are able to harness the values that underpin the concept of charity when they broadcast their appeals. (Drake, 1996, p 156)

While ostensibly remaining committed to social objectives, the VCS organisations are necessarily driven by this environment to adopt a more professional and a strategic and business-like approach. This approach is reflected, for example, by the NCVO and Amicus-MSF (2001) survey, *Employment Policies Survey*, which looked into the scope of employment practices in the sector, finding out that VCS organisations are focusing on "improving employment policies and recognising the value of staff." Almost 75% had a written equal opportunities or diversity policy (NCVO, 2001).

However, VCS organisations are also major service providers, especially in the 'social care' sector. Significant numbers of the larger VCS organisations, generally having charitable status, are in the business of providing employment support programmes for disabled people and in this capacity they have a great potential to impact on the employment prospects of disabled people. For example, the Shaw Trust (2004) describes itself as the largest UK provider of employment services for disabled people, having had 26,795 clients in 2003-04.

There are two major and distinct types of VCS organisations active in relation to disability. Organisations such as the Shaw Trust, and others who may be operating in fields other than employment support, can be called 'disability organisations' in as much as they are operating 'in the field of disability'. They differ from disabled people's organisations in several ways: they have typically not been set up by disabled people and usually have charitable or 'benevolent' roots. Such organisations have not been established on an ethical base which acknowledges the sources of the discrimination that disabled people face, nor have they placed a high premium on employing disabled people in order to provide peer support and draw on lived experience. They differ fundamentally from those organisations that have been set up or are controlled by disabled people and which are operating within the social model of disability developed by disabled people themselves.

'Disability organisations'

Established in 1977 as the Royal Association for Disability and Rehabilitation, RADAR (Calvi, 2004) now describes itself as 'an organisation of disabled people'. At the RADAR 2004 Annual Conference, a key topic for discussion was how the 'disability movement', or organisations operating in the field of disability, could move towards greater 'user control', clearly of increasing importance to disability organisations as the barriers and civil rights approach gains ground. This is a redundant topic in the disabled people's movement, in which organisations are, by definition, controlled by disabled people.

Voluntary and community sector organisations have been active in the field of disability throughout the last century, often beginning as self-help organisations for parents of disabled children (for example SCOPE, originally the 'Spastics Society'); or having benevolent or charitable aims (for example, Guide Dogs for the Blind). Today, the sector is big business. In early 2004, four major charities (Leonard Cheshire, Action for Blind People, Mencap and the MS Society) announced a collaboration to form a 'fundraising club' called Disability United. In 2002/03 these four disability charities had a combined income of over £280 million (financial information collected from the Charity Commission, 2003). Similarly, the newly appointed chair of RADAR has outlined his intention to "get closer to Scope, RNID [Royal National Institute for Deaf People], RNIB [Royal National Institute of the Blind]" (Disability Now, 2003). With such large partnerships developing then, the power and potential of the sector to impact on providing employment for disabled people is huge, especially among these larger organisations.

It is also clear that the role of the VCS in UK disability employment provision is substantial and that it represents some of the most intensive and creative employment programmes currently operating in the UK. Much of the sector provides services under a variety of government contracts, most notably Workstep, the government's supported employment scheme, which is aimed at disabled people who may find it difficult to get or keep a job. Also very important is work funded through the New Deal for Disabled People (NDDP). This has taken the form of 'job broking' contracts introduced by the government in 2001 and as part of the longer run Welfare-to-Work programme. Many others, often local VCS organisations, seek funding through regeneration streams, charitable grants or local authority or NHS contracts. Yet others fund or subsidise their services through charitable fundraising.

The Shaw Trust, Scope and REMPLOY, which was originally set up after the Second World War to provide employment for returning disabled service personnel, are three of the biggest providers of government-funded employment support programmes, although it should be noted that REMPLOY, a major Workstep provider, is neither part of the VCS nor a registered charity, but a private company established and supported by the government.

Other current government programmes to support disabled people into work are Access to Work, Work Preparation, the Job Introduction Scheme and the new Pathways to Work pilots which aim to move Incapacity Benefit claimants into work (DWP, 2002). Apart from Pathways to Work, most of these programmes are contracted out by the Department for Work and Pensions (DWP) to the VCS or REMPLOY. It should be noted, however, that none of these programmes or pilots has so far made much significant impact on the unemployment figures for disabled people. Although there has been a slight rise in the last three years to 2004, and preliminary reports indicate successes for the Pathways to Work pilots in moving people off Incapacity Benefit, the trend in the official figures of 'long-term sick' and claiming benefit is fairly flat, the numbers having fluctuated between 2.1 and 2.2 million since 1998 (ONS, 2004).

While government policy initiatives have typically conformed to the 'rehabilitation of the individual' model of employment support, the environment is perhaps beginning to show early promise of change, as Burchardt (2004, p 749) points out:

> Part 1 of the 'Pathways to Work' Green Paper marks a step change from previous publications produced by the social security department in identifying a range of social barriers to disabled people's employment. ... Unfortunately, the solutions proposed in Parts 2 and 3 of the paper do not match this promising analysis of the problem. In fact the policies outlined are based almost exclusively on exhortations to disabled claimants to try harder.

Changes or no, is the VCS focus on delivering employment support programmes a useful contribution to increasing the employment rate and prospects of disabled people in UK plc? In the absence of published evidence-based evaluation it is not possible to fully examine the overall successes and failures of these programmes: however an increase of around 15,000 'long-term sick' contributed to the annual rise in inactivity to November 2004 (ONS, 2004).

Disabled people's organisations

In contrast to the large VCS organisations, disabled people's own organisations – that is, those controlled and usually staffed by disabled people – are rarely delivering these employment support programmes. Formed usually around an agenda for independent living, and based on a disability and human-rights ethos, these organisations have generally concentrated on capacity building, campaigning, peer support and involvement, as well as developing and delivering the message of the social model of disability. What they are also doing consistently, is successfully employing disabled people.

For example, the British Council of Disabled People (BCODP) was set up in 1981 by six groups of disabled people who wanted a national representative body for disabled people's own organisations. It has since grown to represent some 126 full member organisations with 51% of their voting membership being made up of disabled people. Constitutionally, at least 75% of the BCODP executive body is made up of disabled people. Surviving in the national VC sector for 23 years, BCODP has only ever employed disabled people.

There are many other VCS organisations around the country which are run by disabled people. In Manchester, there are two such significant organisations which are controlled by disabled people: the Greater Manchester Coalition of Disabled People (GMCDP) and Breakthrough UK Ltd.

The Greater Manchester Coalition of Disabled People was set up by disabled people in 1985 to promote the inclusion and independence of disabled people. It has been a landmark organisation, at the forefront of thinking and analysis on disability issues for 20 years. Its Young Disabled people's project is nationally acclaimed while the magazine, *Coalition*, has an international reputation for cutting-edge comment. The coalition has successfully survived the last 20 years in a difficult financial and organisational environment and has only ever employed disabled people, without additional funding from government programmes other than Access to Work.

Breakthrough UK Ltd was set up in 1997 by Manchester City Council (MCC) as a result of consultation with local disabled people over employment support provision in the city. Becoming fully independent from MCC in 1998 and controlled by disabled people, Breakthrough UK Ltd is a leading social model organisation which offers job-related training and employment support to disabled people in Greater Manchester and Liverpool. Breakthrough UK Ltd continues to grow successfully, and in 2003/04 passed the £1 million income mark, having doubled both staff and annual income in five years.

Breakthrough UK Ltd differs from GMCDP through being a service delivery organisation, with an aim to work to the social model of disability and the principles of independent living. With an additional major aim to influence policy and practice, in 2004/05 the chief executive of Breakthrough UK Ltd has been a member of two ministerial advisory committees: the Disability Employment Advisory Committee (DEAC) at the DWP, and the Small Business Council (SBC) at the Department for Trade and Industry, as well as advising the Prime Minister's Strategy Unit (PMSU) on the employer aspects of the PMSU (2004) report, *Life chances of disabled people*.

Using an open recruitment system, and with no specific targets, in 2004 Breakthrough UK Ltd has 65% disabled people at all levels in the staff group of 40. Like GMCDP, the only government programme Breakthrough UK Ltd makes use of is Access to Work. Interestingly, disabled workers nationally have identified Access to Work as a key element of employment support, despite nevertheless citing delays and bureaucracy as major problems with the scheme (Roulstone et al, 2003). Meanwhile, the majority of employers say anecdotally that they are not aware of Access to Work, yet the national budget for this provision rises year on year, seemingly indicating a degree of effectiveness for this programme.

'Disability organisations' as employers

In May 2003, a survey carried out by *Disability Now* magazine looked at the rate of disabled people employed by some of the major 'disability' charities. With 3,891 employees, SCOPE did not fare very well at 3.51%, while the Shaw Trust, although not quoted in this survey, does rather better with over 16% of its 1,017 staff being disabled people (Shaw Trust, 2004). If we look at the number of senior managers who are disabled people, SCOPE does not perform very well at 0.9%. The Shaw Trust percentage is not detailed in this report.

I have chosen these organisations as illustrations because they are both significant VCS organisations delivering in the field of employment support. Would it be simplistic to expect them to apply the principles of the contracted work they deliver to their own practices as employers? Other major VCS organisations also employ low levels of disabled people: Leonard Cheshire, for example, with 8,000 staff, employs 2% of disabled people, with 9% of senior staff being disabled people. Mencap, with around 5,000 staff, employs 2.8% disabled people and 3.7% of senior staff are disabled people.

'Disability organisations' as employment service providers

A variety of provisions exist throughout the VCS in terms of enhancing disabled people's employment chances, although the exact value of the VCS to enhancing disabled people's employment is unknown and unquantified. In the absence of coordinated evidence gathering, it may be helpful to consider examples of provision in terms of the major funding sources behind the services, although an overall evaluation of their effectiveness is not really possible here.

Government contracts disbursed centrally

The current major government programmes are WORKSTEP, NDDP (using the job broker mode), Work Preparation, the Job Introduction Scheme, Access to Work, and the new pilots, Job Retention and Rehabilitation and Pathways to Work. On the horizon is a Vocational Rehabilitation Framework being developed by DWP (see www.dwp.gov.uk/publications/vrframework). Most, but not all of the programmes listed are contracted out to the VCS, with WORKSTEP and NDDP being the largest. Although Access to Work itself is not contracted out, the assessments for support generally are. A defining feature of all these programmes is that they focus primarily on improving the 'employability' of the individual, taking a 'deficit model' approach. A further feature in common is that they are not evaluated within a common framework, so understanding their relative effectiveness is difficult (see Chapters Three and Four of this volume).

Local and regional initiatives

There are many VCS organisations operating locally in the field of disability and employment. The Association for Supported Employment (AfSE) has over 200 member organisations, often raising funds locally through local government, NHS and regeneration sources (see www.afse.org.uk) Additionally, the large charities will often operate locally and resource their services through local funders.

'Organic' services

These are the VCS organisations developed by disabled people themselves; they can be developed in partnership with local funders, or they may be funded through grant applications or resources raised through other means, such as charitable giving. This area of the VCS plays a very diverse role, with some organisations adopting employment research, support and ad hoc projects as part of a much wider brief. Indeed, local disabled people's organisations can of themselves be seen as employment support to disabled people, given their exemplary records in employing only disabled people.

Some examples of activities that are based on a social model approach, taken from my own organisation, Breakthrough UK Ltd, include:

- researching the strategies and supports that *working* disabled people use to gain and retain employment, so as to better inform and develop employment support practices (Roulstone et al, 2003);
- using independent employment advocates to support disabled people through the labyrinth of services intended to provide support but often not working in tandem nor 'joining up';
- focusing on the barriers to work, while supporting the disabled person to identify and achieve their employment goal;
- working with employers to support their recruitment of disabled people and then to identify and tackle the workplace barriers;
- developing a pilot Independent Living Skills course, subsequently mainstreamed in Liverpool, aiming to increase the self confidence and awareness of rights of disabled people who have attended a local authority day centre for many years;
- having a high percentage of disabled staff on our own workforce, including employment support workers and senior managers, thereby providing positive role models for disabled job seekers;
- actively seeking to influence policy and practice in line with a social model approach.

What makes the difference?

What are the different factors or drivers that have led to the three organisations controlled by disabled people mentioned earlier employing all, or a majority of disabled people in their workforce? And are there organisational restrictions that mean that neither SCOPE, the Shaw Trust, Leonard Cheshire nor Mencap can match that performance? Financial resources are clearly not the problem, with SCOPE and the Shaw Trust for example each having respectively for 2003 a gross income of almost £94 million (SCOPE, 2003) and just over £42 million (Charity Commission, 2003). Economies of scale also operate in favour of these larger VCS organisations, in that they have the benefit of centralised human resources functions and their own legal advisers to support good employment practice. Strategic and operational planning surely cannot be a problem for such large and successful organisations? And yet as 'disability organisations', their record in employing disabled people at all levels is not good, while the disabled people's organisations are consistently setting benchmark standards.

My assertion is that what is (or has been) missing is the organisational commitment to adopt inclusive employment practices and to actively recruit and retain disabled staff, a commitment which is at the very core of the three disabled people's organisations mentioned earlier. Interestingly, SCOPE appears to be starting to address this very problem, having recently announced a "reserved posts policy" (Disability Now, 2003) and recognising that "we have yet to practise what we preach". They have set a target of employing 20% of disabled staff by December 2007.

However, what also appears to be missing is a willingness to learn from disabled people's organisations. The collective record of just the three organisations mentioned earlier, of some 50 years experience of employing only or mostly disabled people while operating successfully in a rapidly changing and relatively volatile sector, must surely be valuable 'business to business' learning. Or perhaps the 'disability organisations' feel that they know how to employ large numbers of disabled people, since for some of them this is their core business. And yet they seem to fail to 'practise what they preach'. It surely is not that they lack the expertise to turn strategic learning into successful delivery, being multi-million pound operations? What can explain their failure to be 'good' employers of disabled people, while their 'poor relations', the smaller, disabled people controlled organisations manage it consistently? This returns us to the assertion that any real commitment to employing disabled people is lacking.

How can this situation be remedied and the lessons learned? Three immediate 'early wins' are possible. First, following on from the PMSU (2004) report, *Life chances of disabled people*, the government could commission research which would examine and explain the methods and approaches by which relatively small organisations can demonstrate such good practice. Second, major government funding streams could build in requirements to deliver against these 'good practice benchmarks' so that the major disability organisations could work towards being inclusive employers. And third, organisations which are clearly leading the way in employing disabled people could be actively sought out, supported and resourced in order to expand and develop their activities.

Conclusion

It is reasonable to suggest that the exact value of the voluntary sector in enhancing disabled people's employment is unknown. Despite delivery contracts for a number of government policies and programmes being deliberately aimed at this sector, including building on New Deal for Disabled People, Workstep, Work Preparation, and so on, and despite the huge potential of the VCS itself as an employer, the contribution remains unquantified at both a micro and a macro level. However, we have seen that most 'disability organisations' operating in this field generally perform badly in terms of employing disabled people, while disabled people's own organisations perform extremely well.

The experience of employing disabled people that has been built up by organisations run by disabled people themselves over the last 20 years holds valuable lessons, which have been ignored by policy makers and practitioners alike. There is a clear and pressing need to understand and learn from the actions of the voluntary sector in the area of disability and employment policy and practice, and to make some fundamental changes.

References

BCODP (British Council of Disabled People) (2004) *Welcome to the British Council of Disabled People* (www.bcodp.org.uk).

Burchardt, T. (2004) 'Capabilities and disability', *Disability and Society*, vol 19, no 7, pp 735-52.

Calvi, N. (2004) 'Refocusing the RADAR', *Disability Now*, December, (www.radar.org.uk).

Charity Commision (2003) www.charity-commission.gov.uk.

Disability Now (2003) 'Can charities change?', *Disability Now*, May.

Drake, R. (1996) 'A critique of the role of the traditional charities', in L. Barton (ed) *Disability and Society*, London: Longman, pp 147-66.

DWP (Department for Work and Pensions) (2002) *Pathways to work: Helping people into employment*, Green Paper, London: DWP.

Gooding, C. (1996) *Blackstones' guide to the Disability Discrimination Act 1995*, London: Blackstone.

Miller, J. (2003) *Understanding social security*, Bristol: The Policy Press.

National Council for Voluntary Organisations (NCVO) (2004) *United Kingdom Voluntary Sector Almanac 2004*, London: NCVO.

NCVO and Amicus-MSF (2001) *Employment policies in the United Kingdom voluntary sector*, (www.ncvo-vol.org.uk).

Office for National Statistics (ONS) (2004) *Labour market trends*, November Assessment, London: ONS.

Oliver, M. (1983) *Social work with disabled people*, Basingstoke: Macmillan.

PMSU (Prime Minister's Strategy Unit) (2004) *The life chances of disabled people. An interim report*, London: Cabinet Office.

Rickell, A. (2004) 'First class post', *Disability Now*, December.

Roulstone, A., Gradwell, L., Price, J. and Child, L. (2003) *Thriving and surviving at work: Disabled people's employment strategies*, Bristol: The Policy Press.

SCOPE (2003) *Annual report 2002/03*, London: Scope, (www.scope.org.uk).

Shaw Trust (2004) *Facts about Shaw Trust*, (www.shaw-trust.org.uk).

UPIAS (Union of the Physically Impaired Against Segregation) (1976) *Fundamental principles of disability*, London: UPIAS.

VSNTO (Voluntary Sector National Training Organisation) (2004) *Voluntary sector key facts*, London: NCVO, (www.vsnto.org.uk).

TWENTY

Professional barriers and facilitators: policy issues for an enabling salariat

Bob Sapey and Jeannine Hughes

Introduction

Using social work as a case study, this chapter explores the barriers and facilitators that operate within a number of human services professions in relation to disabled people's access to those occupational groups. In particular, we are interested in examining how the current legislative context in the UK relates to the tendency to define the skills and knowledge of those entering professions through competence standards. Do these provide a means of greater or fairer access to disabled people or do they constitute an additional barrier?

Disabled people working in professions

There is a distinct lack of a comprehensive analysis in relation to disabled workers in the UK (Jones et al, 2003). It is unsurprising, therefore, that limited data is available in relation to disabled people working specifically in a professional capacity. That which is available, raises difficulties in relation to definitions of disability used to collect data (Smith and Twomey, 2002). Thus, not only is there inconsistency in how data is collated, the potential usefulness of the data is also somewhat limited. Some agency-led studies utilise self-reported disability statistics focusing on specific roles within an organisation (for example, Higher Education Statistics Agency (HESA), 2003; NPS, 2004). Staff included in these surveys are not necessarily obliged to report a disability, even if they are aware of the definitions used by their employers. Employees may therefore make an active choice not to disclose a disability, therefore under-reporting and non-reporting impacts upon the generalisability of the available statistics. Both the

National Probation Service (NPS, 2004) and HESA (2003) have identified this as a major flaw in their data collection. A lack of robust, standardised human resource systems within human services organisations may also impact on the reliability and reporting of relevant data, particularly in relation to professional occupations.

Utilising the Disability Rights Commission's (DRC, 2004a) analysis of the 2003 Labour Force Survey, 19% of working-age people living in private households had a current long-term disability, a total of 6.86 million people. Of these, less than half were employed in summer 2003. For non-disabled people the employment rate at that time was 81%, for disabled people that figure is 49%. The same survey also identified that disabled people were under-represented among management and professional occupations while being over-represented in personal services, process, plant and machine operatives, and elementary occupations.

This higher prevalence of disability among social classes associated with manual and unskilled work was also observed in the *Health Survey for England – Disability*, although the Department of Health (DH, 2002a) also reported a significant fall in disability prevalence in social classes II and V from the previous health survey undertaken in 1995. This perhaps highlights the need for further analysis to be undertaken in relation to the effects of the 1995 Disability Discrimination Act (DDA) upon the employment of disabled people:

Table 20.1: Prevalence and severity of disability by social class[a]

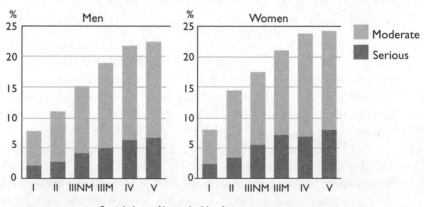

Social class of household reference person

[a] Table reproduced from *The Health Survey for England* (DH, 2002a) by kind permission, showing how those with a disability are less likely to occupy social class I and II. Social classes were defined as follows: I (professional), II (managerial and technical), IIINM (skilled non-manual), IIIM (skilled manual), IV (partly skilled), and V (unskilled).

The Department of Health (2002a) also highlighted the under-representation of disabled people when examining levels of qualification:

> ... within each age group the proportion [of people] without qualifications was significantly higher for those with a disability than for those without.

Less than half of disabled men with formal qualifications were found to possess higher levels of qualification. However, 79% of men without a disability had a qualification, three in five of whom had a higher qualification. The pattern among women, although similar, was not as significant.

The current focus of official statistical data gathering appears to be solely on the numbers of disabled people participating in employment, rather than the types of employment that are accessible to disabled people. However, what is evident from the available data, irrespective of the initial definitions used to collate them, is that when disabled people are compared to the overall population, unemployment rates are higher and average earnings are significantly lower (Jones et al, 2003), while qualifications gained are of a lower standard and there is clear under-representation within professional and managerial

Table 20.2: Educational attainment by disability status, age and sex (2001) (%)

Age 16 and over (2000-01) Educational attainment	16-44 ND	16-44 WD	45-64 ND	45-64 WD	65-74 ND	65-74 WD	75+ ND	75+ WD	Total ND	Total WD
Men										
A-Levels or higher	54	38	46	27	31	17	21	14	48	23
O levels or equivalent	34	37	25	24	21	23	21	18	29	25
Vocational/Trade	1	2	3	4	4	4	6	4	2	3
No qualification	11	24	26	45	45	57	52	64	21	49
Women										
A-Levels or higher	46	28	32	17	19	10	12	8	37	15
O levels or equivalent	40	42	26	20	14	9	10	7	32	18
Vocational/Trade	2	2	9	9	9	8	10	8	5	7
No qualification	12	29	33	55	58	73	68	76	26	61
Bases										
Men	4,717	317	2,712	633	871	446	443	407	8,743	1,825
Women	5,768	424	3,231	710	1,031	493	579	730	10,609	2,357

Notes: ND = No disability; WD = With disability
Source: Reproduced from Health Survey of England – Disability (2001)

occupations. Jones et al (2003) take the view that legislative and policy-related changes aimed to assist disabled people, including the DDA, have had little if any effect in counteracting discrimination faced by disabled workers.

In light of this, it is therefore essential that additional barriers, in the form of National Occupational Standards and Benchmarking statements, are not constructed to further deny disabled people access to professional roles.

Disability Discrimination Act (1995)

Part Two of the DDA makes it illegal for any employer, except the armed forces, to discriminate against a disabled person in relation to either recruitment or retention of staff. In its (2002) *Code of practice on employment and occupation*, the DRC (2002) promotes a social model understanding and make clear the need to re-examine employment and occupation practices.

> The concept of discrimination in the Act reflects an understanding that functional limitations arising from disabled people's impairments do not inevitably restrict their ability to participate fully in society. Rather than the limitations of an impairment, it is often environmental factors (such as the structure of a building, or an employer's working practices) which unnecessarily lead to these social restrictions. This principle underpins the duty to make reasonable adjustments …. It is as important to *consider which aspects of employment and occupation create difficulties for a disabled person* as it is to understand the particular nature of an individual's disability. (DRC, 2004b, para. 2.2, emphasis added)

Part Four of the DDA, as amended by the Special Educational Needs and Disability Act 2001 (SENDA), also makes it illegal for education institutions to discriminate against disabled students. The provision and arrangements for compulsory work placements, which are an integral part of many professional courses, are covered by this legislation.

Discrimination can occur either when a responsible body treats a disabled person less favourably on grounds of their disability than they would treat a non-disabled person, or when a responsible body fails to make a reasonable adjustment so that a disabled student is placed at a substantial disadvantage compared with a non-disabled person. Furthermore, in relation to education an important duty is that of planning ahead, anticipating:

> Responsible bodies (ie HE institutions) should not wait until a disabled person applies to a course ... before thinking about what reasonable adjustments they could make. Instead they should continually be anticipating the requirements of disabled people or students and the adjustments they could be making for them. Failure to anticipate the need for an adjustment may mean it is too late to comply with the duty to make the adjustment when it is required. (DRC, 2002, para 1b)

Since October 2004, the DDA 1995 (Amendment) Regulations 2003, have placed responsibilities on qualifications bodies not to discriminate against disabled people. This covers:

- the arrangements it makes for the purpose of determining upon whom to confer a professional or trade qualification, or
- the terms on which it is prepared to confer such a qualification, or
- refusing or deliberately omitting to grant any application by him for a professional or trade qualification, or
- withdrawing such a qualification from him or varying the terms on which he holds it. (DRC, 2004c, para 3.19)

One of the keys to whether a qualifications body is acting legally is whether, in making decisions, it is applying competence standards that are necessary for a person to have achieved in order to qualify for that occupation. Hence the *Code of practice for trade organisations and qualifications bodies* (DRC, 2004c) discusses the meaning and application of competence standards at length. Section 14A(5) of the DDA defines a competence standard as "an academic, medical or other standard applied by or on behalf of a qualifications body for the purpose of determining whether or not a person has a particular level of competence or ability". However, it is necessary to distinguish between the application of a standard and the process by which it is applied, so, for example, the code suggests it is perfectly legitimate for a foreign language interpreter to be expected to undertake an oral examination, but it would be illegal not to permit a person with dyslexia to have additional time within a written examination – the latter would be a reasonable adjustment.

In respect of the application of the standard itself, this is only likely to be illegal if the qualifications body cannot show that the standard is applied equally to others and that "its application is a proportionate means of achieving a legitimate aim" (DRC, 2004c, para 8.36). The DRC give an example of someone who fails a fitness test which is applied to all other applicants, but which is not consistently applied after people have joined that profession, thereby demonstrating that it is not proportionate.

These rules could be quite important within many human services professions, particularly where stereotypical assumptions are made about the impact of particular impairments on a person's ability to undertake certain tasks. Within social work for example, assumptions may be made about the ability of blind people to undertake child protection duties due to their inability to observe bruising on a child (James and Thomas, 1996). If a blind person were to be refused entry to the occupation on these grounds, presumably it would be necessary to show that all social work students are assessed in relation to their ability to observe and interpret such bruising, which is not the case. What happens in practice is that if a student can demonstrate the ability to transfer their learning between two different groups of people, neither of whom have to be children, then it is assumed they are able to do this with others. This is what the occupational bodies for social work appear to have always accepted as proportionate. However, in this case an additional post-qualification assessment is undertaken by social workers to be eligible to undertake child protection work and it may be that the qualifications body could require all applicants for this specialised status to meet such a competence standard.

The *Code of practice* states that if qualifications bodies are to avoid discrimination, they need to show two things:

> First, it will have to show that the application of the standard does not amount to direct discrimination. Second, it will be necessary to show that the standard can be objectively justified. (DRC, 2004c, para 8.41)

The DRC go on to argue that "this is more likely to be possible where a qualifications body has considered the nature and effects of its competence standards *in advance* of an issue arising in practice" (emphasis added, para 8.41). The DRC advises on a review and evaluation of such standards including:

- Identifying the specific purpose of each competence standard which is applied, and examining the manner in which the standard achieves that purpose
- Considering the impact which each competence standard may have on disabled people and, in the case of a standard which may have an adverse impact, asking whether the application of the standard is absolutely necessary
- Reviewing the purpose and effect of each competence standard in the light of changing circumstances – such as developments in technology
- Examining whether the purpose for which any competence standard is applied could be achieved in a way which does not have an adverse impact on disabled people, and
- Documenting the manner in which these issues have been addressed, the conclusions which have been arrived at, and the reasons for those conclusions. (DRC, 2004c, para 8.41)

Occupations, professions and competence standards

A conventional view of the formation of professions would suggest that, over time, certain occupational groups come together to satisfy needs in the social structure. They identify a body of knowledge that is necessary for others to join; they develop courses in universities, professional associations and codes of ethics, and their members profess an allegiance to the standards that have been laid down (Hall, 1968). Early professions such as medicine and the law may even have involved some form of commitment to serve others regardless of recompense.

While in sport the distinctiveness of professionals is that they are paid, in other occupational areas it may be their exclusivity and protection of self-interest. Professions were, and to some extent still are, self governing, although the degree to which they have become reliant on public sanction has led to considerable control over their activities by successive governments. The rise of managerialism in the 1980s was seen by many as a concerted attempt to overthrow the power of professional associations and to de-professionalise public services. For example, Clarke (1995) has argued that quality assurance ceased to be solely concerned with the "production and dissemination of good practice and the delivery of service" (p 10) and became a "central mechanism for disciplining professional autonomy" (p 10).

Managerialism also made use of the notion of competence in its effort to undermine professional authority. The initial introduction of vocational qualifications had two key features. First, they were methods of assessing competence rather than courses of study and as such they needed to be very precise about what competence was in any occupation. The resulting 'units, elements, performance criteria and critically enabling knowledge' statements were developed through a process of functional analysis in which occupational activities were deconstructed and the parts of those activities reconstructed into assessable forms, often losing the gestalt of the whole. Second, as these standards were not linked to any particular course of study, but were intended to validate experienced, unqualified workers, the assessors would be the managers of those being assessed. This fundamentally shifted the authority to determine access to many occupations from colleges and universities to employers. As the DDA now illustrates, competence standards have gained such a status that they are defined within our legislation and even provide a basis for determining whether a qualifications body is acting lawfully in relation to disability discrimination.

What is also interesting about the rise of managerialism is the extent to which many professions and occupational groupings have succumbed by handing over much of their responsibility for self-government and embracing the new more technocratic approaches. Finkelstein (1999, p 2) addresses this issue from the viewpoint of disabled people's experience of professions allied to medicine:

> Is de-professionalising the statutory education, health and welfare services, while maintaining worker illusions about who and what they are, the hidden agenda behind modernising public services? Transforming professionals into rule-following technicians who rigidly follow a covert cost-cutting agenda appears to be an extraordinarily effective way of making changes that otherwise would be instinctively resisted.

The DRC, through its codes of practice, encourages employers, educational institutions, trade organisations and qualifications bodies to take a social model approach to understanding and dealing with disabling barriers. However, as Oliver (1983) has argued, changing from an individual model of disability to a social model involves a paradigm shift and this, as Kuhn (1962) has pointed out, is not achieved without the introduction of some revolutionary ideas. These are likely to meet resistance within professions, not simply due to the protection of power, but also due to the nature of professionalism and the attributes of professionals. On entering a profession, people express an allegiance to the knowledge base and codes of ethics of that profession. They become part of what Kuhn (1962) referred to as 'normal science'. In effect, they become normal scientists who share an understanding of their occupation; that is, they operate within the existing paradigm. In human service professions that have traditionally operated on an individual model understanding of disability, there will be some difficulties therefore in getting occupation bodies to adopt a social model, and therefore the review and evaluation of their own competence standards that the DRC has advised, may be a rather futile exercise.

Some may cast doubt on this criticism of professions, especially those within the human services, so perhaps it is necessary to recall some of the exclusion policies that have operated in the recent past. Following the 1994 Clothier and 1997 Bullock reports, people were required to be free of treatment for psychiatric illness for two years before they could be considered safe to work in health settings. This guidance was not rescinded until 2002 (DH, 2002b) due to the requirements of the DDA. Similarly people with skin diseases have been excluded from nursing and prospective teachers have been required to declare if they have facial disfigurements. Until quite recently, the Church of England refused to accept applicants for the clergy if they had a history of epilepsy, while the new rules for social work degrees require applicants to be able to speak English, thus potentially disbarring people for who British Sign Language is their only language, despite the fact that they could undertake the earlier qualification for entry.

In reviewing the literature about disabled people within social work, Sapey et al (2004) found that a consistent theme was that disabled people were considered to be clients, not colleagues. This reflects a paradigm of thinking and it arises from what Oliver (2004) has described as the humanitarian and compliance approaches that have dominated social work. He doubts if social work has a future and calls for disability services to be delivered with a citizenship approach. Finkelstein (1999) also argues that we do not simply need a paradigm shift within existing professions, but that we need a new profession. He claims that professions allied to medicine which dominate the disability industry have been educated within an 'intellectually bankrupt care philosophy' and that what is needed now is a new profession allied to communities. Such professionals would be allied to disabled people and concerned with aspirations, not needs.

The National Occupational Standards for Social Work

The National Occupational Standards for Social Work were devised by the Training Organisation for the Professional Social Services (TOPSS) in 2002, in consultation with employers, people who use services, carers, practitioners, government officials and representatives from further and higher education, and from professional bodies. They are designed to raise practice standards, by providing a baseline to measure the performance of both social work organisations and individual staff within these organisations. For those aiming to enter the profession of social work, National Occupational Standards will form the basis of the assessment criteria upon which their ability to practise will be based. These standards do not stand alone, but are part of a wider regulatory framework for social work education (Sapey et al, 2004). Within this overall framework, there are numerous potential barriers to qualification for disabled people. However, for the purpose of this chapter, we will be focusing on the National Occupational Standards for Social Work. In examining these, it is pertinent to consider the potential for the criteria, laid down for assessing those entering the social work profession, to be either intrinsically flawed in design or having the potential to be poorly implemented. Sapey et al (2004) argue that the former does not appear to them to be the case, while the latter is a common experience of disabled students.

The National Occupational Standards for Social Work are divided into six 'key roles', which are subdivided into 21 'units', with each unit further subdivided into 77 'elements'. Currently, a student must be assessed as successfully passing each element to enable a social work qualification to be awarded. Each of these elements has a number of performance criteria or indicators, which provide practice assessors and students with examples of how the specific element may be met. While it is not essential for students to demonstrate each of these 300+ indicators, it is imperative that these indicators are used in a consistent manner, with reasonable adjustments being made as appropriate to ensure that discrimination does not occur (DRC, 2004c).

Sapey et al (2004, p 30) highlight that the potential for discrimination is most likely to occur where:

> those involved in the provision of practice learning fail to either provide appropriate opportunities ... or are too restrictive in the way they think standards should be met.

Unimaginative application of the performance criteria associated with each unit of the National Occupational Standards perhaps provides the greatest potential for discrimination. Thus, how individual practice assessors interpret these standards is crucial. The knowledge, training and experience of each practice assessor will inevitably impact upon their assessments of disabled students and given the under-employment of disabled people in professional occupations it is more likely that practice assessors will be non-disabled people. In this chapter, we highlight some problems that may occur in different 'key roles', but it is important to note that the examples provided could be applied to many of the key roles, units, elements or performance criteria.

Within Key Role 1, performance criteria indicate that students need to demonstrate their ability to:

a. Identify and access case notes and relevant information
b. Read and review information ... (for a variety of purposes)

It should not be assumed that a person who is visually impaired could not achieve these criteria; rather, that reasonable adjustment should be made to enable a disabled student to access this information differentially. A practice assessor working from an individual model of disability may see the student's impairment as the problem. Appropriate training provided for the practice assessor prior to the commencement of the practice learning opportunity would limit the possibility of this occurring.

Within Key Role 2, a reasonable adjustment for a hearing impaired student may be that an interpreter is employed to enable the following performance criteria to be met:

Involve individuals, families, carers, groups and communities in the discussions, debates and proceedings, wherever possible.

However, financial provision for this facility throughout the required 200 days of practice learning required for a degree in social work remains a barrier to deaf students (Sapey et al, 2004). Therefore, even with the most skilled practice assessor assessing a student, other barriers exist that may deny disabled students access to the profession of social work.

A practice assessor failing to see the impact of a student's particular impairment, as highlighted by Green (2003) who was then a physiotherapy student, has the potential to lead to discrimination in relation to the assessment of Key Role 3 which requires social workers to 'support individuals to represent their needs, views and circumstances':

> People either may not notice or overlook any mistakes I
> make and assume it is due to something else and not my
> deafness. (Green, 2003, p 1)

Where concern exists about a student's ability in relation to this key
role, the skilled use of supervision and constructive feedback from the
practice assessor will usually bring about the changes required to
achieve the pass standard. The supervisor, however, must have
undertaken and understood relevant training in relation to both the
social model of disability and the supervision of disabled students
from this perspective.

The potential for disabled people to be viewed as clients rather than
colleagues (Sapey et al, 2004) could impact negatively on disabled
students attempting to demonstrate their competence in relation to
Key Roles 4 and 5, specifically the need to "manage risk to individuals,
families, carers, groups and communities and self and colleagues" and
to "manage and be accountable with supervision and support, for
your own social work practice within your organisation". Should
practice assessors exhibit negative assumptions when assessing a disabled
student's competence in these areas, a student may be perceived, as
clients frequently are, as failing to manage their situation.

The divisive presumption of superiority in favour of the dominant
group, in this case non-disabled people, may lead to the assumption
that disabled students commence practice learning opportunities with
more to learn than their non-disabled peers. This may particularly
impact upon Key Role 6, which requires a student to demonstrate
"professional competence in social work". A future area for research
would be the examination of practice learning documentation for
indicators of disabled students being required to undertake a longer
time to be assessed as meeting the set standards.

Conclusion

Although the DRC make very clear recommendations on how trade
organisations and qualification bodies should review the competence
standards for entry into professions, the DDA 1995 also makes it very
clear that such standards are sacrosanct. It is the application of the
standards that needs to be fair. However, as we have argued, the bodies
responsible for both reviewing and applying the standards will in most
cases be closely associated with occupations that have shown themselves
to be less than responsive to the challenges of the disabled people's
movement (Thompson, 2002). Indeed, some would argue (Gibbs, 2004;

Gilson and DePoy, 2002) that the models of education and service provision that dominate the human services amount to a disciplining process which focuses only on the deficits of disabled people. To achieve any degree of equality in either the review or assessment of competence standards, it will be necessary for qualification bodies to think in revolutionary ways (Kuhn, 1962) about the standards they are charged with upholding.

References

Clarke, J. (1995) *Doing the right thing? Managerialism and social welfare*, paper presented to the ESRC seminar, 'Professionals in Late Modernity', Imperial College, 26 June.

DH (Department of Health) (2002a) *Health survey for England – 2001 series*, London: The Stationery Office (TSO).

DH (2002b) *Mental health and employment in the NHS*, London: DH.

DRC (Disability Rights Commission) (2002) *Code of practice post-16, Disability Discrimination Act 1995: Part 4*, London: TSO.

DRC (2004a) *DRC Disability Briefing*, (www.drcgb.org/publicationsandreports/completed.asp).

DRC (2004b) *Disability Discrimination Act 1995. Code of practice, employment and occupation*, London: The Stationery Office.

DRC (2004c) *Disability Discrimination Act 1995. Code of practice, trade organisations and qualifications bodies*, London: The Stationery Office.

Finkelstein, V. (1999) *Professions allied to the community (PACs) I*, Leeds: Disability Archive, (www.leeds.ac.uk/disability-studies/archiveuk).

Gibbs, D. (2004) 'Social model services: an oxymoron?', in C. Barnes and G. Mercer (eds) *Disability policy and practice: Applying the social model*, Leeds: The Disability Press.

Gilson, S. and DePoy, E. (2002) 'Theoretical approaches to disability content in social work education', *Journal of Social Work Education*, vol 38, no 1, pp 153-65.

Green, V. (2003) *See your voice: Practicalities, problems and possible solutions for deaf students accessing learning within a health profession course, with specific reference to physiotherapy*, (www.health.ltsn.ac.uk/publications/studentessay/veritygreen).

Hall, R. (1968) 'Professionalisation and bureaucratisation', in G. Salaman, K. Thompson and M. Speakman (eds) (1973) *People and organisations*, Milton Keynes: Open University Press.

HESA (Higher Education Statistics Agency) (2003) *Resources of higher education institutions 2002/03*, London: HESA.

James, P. and Thomas, M. (1996) 'Deconstructing a disabling environment in social work education', *Social Work Education*, vol 15, no 1, pp 34-45.

Jones, K., Latreille, P.L. and Sloane, P.J. (2003) *Disability, gender and the labour market*, Swansea: University of Wales.

Kuhn, T. (1962) *The structure of scientific revolutions*, Chicago, IL: University of Chicago Press.

NPS (National Probation Service) (2004) *Human resources workforce profile report*, London: NPS.

Oliver, M. (1983) *Social work with disabled people*, Basingstoke: Macmillan.

Oliver, M. (2004) 'The social model in action: if I had a hammer', in C. Barnes and G. Mercer (eds) *Implementing the social model of disability: Theory and research*, Leeds: The Disability Press.

Sapey, B., Turner, R. and Orton, S. (2004) *Access to practice: Overcoming the barriers to practice learning for disabled social work students*, Southampton: Social Work and Social Policy Learning and Teaching Support Network (SWAPltsn).

Smith, A. and Twomey, B. (2002) 'Labour market experiences of people with disabilities', *Labour Market Trends*, August, pp 415-27.

Thompson, N. (2002) 'Social movements, social justice and social work', *British Journal of Social Work*, vol 32, 711-22.

TOPSS (Training Organisation for the Personal Social Services) (2002) *National occupational standards for social work*, (www.topss.org.uk/uk_eng/standards/cdrom/Index.htm).

TWENTY ONE

Disabled people, the state and employment: historical lessons and welfare policy

Jon Warren

This chapter seeks to show how the social policies of the past have shaped and still inform the current strategies that are being both pursued and proposed in the field of disability, employment and welfare. It focuses on the relationship between the individual the state and the question of employment. The social policy of New Labour can be typified by the proposition that 'Work is better than welfare'. Since 1997, the welfare-to-work principle and New Deal programme have been applied to young people, lone parents, the long-term unemployed and of course disabled people. This targeted approach to certain sections of the population is in itself novel on the scale it has been pursued, rather than seeing the 'unemployed' as an indistinct mass as had been the case since the early 19th century.

What makes this approach possible are arguably structural changes in the labour market and a redefinition from government's point of view regarding who is employable. It shares British social policy's traditional view of work. This tradition, which has its origins in the 1834 Poor Law Amendment Act and can be traced via the Employment White Paper and the Disabled People's Employment Act (both 1944) to the present day, conceptualises 'work' within very narrow margins. Work is equated with wage labouring, nothing more or nothing less.

What is perhaps more enlightening is what it neglects. This discussion will explain how the British social policy tradition has at best failed to understand and at worst ignored the possibility of seeing work in any terms other than income. This approach has implications for disabled people. Paradoxically, this runs in parallel to another tradition, that of 'citizenship' within which being in employment and being a legitimate citizen are densely intertwined. This discourse while being fiercely expressed since 1979 in the guise of the 'property-owning democracy' in the Thatcher years, and more recently albeit in its softer New Labour form as 'a stakeholder society' can again be traced back to 1834. What they hold in common, however, is their conceptualisation of the individual. In policy terms, government has rarely attempted to venture far beyond the 'factory gates', and has largely left questions of the economic and social relations of the workplace to employers and workers, or the latter's collective representation via trade unions.

In terms of citizenship, government has placed the onus of seeking and maintaining employment largely upon individual workers, while providing opportunities to enable them to do this. Those who fail to find work or use the schemes provided for whatever reason forfeit their social status to a large degree. Disabled people have been caught at the nexus of these two traditions. The transformation of working life which occurred during the industrial revolution and which was exemplified by what became known as the 'factory system', revolutionised not only the workplace, but also the entire social fabric of Britain. Work became essential to survival in new urban areas, and what is often neglected is the fact that agriculture was also increasingly industrialised, and the 'peasant farmer' had been progressively eradicated by the enclosure acts from the 17th century onwards.

Thus, in town or country the relations of production had been redrawn. The consequences of this for disabled people and the emergence of a discourse of 'able-bodiedness' have been established by writers such as Finkelstein (1980), Stone (1985) and Gleeson (1991).

The state via its responses played a highly important role in the establishment of hegemony of wage labour and able-bodiedness that persists to this day. As John Ditch (1991, in Loney et al, 1991, p 24) points out:

> A dominant theme running through the history of social policy and still current in much social welfare thinking and practice is the distinction between the deserving and undeserving poor.

While this distinction is clear in the New Poor Law of 1834, it is not explicit. Disabled people were viewed as 'deserving' because the poor law's administrators – the local 'boards of guardians' – did not view them as being 'idle'. Idleness was seen as the result of moral defect within the individual; hence 'the idle' were seen as undeserving of relief. By this logic, the undeserving were morally defective and thus not capable of the duties of citizenship and consequently not worthy of any rights it might bestow. But what of the deserving poor? Deserving in this sense means deserving of relief and little else. Those receiving relief also became second–class citizens, not because of moral laxity, but because of their inability to work, as opposed to the undeserving poor's unwillingness to work.

The principle that made this a reality and applied to all those who sought relief, regardless of their situation, was that of 'less eligibility'. This central tenet of the poor law, as Ditch (1991, in Loney et al, 1991, p 25) explains, meant that:

> Under this principle no unemployed person could receive assistance (and thereby a standard of living) which was greater than that which could be achieved by the lowest paid labourer in the immediate locality.

Although guardians had the power to vary relief especially to the 'deserving', the principle of less eligibility demonstrates; first a minimalist approach from the state towards welfare; and second the importance of the activities of work and consumption as conditions for full citizenship.

The relationship between legislators and employers in Britain from the 19th century until the present day has operated along the lines of what Brian Inglis termed "laissez–nous–faire":

> the capitalism which developed in Britain was not laissez–faire in the original sense; but what the employers preferred to call "laissez–nous–faire". In other words they were asking not that the economic system be left alone, but that they should be. (Inglis, 1972, p 32)

This meant that government, while championing the need for work, has historically acted to enable workers to access employment via a variety of 'carrots' and 'sticks', while it has done little to intervene in the work place directly. Objections and exceptions to this can of course be found. However, it can be contended that they are precisely that – exceptions to the dominant tradition.

For example, at first glance the Factory Acts of the 1840s appear to be and have often been characterised as progressive pieces of pioneering health and safety legislation. However, if we look again they can be seen as regulating workers and opportunities for work. The Factory Acts, for instance, banished women from the mines, not out of altruism but due to issues of gendered constructions of morality. Thus they can be seen as an attempt to further the emergent hegemony of the workplace as male adult and able-bodied (Cockburn, 1985).

The limitation of working opportunities for all outside this definition, further entrenched their position of economic, civil and political inequality. The exclusion of 'other' types of labour was also vigorously pursued by the trade unions who saw the widening of the potential workforce as an opportunity for the employer to undermine the wages and conditions of their members (see Cockburn, 1985; Bradley, 1989).

The introduction of Wages Councils by Asquith's 1908-16 administration can again be seen as the state acting in the absence of strong collective structures rather than an early attempt to introduce a minimum wage, as it has so often been portrayed. Had these areas been strongly unionised, it can be argued the state would have left matters alone. The inadequacy of relying on market mechanisms alone to provide and regulate employment, particularly in a world economy in which Britain no longer dominated became apparent in the slump of the 1920s and 1930s. As did the shortcomings of the Liberals insurance based scheme. Indeed, as Ditch (in Loney et al, 1991, p 29) points out, the system began to look increasingly like the Poor Law, with the administrators determining who was 'deserving' via moral judgement, albeit dressed in the bureaucratic clothing of 'regulations':

> The administration of the National Insurance scheme was complicated by regulations designed to determine that the claimant was 'genuinely seeking work'. Some 3 million claims were refused during the 1920s on the grounds that this condition had not been satisfied.

The only option for many was of course the Poor Law and the 'means test'; it is all too easy to forget that this system of 19th century welfare persisted in practice for the first half of the 20th century.

Arguably, by the 1930s, disabled people found themselves more excluded from employment than they had been a century before. While women had secured the vote as working class men had 50 years earlier, the structures of welfare that marginalised all non-workers were well established and showed very few signs of imminent change. However, the establishment of an ideology of work based on assumptions of able-bodiedness and masculinity had been established in the mindset of politicians and the population at large. Disabled people remained excluded and in segregated institutional structures that had developed apace during the early decades of the twentieth century. For example, more 'protective legislation' was passed regarding mental health between 1900 and 1930 and this took place in a society where eugenic ideas about refining the genetic stock of the nation were increasingly fashionable (see Pilgrim and Rogers, 1993; Bornat et al, 1993).

It was wealth, of course, that made the critical difference and gave substance to any civic-based notions of citizenship. Disabled people remained at the margins increasingly less characterised by being unemployed, rather they had become the unemployable. It is interesting that to this day the archetypal image of British unemployment in the 1930s remains that of the Jarrow marchers, able-bodied, male and working class. However, what Roulstone (2000) has described as "the effective autonomy of capital and business" was about to be challenged.

The Second World War transformed the social and economic landscape of Britain. The nature of the conflict was in the words of Peter Calvorcoressi and Guy Wint (1972) termed a 'Total War'. The war forced government to rethink its role and purpose, as the war effort involved the entire population, almost without exception. Government was forced into action in 1940, and it led it into areas it had never previously ventured, and indeed in some of those areas it has remained as the prime mover until this day. Calvocoressi and Wint (1972) argue that, first, the war forced the highly stratified and class conscious to fraternise and break down barriers due to necessity; second, and more significantly:

> ... by creating an emergency which required the mobilization of the whole nation, war forced government to take note of the whole nation. (Calvocoressi and Wint, 1972, p 407)

This meant a fundamental rethink of government's function and its relationship with its citizens. 'Laissez-nous-faire' was abandoned. Government, rather than reluctantly intervening when problems arose, was of necessity to set the agenda and take the lead.

Perhaps more significantly these actions had redefined the nature of work and the relations of it in Britain (Barnes, 1991). The conditions of wartime and the actions taken by government effectively abandoned the idea that employment was simply a matter for the individual to negotiate with the employer either on an individual or on a collective basis (Lowe, 1993, Glennerster, 1995). Instead, employment had become a matter of 'national good'; the state had accepted not only that it could play a role in employment policy, but also and perhaps crucially that it was in the interests of the nation and desirable for it to do so. This became clear in the Employment White Paper of 1944, which stated that:

> The Government accept as one of their primary aims and
> responsibilities the maintenance of a high and stable level
> of employment after the war ....A country will not suffer
> from mass unemployment so long as the total demand for
> its goods and services is maintained at a high level. (Cited
> in Lowe, 1993, p 100)

The second sentence is essential, as the state recognised that one of its
functions was to regulate, stimulate and control demand, via 'Keynesian'
economic principles. For the first time, British economic and social
policy accepted that the market alone could not produce stable and
just conditions of employment and it committed itself to achieving
those ends. This extension of the state's duties can be argued by its
very nature to modify the nature of citizenship and extend the social
rights of the individual.

The Disabled Persons (Employment) Act 1944, which followed the
recommendations of the Tomlinson Committee on the rehabilitation
of disabled people, can be viewed as a landmark in several ways. First,
government was directing employers to act in a particular way, not
just as to support the interests of capital as outlined previously above,
but for a wider social good. To use today's idiom, it was 'promoting
inclusion' by directing business. Second, it is a piece of legislation that
does not directly relate to matters of medical intervention and
supervision nor the social segregation of disabled people. This
legislation recast disabled people from being 'unemployable' to being
'employable' (Stone, 1985) and hence recognised disabled people's
potential to be useful citizens. Third, this shift in what Stone (1985)
terms the 'disability category' happens at a time when disabled people
were becoming more visible in British society as the way they had
acquired their impairments could not be easily ignored or misread.

The inadequacies of the quota system, one established in the 1944
Act to ensure greater employment opportunities for disabled people,
are well known and have been discussed at some length by writers
such as Thorton and Lunt (1995) and Roulstone (2000). However, its
limited impact was not evidence that the corporatist principles that
lay behind it were flawed or misguided. The system failed to function
as the government quietly abandoned it until it could be dismissed as
ineffective and outdated (Barnes and Oliver, 1995). The questions of
political vision and the political will to make these visions real are
central to understanding disability and employment policy in the 60
years which have passed since 1944.

Arguably, the immediate post-war era made both governments and its intellectual supporters (Marshall, 1950) somewhat complacent. There was broad agreement on the state's role as a key economic player via commitment to demand led economic measures and its involvement with the nationalised industries. In effect, the state's wartime role continued but diminished. While military conscription remained in the form of National Service until 1960, industrial conscription had ceased abruptly in 1945. Peacetime allowed the state to relinquish its role as a prime mover in the area of employment policy, the relative prosperity and full employment of the 1950s and 1960s left it with little to do apart from acting as a planning consultant and a general underwriter. Arguably, this was an opportunity missed as it allowed the pre-war norms to re-emerge, with employment matters being left to employers and a revitalised trade union movement. Instead government concerned itself with matters of welfare and social security. There can be no doubt that great advances were made. By the early 1960s, old assumptions about disability and segregation were being questioned. Powell's famous 'water-tower' speech in 1959 seemed to herald the prospect of an end to segregation and offer a vision of 'care in the community' (see Barnes, 1997; Bornat et al, 1993).

Indeed as Thornton and Lunt (1995) report, by 1961, 61.4% of employers were fulfilling their employment quotas for disabled people under the provisions of the 1944 act. Superficially, to borrow a famous phrase of that time, disabled people and Britain in general had 'Never had it so good'. However, this was an illusion, created by favourable economic conditions and a scarcity of labour. It faded as quickly as it had appeared. Ironically it was undermined by post-war social policy itself. When Aneurin Bevan remarked in 1948 that, "We have finally buried the body of the poor law", he did not imagine that its ghost would continue to haunt British social policy into the 21st century.

The welfare state as envisaged by Beveridge, while undoubtedly more comprehensive and generous than any previous attempt at a system of social security in Britain, was based around one central assumption: full employment for able-bodied, male breadwinners (see Williams, 1989). This central assumption undermined the measures in the 1944 Disabled Persons (Employment) Act, as the priority for any government in times of economic downturn would of course be able-bodied male workers in order to mitigate the costs of the subsequent Social Security Bill. This, of course, was detrimental to the employment prospects of not only disabled people but also women and younger and older workers.

The abandonment by government of its role as an underwriter of a full employment policy for able-bodied male workers can be traced to the 1970s. This occurred, first, with reluctance by the Wilson and Callaghan administrations. However, the changing nature of global capital had made the demand led economics of classical Keynesianism increasingly 'impractical' and ineffective for individual nation states to pursue. The government instead concentrated on salvaging what they could of Britain's industrial capacity (for example, the hurried nationalisations of shipbuilding and aircraft construction in 1976). The state's role was now that of a broker trying to mitigate the consequences of unemployment, and it was attacked by employers and trade unions alike.

'Labour isn't working' (Saatchi and Saatchi) was one of the main Conservative poster campaigns of the 1979 General Election. As official unemployment neared one million, it was again a mainstream political issue after a 40-year absence. It is also worth pointing out that famous poster depicting a dole queue again conforms to and helped to reinforce the idea of who the 'legitimate' unemployed were. Yet again those depicted are overwhelmingly male and able bodied. Disabled people are absent.

If the Labour government of the late 1970s can be said to have reluctantly retreated from the state's role in employment policy, the Conservative government from 1979 onwards sought to make a virtue of its abandonment, under the ideological banner of 'market forces'. The economic policies of the first Thatcher government led to the return of mass unemployment on the scale of the 1930s, with the official claimant count passing two million by the end of 1981. The state was back to its pre-war stance, of allowing collective bargaining between employers and unions. However, it did not act in a 'laissez-faire' manner. The Thatcher administration was not only ideologically pro-market; they were also ideologically opposed to organised labour and determined to emasculate it, viewing it as the 'enemy within'. The Employment Acts and Industrial Relations Acts curbed the power of trade unions; in effect, government was not only returning to a policy of 'effective autonomy of capital and business' but actively promoting it.

During the 1980s, employment policy was effectively subsumed by Social Security to provide basic relief for those not in employment and the newly created Department of Trade and Industry (DTI), which promoted trade. By the mid-1980s employment had become a matter for individuals once more rather than a responsibility of the state. The onus now was for the unemployed to 'get on their bikes and look for work' as Norman Tebbit so crudely but concisely put it in 1981. Even this comment was aimed at able-bodied males; disabled people were marginalised even further as the state began to differentiate between those who were 'legitimately' unemployed and those who were not.

By 1986, despite numerous government directives reducing the way in which the official unemployment rate was calculated, unemployment was in excess of three million. The 1980s also saw the establishment of the idea of the citizen in terms of consumption. In effect, political and civil rights in Britain were now 'index linked' to individual's incomes. So where did this leave disabled people? Clearly, by 1990 the quota system was not functioning as its founders intended, and it was increasingly regarded as an anachronism by government. In 1990, only 21.8% of employers were meeting their statutory requirements (Thornton and Lunt, 1995). The 1980s can also be seen as the decade within which disability again became equated with 'unemployability', this occurred out of the need to reduce the headline rate of unemployment. For example, in the North East of England, redundant workers from heavy industry who had no realistic prospect of ever finding work again were encouraged to leave 'the dole' and were reclassified as 'long-term sick' with the consequence that they no longer appeared in official out of work and claiming benefit statistics. Whiteside (in Ellison and Pierson, 1998, p 98) notes:

> Since 1979 the economic activity rate of men over the age of fifty has dropped dramatically; those losing work are more likely to be seen as in early retirement or as suffering from long term sickness whose incidence has risen by a factor of five.

However, what had become apparent by this time, even though Stone's 'disability category' (1985) was shifting, was the fact that disabled people now had their own collective structures through which to lobby government, employers and service providers. This was undoubtedly beneficial as the government could now be taken to task on the basis of failing to provide adequate services to welfare 'consumers'. The Major governments of 1990-97 attempted to make state welfare more consumer-orientated via a number of initiatives most notably the 'Citizens Charter'. The name of this initiative demonstrates the increasing dominance of the idea of the citizen as first and foremost a consumer, and a social policy geared toward providing individual services while ignoring broad collective social needs. This of course complies with what Oliver (1990) characterised as the 'individual model of disability'.

However, getting disability onto the policy agenda as a collective and civil rights issue is an ongoing problem. The Disability Discrimination Act (DDA) of 1995, while recognising that discrimination exists and providing a legal mechanism for its redress, operates within an individual model: the onus is upon the disabled person to prove their case against the employer. Individualism is thus reinforced (Gooding, 1996; Roulstone, 2002). The introduction of the DDA saw the final abandonment of the quota system introduced by the 1995 Act. That the option of abolition rather than that of reform was taken serves to illustrate the completion of the shift of emphasis from the state back to the individual in matters of employment.

The Blair governments of 1997 and 2001 have taken a modified but still essentially 'individualist' view of employment. Having enjoyed relatively good economic conditions during its time in office, Labour claims success in reducing unemployment. For example, a Party Political Broadcast by Labour recently proclaimed, 'Britain is working'(November 2004). Its strategy has been to attempt to modify the unemployed and those previously seen as unemployable: young people, disabled people, lone parents, the long term unemployed and older workers via the Various New Deal schemes. The New Deals are an interesting development as they can be seen as targeting and offering extra 'assistance' to traditionally marginalised groups. However, the emphasis is largely upon what individuals can do to make themselves more marketable rather than how employers might make work a more viable prospect for these groups. Government has promoted the virtues of work as opposed to welfare, and the tax credit system, despite its operational deficiencies, can be seen as a genuine attempt to remove some of the perversities of the welfare state which for many meant that 'work would never pay'. It can also be seen as furthering and reinforcing the ideal of the 'consuming citizen'.

To return to an earlier theme of this chapter, the 'deserving poor' can now be characterised as those individuals who are prepared to modify their lives, behaviour and aspirations in line with the directives of government through schemes such as New Deal. The key problem for disabled people who are within the scope of such schemes is that while employers are able to argue what they consider to be a reasonable adjustment from a position of strength, disabled people are being asked to make such adjustment to themselves from a disempowered position. This also reflects how welfare systems and social policy in Britain in general are assuming more overt surveillance functions in addition to the administrative powers they have long held. This, of course, is beneficial to government as it promotes work and consumption and stigmatises and marginalises those who will not seek it. However, it fails to take full account of the fact that barriers to employment are not always due to a lack of flexibility on the part of disabled people or the refusal to make relatively cheap and easy modifications on the part of employers. A recent report by the Prime Minister's Strategy Unit (PMSU) recognises the extent to which disabled people are excluded from the labour market and encouragingly recognises that work is not just about income, but an activity whose absence impacts upon individuals' social status, self esteem and social inclusion. It also recognises that collective action is required:

> Society needs to remove the barriers to the inclusion of disabled people. Barriers that mitigate against the full inclusion of disabled people must be tackled collectively – it is society's responsibility to promote the full inclusion of disabled people by removing these barriers. (PMSU, 2004, p 33)

This is swiftly countered by a shift back to the individual, which emphasises the need for self modification, noting:

> Individuals need to be supported to fulfil their own potential. (PMSU, 2004, p 33)

The report also asserts that:

> Every individual has a responsibility to ensure that they play a full part in fulfilling their own potential. (PMSU, 2004, p 33)

The question is, who defines the scope and boundaries of that potential? If real progress is to be made towards equality for disabled people the issue of employment must be addressed and government must play a key role, not as an encouraging cheerleader on the sidelines but as a campaigning advocate determined to provide tangible equality for disabled people. It is above all a question of vision and political will:

> If we talk about equality we really can't mean it unless those with a disability are provided first of all with a practical means, and then are able to operate in a world where people's attitude has changed positively. (David Blunkett, 2004)

References

Barnes, C. (1991) *Disabled people and discrimination*, London: Hurst and Co.

Barnes, C. and Oliver, M. (1995) 'Disability rights: rhetoric and reality in the UK', *Disability and Society*, vol 10, no 4, pp 111-16.

Barnes, M. (1997) *Care, communities and citizens*, London: Longman.

Bevan, A. (1948) www.sochealth.co.uk/history/nye.htm.

Blunkett, D. (2004) *BBC News*, 26 May, (news.bbc.co.uk/2/hi/uk_news/3746893.stm).

Bornat, J., Johnson, J., Pereira, C., Pilgrim, D. and Williams, F. (1993) *Community care: A reader*, Buckingham and Oxford: Macmillan/Oxford University Press.

Bradley, H. (1989) *Men's work, Women's work. A Sociological History of the Sexual Division of Labour in Employment*, Cambridge: Polity.

Calvocoressi, P. and Wint, G. (1972) *Total War*, London: Penguin.

Cockburn, C. (1985) *Machinery of dominance: Women, men and technical knowledge*, London: Pluto.

Ellison, N. and Pierson, C. (eds) (1998) *Developments in British social policy*, London: Macmillan Press.

Finkelstein, V. (1980) *Attitudes and disabled people: Issues for discussion*, New York: World Rehabilitation Monograph.

Glennerster, H. (1995) *British social policy since 1945*, Blackwell: Oxford.

Gleeson, B. (1991) *Notes towards a materialist history of disability*, Occasional Paper, Department of Geography, University of Bristol.

Gooding, C. (1996) *Disability Discrimination Act 1995*, London: Blackstone Press.

Inglis, B. (1972) *Poverty and the industrial revolution*, London: Granada.

Loney, M., Bocock, R., Clarke, J., Cochrane, A., Graham, P. and Wilson, M. (eds) (1991) *The state or the market: Politics in welfare in contemporary Britain*, London: Sage Publications.

Lowe, R. (1993) *The welfare state in Britain since 1945*, London: Macmillan.

Marshall, T. (1950) *Citizenship and social class*, Cambridge: Cambridge University Press.

Oliver, M. (1991) *The politics of disablement*, London: Macmillan.

Pilgrim, D. and Rogers, A. (1993) *A sociology of mental health and mental illness*, Buckingham: Open University Press.

PMSU (Prime Minister's Strategy Unit) (2004) *Strategy Unit disability project analytical report June 2004*, London: PMSU.

Roulstone, A. (1998) *Enabling technology: Disabled people and new technology*, Buckingham: Open University Press.

Roulstone, A. (2000) 'Disability, dependency and the New Deal for Disabled People', *Disability and Society*, vol 15, pp 427-44.

Roulstone, A. (2002) 'Disabling pasts, enabling futures? How does the changing nature of capitalism impact on the disabled worker and jobseeker?', *Disability and Society*, vol 17, no 6, pp 627-42.

Stone, D. (1985) *The disabled state*, London: Macmillan.

Thornton, P. and Lunt, N. (1995) *Employment for disabled people: Social obligation or individual responsibility?*, York: Social Policy Research Unit, York Publishing.

Williams, F. (1989) *Social policy: A critical introduction: Issues of class, race and gender*, Cambridge: Polity Press.

TWENTY TWO

'Work' is a four-letter word: disability, work and welfare

Colin Barnes and Alan Roulstone

Introduction

This chapter suggests that to overcome the problem of disabled people's ongoing disadvantage in mainstream employment and, therefore, society, a radical alternative strategy is required that poses a direct challenge to orthodox thinking on work, and associated policies that centre almost exclusively on disabled workers. Building on longstanding analyses from within the disability studies literature, it is argued that an holistic approach is needed that includes:

- the reconfiguration of the meaning of work for disabled people;
- the de-stigmatisation of associate welfare provision;
- that the theoretical and practical foundations for such an approach have already been laid (Barnes, 2000, 2003; Abberley, 2002: Oliver and Barnes, 1998).

This chapter begins with an overview of theoretical considerations with reference to the concept of 'independent living' for disabled people and the social model of disability. Attention will then centre on the organisation of labour, the reconfiguring of work for disabled people, and its implications for work and welfare in the 21st century.

Theoretical considerations

As the contributions to this book indicate, disabled people are disproportionately disadvantaged in the labour market. This is because in western society since at least the eighteenth century, work has been organised around a particular set of values and principles; namely, the pursuit and maximisation of profit and competition between individual workers, both of which effectively disadvantage, or disable people with any form of perceived functional limitation/impairment, whether physical, sensory or intellectual. The more overt the impairment, the more severe the disadvantage or 'disability' (Finkelstein, 1980; Oliver, 1990; Barnes, 1991; Hyde, 1995; Stiker, 1998; Gleeson, 1999). Hence, in his recent review of work, disability and European social theory Abberley (2002, p 136) has argued that to address the problem of disabled people's exclusion from mainstream society:

> We need to develop theoretical perspectives that express the standpoint of disabled people, whose interests are not necessarily served by the standpoint of other social groups, dominant or themselves oppressed, of which disabled people are also members.

The thrust of Abberley's argument is based on three main points:

- that the eradication of environmental and cultural barriers associated with capitalism, will not generate a society in which all people with impairments are able to 'work';
- that previous social theories; functionalist, Marxist and feminist, cannot provide an appropriate framework for the development of policies that give disabled people equity in terms of either employment or living standards;
- that paid 'work' need no longer be a key organisational feature of western 'developed' nations in the future.

The theoretical perspectives that reflect the standpoint of disabled people are expressed in the concepts of 'independent living' and the 'social model of disability'.

Independent living

The phrase 'independent living' first entered the English language in the 1970s following its adoption by disability activists in the US. What became known as the American Independent Living Movement (ILM) emerged partly from within the campus culture of American universities and partly from repeated efforts by disability activists to influence disability legislation. Due to the lack of community based support services for disabled people across the US, several American universities developed various self-help programmes to enable students with 'severe' physical impairments to attend mainstream courses. These later evolved into what became known as Centres for Independent Living (CILs).

These new CILs were self-help organisations exclusively run and controlled by disabled people themselves. In contrast to other professionally dominated provision that focused almost exclusively on medical treatments and therapies within institutional settings, CILs provided a new and innovative range of services designed to enable people with impairments to adopt a lifestyle of their own choosing within, rather than apart from, the local community. Subsequently, these ideas had a considerable impact on disabled people's organisations and disability policy throughout the world. There are now CILs or similar user controlled organisations providing services and support for disabled people and their families in many countries across the globe (Alonso, 2003).

Part of the reason for this unprecedented success is the almost universal appeal of the concept of independent living within western culture. It is apolitical in that it appeals directly to advocates of the politics of the right and of the left, and is political in that the environmental and cultural changes needed to facilitate meaningful independent living for disabled people will benefit everyone regardless of impairment or status.

Early exponents of independent living allied themselves with the 'radical consumerism' of the 1960s and 1970s. Therefore, it has a particular appeal to proponents of the ideological cornerstones of capitalist development such as economic and political freedom, consumer sovereignty, and self-reliance. This realisation prompted some critics to suggest that the philosophy and policies of the ILM favoured only a relatively small section of the disabled population: notably, young intellectually able, middle-class white males (Williams, 1984).

However, this is a misrepresentation of what the phrase 'independent living' represents. Although they are often characterised as providing services for people with physical impairments only, historically, CILs have struggled to provide services for all sections of the disabled community. Where they have not, this is usually due to limited resources, material and human, and/or entrenched opposition from vested interests within traditional disability service provider organisations (Morgan et al, 2001; Glasby and Littlechild, 2002).

Furthermore, in view of the dangers of misinterpretation, some disability activists particularly in the UK, have adopted the terms 'integrated' or 'inclusive' living rather than the original 'independent' living to characterise the philosophy on which their activities are based. Such terms have a far greater appeal to the left of centre elements within Britain's disabled people's movement who recognise that humans are by definition 'social' beings, and that *all* humans, regardless of the degree and nature of impairment, are interdependent and, therefore, that a truly 'independent' lifestyle is inconceivable.

From this perspective, the ideologies and practices that justify the systematic oppression of people with impairments within capitalist society are similar to those that legitimise the oppression of other disadvantaged sections of the populations such as women, minority ethnic groups, lesbians and gay men, and older people. Taken together they represent an increasingly costly and complex barrier to the development of a truly meaningful inclusive representative democracy.

The social model of disability

The social model of disability emerged from within Britain's disabled people's movement. In contrast to previous individual medically based definitions the Union of the Physically Impaired Against Segregation (UPIAS, 1976) re-defined 'disability' as something imposed on top of people with impairments' lives by a society intolerant of any form of biological flaw. Originally associated with physical conditions this reinterpretation was later expanded to include all impairments: physical, sensory and intellectual, by the wider disabled people's movement: both nationally and internationally (Barnes, 1991).

Integral to this re-assessment is the assertion that all physiological conditions have psychological implications and that all psychological problems have physical consequences. Therefore, it is an inclusive concept that encompasses all sections of the disabled community including, for example, mental health systems users and survivors. This is in recognition of the fact that labels are generally imposed rather than chosen, and, therefore, socially and politically divisive, and that the values and attitudes that generate labels are historically, culturally and situationally variable. Moreover, as the social model is frequently misrepresented in academic circles (see, for example, Shakespeare and Watson, 2002), it is important to remember what it constitutes. A model is what social scientists call a 'heuristic device' or an aid to understanding. Thus:

> A good model can enable us to see something which we
> do not understand because in the model it can be seen
> from different viewpoints… it is this multi-dimensioned
> replica of reality that can trigger insights that we might not
> otherwise develop. (Finkelstein, 2002, p 13)

The social model has been the catalyst for the increasing politicisation of large numbers of disabled people and their allies in the UK (Hasler, 1993; Campbell and Oliver, 1996), and provided a firm foundation for the development of a fully formed 'materialist' account of the social creation of disability in the modern world (Oliver, 1990; Gleeson, 1999), as well as a workable analytical framework with which to understand and explain the particular type of institutional discrimination encountered by people labelled 'disabled' because of perceived impairment (Barnes, 1991).

In contrast to conventional individualistic medical approaches, the social model is a deliberate attempt to switch the focus away from the functional limitations of impaired individuals onto the problems caused by disabling environments, barriers and cultures. It is not a denial of the importance or value of appropriate individually based interventions, whether they are medically, re/habilitative, educational or employment-based, but draws attention to their limitations in terms of furthering disabled people's empowerment and inclusion in a society constructed by 'non-disabled people' for 'non-disabled' people. It is an holistic approach, therefore, that explains specific problems experienced by disabled people in terms of the totality of disabling environments and cultures. It is therefore a tool with which to gain an insight into the disabling tendencies of modern society in order to generate policies and practices to facilitate their eradication (Oliver, 2004).

Consequently a social model analysis of the labour market raises several important points. One, disabled people's individual and collective disadvantage in the realm of paid employment is linked directly to the social organisation of work. Two, a social model account rejects the notion that unemployment and underemployment among disabled workers can be explained in isolation from other factors such as education, transport, the built environment, access, ideology and culture. Three, it recognises that within the present context, policy developments in the employment field can have only a limited impact on the employment problems of disabled people. Finally, that as a consequence of all this, meaningful change is only likely through a radical reformulation of the meaning and the organisation of work (Barnes, 2000).

Disability, work and welfare

There is substantial historical and anthropological evidence that the combination of industrialisation, urbanisation, and associated ideologies: liberal utilitarianism and medicalisation, provided 'scientific' legitimacy for the gradual but intensifying commodification of everyday life. Hence, work became almost exclusively associated with wage labour and an employment infrastructure geared to the needs of those capable of engaging in this type of activity, and exclusion for those who could not (Finkelstein, 1980; Oliver, 1990; Gleeson, 1999).

Nonetheless, when work is organised around a different set of principles, such as social necessity and interdependence, for example, employment becomes less exclusionary. For instance, in Britain during the 1939/45 conflict many hitherto excluded groups such as women and disabled people were drafted into the labour force at various levels to aid the war effort. Immediately following the cessation of hostilities considerable government effort was put into maintaining this situation due to the 'social obligation' (Thornton and Lunt, 1995) felt towards these workers. Subsequently, government priorities changed and so did their labour market policies (see Chapter One of this volume). Similar patterns are evident in other western countries such as the US, for example (Russell, 2002). Clearly, as with perceptions of disability, the meaning and organisation of work is a social creation and subject to change (see also Chapter Twelve of this volume).

Moreover, many commentators are now suggesting that the meaning and organisation of work has undergone changes that are as fundamental as those that accompanied Industrialisation. The intensifying globalisation of the world economy along with unprecedented technological development in the post-1945 period has meant that many western societies have shifted from what Wolfensberger (1989) termed 'a primary' to a 'post-primary production' economy. In short, agricultural and manufacturing industries have given way to human services as the main source of employment.

More recently, Beck (2000) argues that the traditional work environment and lifelong working, has given way to a much less stable situation in which skills are devalued, jobs lost, and welfare reduced or eliminated. He maintains that to offset the social and political instability that will inevitably ensue, new ideas and models must be developed. The way forward requires democratically organised local, national and trans-national networks of active citizens. Everyone, he maintains, must have the right to be included in a new definition and distribution of work in order to address the threat of large-scale social exclusion. This will include movement in and out of paid employment and forms of self-organised artistic, cultural and political 'civil labour' involving equal access to comprehensive social protection.

However, while much is made of the role of active citizens in this and similar analyses, little is said about the role of government, disabled people and their organisations. This is important since the experience of work instability and social exclusion has characterised disabled people's work experiences for much of the last century, and that if this situation is to be resolved government intervention is fundamental. It is important to remember, too, that government involvement in the way the labour market operates is not new nor is it confined to policies for disabled people. Throughout modern history governments throughout the world have played a major role in structuring and restructuring the labour market through grants and tax concessions for industrialists and employers in order to sustain economic growth and maintain political stability. With regard to the employment of disabled people, as noted earlier, in the UK various 'demand-side' initiatives were implemented during and immediately following the Second World War to facilitate their inclusion into the workforce.

Hence, if governments are serious about getting disabled people into paid work then similar policies might be reintroduced. In Britain for example, ministers could set targets for all government departments and state organisations, including the NHS, local authorities, universities and so on, to achieve in respect of employing disadvantaged workers. In its dealings with the private sector they could use similar targets to enforce contract compliance. They could also divert the grants they give to the voluntary sector to organisations controlled by disabled people whose record in employing people with perceived impairments puts the traditional voluntary sector to shame (Calvi, 2003; Oliver and Barnes, 1998).

Certainly politicians and policy makers have recently adopted the language of inclusion, and posited what at first glance may seem like social model solutions to the problems associated with disability in the workplace. The rhetoric surrounding the introduction of the Disability Discrimination Act (DDA)1995, the setting up of the 'Disability Rights Task Force', the development of the 'New Deal' programme, and the recent proposed benefit changes provide a wealth of examples. However, rhetoric rarely accords with reality and policy remains centred largely on the supply rather than the demand side of labour. As a consequence, policies which target and highlight the functional limitations of individuals with perceived impairments are prioritised and supported at the expense of those which draw attention to and seek to resolve the stark inequalities of the social organisation of work (Roulstone, 2002; OECD, 2003). The rhetoric has changed but, on the whole, the policies have not.

Indeed, the Blair government's avowed commitment to getting more disabled people into employment through 'welfare-to-work' type schemes and the development of more flexible and less demeaning 'benefit' systems is, in broad terms, commensurate with the ongoing demands of the disabled people's movement. In many ways, however, these policies are not really new and their impact will be significantly tempered by the fact that, as yet, politicians remain reluctant to tackle the very real environmental and social barriers disabled people encounter daily. Equally important, if people with perceived impairments are to be encouraged into paid work then employment must be made far more socially and financially rewarding. All too often the type of jobs offered to disabled people are low status, low waged occupations with poor working conditions and few opportunities for advancement. The 'tax credit' scheme for disabled workers and the introduction of the minimum wage may be seen as a partial recognition of this problem. However, the impact of such policies in the current work environment is limited. Institutional discrimination against disabled people in British society remains largely unchecked.

Consequently, where legislation exists, enforcement must be properly funded and made highly visible, naming and shaming those who act in discriminatory ways. Where legislation is currently being considered, again governments must make the appropriate arrangements to ensure enforcement commissions are properly in place and that individual responsibility is not left to disabled people themselves. It is important to point out here, however, that this is not to suggest that everyone with an accredited impairment can or should be expected to work at the same pace as non-disabled contemporaries, or that all disabled people can or should work in the conventional sense (Oliver and Barnes, 1998).

It may be argued of course that this is recognised by government ministers by the use of the phrase "work for those who can and security for those who cannot" (DWP, 1998, p iii). However, in a cultural environment that generally only values and recognises paid employment as the norm, such a phrase fails to address the stigma associated with unemployment and the social and psychological consequences for those excluded from the workplace. Rather, it compounds them since it implies that those excluded from employment cannot and do not work. But this is not the case. Therefore, to overcome this problem a radical re-appraisal of the meaning of work for disabled people that goes beyond the rigid confines of paid employment is long overdue. With reference to domestic labour, feminists have adopted a similar strategy in their attempts to assert women's citizenship in a predominantly patriarchal society (Lister, 1997). For disabled people, however, this re-conceptualisation must go much further because although many unemployed disabled people, both female and male, do housework, and have childcare, and/or 'caring' responsibilities many do not.

Thus, the re-configuring of work must include the every day tasks that non-disabled people take for granted such as getting out of bed, washing, dressing and so on. This idea is not unprecedented within the social sciences. For example, Corbin and Strauss (1988) identified three types of work associated with 'illness' management:

- *illness work*, including activities like organising and administering medication, doing physiotherapy, and so on;
- *everyday work*, such as household tasks and interactions with family and professionals;
- *biographical work*.

The latter involves strategies that disabled people adopt in order to incorporate impairment into their everyday lives. This might involve developing ways of making sense of their condition and explaining it to others.

Further, disabled people and their organisations have long since recognised that living with impairment in a disabling society involves a great deal of effort and work. This is clearly evident in the various guides and handbooks now available for the recruitment of personal assistants (PAs) to enable people with 'severe' impairments to achieve an independent lifestyle. For example, Carl Ford and Richard Shaw (1993) divide the work that PAs might have to do into three distinct but related categories: personal, domestic and social. Personal work might include getting the disabled person out of bed, dressing them, feeding and so on. Domestic work includes things like housework, shopping, cooking. Social tasks could include accompanying the disabled person on social occasions like going out for a meal, to the cinema or the pub. The point is that all these activities have been defined in one way or another as work.

Notwithstanding that since the emergence of the disabled people's movement, independent living, disability arts and culture, the concept of a 'disabled identity' has taken on a whole new meaning that in many ways challenges traditional assumptions about disability and work. In particular, the disability arts movement has generated a range of cultural activities involving both disabled and non-disabled individuals which, taken together, constitute a meaningful alternative to the various non-disabled cultures that permeate late capitalist society (Finkelstein, 1996; Peters, 2000).

The development of direct and indirect payment schemes has meant that many disabled people, although technically 'unemployed' themselves, are now employers. Many PA users employ as many as five or six people over the course of a week. Furthermore, the recent expansion of user led involvement in the development and delivery of services has also meant that more and more disabled people spend their 'free' time actively involved in service provision of one form or another. Interestingly, although successive governments since the 1980s have actively sought to encourage service user involvement, none have recognised this type of activity as a meaningful form of work that warrants a suitable financial reward.

A further corollary of these developments is the need for a re-evaluation of disability related benefits and welfare systems within the workings of the economy. Escalating welfare costs are due to a variety of factors: demographic, economic, political and cultural; not least of which is the on going government failure to address the structural barriers to disabled people's meaningful involvement in the conventional workplace. As a result, disability-related premiums and welfare systems are fundamental to societies geared almost exclusively to non-disabled lifestyles. However, rather than being viewed as a drain on the national economy they should be considered an indicator of collective social responsibility and social justice. It should also be remembered that disability and related benefits are not passive in the sense that they go straight into the recipient's pockets; rather, they are circulated throughout the economy in terms of generating employment, goods and services. As noted earlier in the UK and elsewhere, increasingly large sections of the workforce are employed in the human service sector. They are therefore dependent on disabled people and other disadvantaged groups for their very livelihood. Rather than stigmatise and penalise those in receipt of disability or related benefits and services, politicians and policy makers should be striving to develop a more equitable and less stigmatising distribution system.

This re-configuration of the concept work should not be construed as an alternative to the on-going struggle for disabled people's participation in the workplace rather it should be seen as complementary to it. It draws on and is commensurate with disabled people's standpoint, as represented by the philosophy of independent living, and a social model analysis of the oppression of disabled people in late capitalist society. This is because it constitutes more than simply a reaction to existing inequalities, but represents a concerted attempt to challenge and overturn one of the key cultural values upon which those inequalities rest.

Discussion

This discussion may be located within the growing realisation among academics and policy makers that the continued development and, therefore, future stability, of a western style economy such as the UK is inextricably linked to the complex and ever changing relations between production and consumption (Bauman, 1998). This should be coupled with the recognition that, regardless of their role within the orthodox work environment, disabled people are both producers and consumers of a vast array of services upon which many non-disabled people depend; they are, therefore, a fundamental component within this equation. Moreover, as the boundaries between what is and what is not considered a socially acceptable condition become ever more blurred, as they most surely will if only because of the changing demography of the UK, and recent developments in genetic medicine, changes that are evident throughout much of the 'western' world, the significance of this realisation will become ever more important.

References

Alonso, J.V.G. (ed) (2003) *El movimento de vida independendiente: Experiencias internacionales*, Madrid: Foundacion Luis Vivas.

Abberley, P. (2002) 'Work, disability and European social theory', in C. Barnes, M. Oliver and L. Barton (eds) *Disability studies today*, Cambridge: Polity Press, pp 120-38.

Barnes, C. (1991) *Disabled people in Britain and discrimination: A case for anti-discrimination legislation*, London: Hurst and Co, in association with the British Council of Organisations of Disabled People.

Barnes, C. (2000) 'A working social model? Disability, work and disability politics in the 21st century', *Critical Social Policy*, vol 20, no 4, pp 441-57.

Barnes, C. (2003) 'Vida independiente: socio-politica [Independent living: politics and implications]', in V.G. Alonso (ed) *El movimento de vida independendiente: Experiencias internacionales,* Madrid: Foundacion Luis Vivas, pp 61-8.

Barnes, C. and Mercer, G. (2003) *Disability*, Cambridge: Polity Press.

Barnes, C. and Oliver, M. (1995) 'Disability rights: Rhetoric and reality in the UK', *Disability and Society*, vol 10, no 1, pp 110-16.

Bauman, Z. (1998) *Work, consumerism and the new poor*, Buckingham: Open University Press.

Beck, U. (2000) *The brave new world of work*, Cambridge: Polity Press.

Calvi, N. (2003) 'Can charities change', *Disability Now*, May, p 17.

Campbell, J. and Oliver, M. (1996) *Disability politics: Understanding our past, changing our future*, London: Routledge.

Corbin, J. and Strauss, A.L. (1988) *Unending work and care: Managing chronic illness at home*, San Francisco (CA): Jossey-Bass Publishers.

DWP (Department for Work and Pensions) (1998) *A new contract for welfare: Support for disabled people*, Cm 4103, London: The Stationery Office (TSO).

Finkelstein, V. (1980) *Attitudes and disability*, Geneva: World Rehabilitation Fund.

Finkelstein, V. (1996) 'We want to remodel the world', Paper presented at the 10th anniversary of the founding of the *Disability Arts in London* magazine (www.leeds.ac.uk/disability-studies/archive.uk/index).

Finkelstein, V. (2002) 'The social model of disability repossessed', *Coalition: The magazine of the Greater Coalition of Disabled People*, Manchester: GCDO, February, pp 10-16.

Ford, C. and Shaw, R. (1993) 'Managing a personal assistant', in C. Barnes (ed) *Making our own choices*, Derby: British Council of Disabled People, Ryburn Press, pp 19-24.

Glasby, J. and Littlechild, R. (2002) *Social work and direct payments*, Bristol: The Policy Press.

Gleeson, B. (1999) *Geographies of disability*, London: Routledge.

Hasler, F. (1993) 'Developments in the disabled people's movement', in J. Swain, S. French, C. Banes and C. Thomas (eds) *Disabling barriers – Enabling environments*, London: Sage Publications in Association with the Open University.

Hyde, M. (1996) 'Fifty years of failure: employment services for disabled people in the UK', *Work, Employment and Society*, vol 12, no 4, pp 683-700.

Lister, R. (1997) *Citizenship: Feminist perspectives*, New York: New York University Press.

Morgan, H., Barnes, C., Mercer, G. (2001) *Creating independent futures: An evaluation of services led by disabled people. Stage Two Report*, Leeds: The Disability Press.

OECD (Organisation for Economic Cooperation and Development) (2003) *Transforming Disability into Ability*, Paris: OECD.

Oliver, M. (1990) *The politics of disablement*, Basingstoke: Macmillan.

Oliver, M. (2004) 'If I had a hammer', in J. Swain S. French, C. Banes and C. Thomas (eds) *Disabling barriers, enabling environments*, London: Sage Publications.

Oliver, M. and Barnes, C. (1998) *Disabled people and social policy: From exclusion to inclusion*, London: Longman.

Peters, S. (2000) 'Is there a disability culture: a synchronisation of three possible world views', *Disability and Society*, vol 15, no 4, pp 583-602.

Roulstone, A. (2002) 'Disabling pasts, enabling futures? How does the changing nature of capitalism impact on the disabled worker and job seeker?', *Disability and Society*, vol 17, no 7, pp 627-42.

Russell, M. (2002) 'What disability civil rights cannot do: employment and political economy', *Disability and Society*, vol 17, no 2, pp 117-37.

Shakespeare, T. and Watson, N. (2002) 'The social model of disability: an outmoded ideology', *Research in Social Science and Disability*, vol 2, pp 9-28.

Stiker, H.J. (1998) *A history of disability*, Michigan (IL): Ann Arbor, The University of Michigan Press.

Thornton, P. and Lunt, N. (1995) *Employment for disabled people: Social obligation or individual responsibility*, York: Social Policy Research Unit, University of York.

Williams, G. (1984) 'The movement for independent living: an evaluation and critique', *Social Science and Medicine*, vol 17, no 15, pp 1000-12.

Wolfensberger, W. (1989) 'Human service policies: the rhetoric versus the reality', in L. Barton (ed) *Disability and dependency*, Lewes: Falmer, pp 23-41.

UPIAS (Union of the Physically Impaired Against Segregation) (1976) *Fundamental principles of disability*, London: UPIAS.

*Also see: www.leeds.ac.uk/disability-studies/archiveuk/index.

TWENTY THREE

Conclusions

In this brief postscript, we reflect on some of the key policy insights to flow from this book's chapters. These empirical and theoretical insights have provided a detailed appraisal of a range of key disability and employment policies and have established the benefits and limitations of current policies. Given the broader objectives of translating new ideas into changing policy and practice the key policy points are laid out later in this chapter.

Working futures? makes clear both the continuities and changes that marked the shift from neo-Conservative to New Labour governments. A continued commitment to making welfare conditional upon certain types of active labour market behaviour characterises the links between these approaches. There is once again continuity between these political and policy responses to the challenge of employing more disabled people. However, the old distinctions between deserving and undeserving have been shifted to reflect the alterations to the 'disability category', which are at the heart of New Labour's dichotomous treatment of work for those who can and support for those who cannot. In practice, while this commits far more than governments of the 1980s and early 1990s, it does oversimplify the relationships between paid work, disability, impairment and perceptions of the value of paid work for disabled people.

While the Conservative governments of 1979-97 made efforts to distinguish between levels of support in terms of daily disability support (Disability Living Allowance mobility and care components), it has been New Labour that has looked more fully at the range of disability employment programmes with the aim of more targeted support.

There is evidence in this book's chapters that some policy and programme improvements have taken place, and these are clearly to be welcomed. Specifically, more flexible benefit linking rules, a less fragmented employment and benefits service and the mainstreaming of disability tax credits. The emphasis in WORKSTEP, the new supported employment programme is philosophically and practically on open as opposed to segregated or subsidised employment, this too has to be welcomed for many disabled people for whom this represents a further step towards social integration.

There are many continued limitations and concerns, however, about current disability and employment policy and programmes. The lack of user involvement, service-led philosophies, the continued dominance of medical model definitions of disability, the apparent weaknesses of the Disability Discrimination Act (DDA) 1995 and the funding formulae that encourage a quantitative emphasis on programme throughput all raise doubts about the scope for enhancing disabled people's longer-term working futures. In a global context, welfare retraction, poverty and labour market rigidities all add to the pervasive sense of the weight of barriers that remain. Within Europe, the evidence suggests that while there are particular merits in certain policy options, there is no evidence of a policy panacea simply waiting to be uncovered. Transnational corporate activity, while viewed in diverse ways by disability commentators, seems to add an additional layer of planning uncertainty as decisions to employ, invest and disinvest may impact locally but be taken globally. There is little evidence from Africa, Europe and Anglophone countries that social and cultural prejudices are declining in a way that makes policy choices merely of a technical nature. Persuasion, packaging of disabled people and increasingly business cases seem more pervasive globally than a moral or human rights *weltanschauung* (worldview).

It is not surprising, given then that specific attention was paid in a number of chapters to the imperative need for greater demand-side governmental and employer activity and the need to value wider social activity outside of paid work to broaden and enhance disabled people's social inclusion outside of paid work. The need to question the economic and cultural values that pervade post-industrial capitalist society, how they continue to construct disability as inability to work needs urgent attention.

One way of ensuring a shift away from an individual model of rehabilitation is the greater user involvement of disabled people in policy making and review in the area of employment and pre-employment policy. Given the complexity of disability, employment and the policy context this would involved disabled people and policy/programme makers working together as has characterised work around integrated and now inclusion in UK Centres for Independent Living (CILs). There is a need to go beyond the 'work for those who can' mantra to look at ways of reaching those disabled people furthest from the labour market but who might want paid work and for a full appraisal of just what workable is taken to mean in current policy terms. An investment model needs to be nurtured to ensure benefits savings are seen as only one plank of policy reform.

The issue of trust was seen as important if disability and employment policy are to succeed more fully. This translated into the need to avoid coercion in policy and programme terms, and the view that coercion fosters suspicion in client groups that may be very difficult to transform.

It is perhaps unexpected that a focus on epistemological and definitional issues should feature so fully in a policy book of this kind. However, some felt there was an urgent need for clarification of key terms: disability, impairment, illness which at present are not used in any clearly defined way in key policy documents, benefit regulations and eligibility. This leads to policy muddle and a further fragments an already complex system. The recent emphasis in the UK government report (PMSU, 2005), *Improving the life chances of disabled people*, on single assessment protocols has to be a welcome development and its impact will be eagerly awaited. The perceived complexity of the UK benefits system requires both an appraisal of the 'fit' between current benefits and the feasibility of a 'Benefits Bill' designed to streamline the current bewildering and fragmented benefits system. The current use of 'incapacity' as the basis of employment and benefits policy was severely questioned by some contributors. A joined-up benefits and employment support system was seen to require the broadening of direct payments to the field of employment, for example in the Access to Work scheme. Of note, the recent PMSU report (2005) commits in principle to greater use of direct payments, but unlike employee activation policies such as pathways to work and job retention programmes, no target datelines are given.

The role of law in enhancing the social position of disabled people featured explicitly or in passing in a number of chapters. There was general agreement that the limitations of the DDA require a longer-term monitoring of its defining terms, case law handling, tribunal system and the need for disability equality training for all involved in the legal process. The relationship between the DDA and the proposed Disability Discrimination Bill 2006 have to be carefully monitored to best afford a complementary role for each statute. Clearly disability law has to be measured both in terms of its keynote successes, but also in terms of the discrepancy between those seeking support and those receiving it. Currently the UK Disability Rights Commission (DRC) limits its legal representation to 75 cases per year. There is much evidence of a 'discrimination iceberg', which the current arrangements are unable to respond to. In this context the impact of the proposed Equality and Human Rights Commission needs to be carefully monitored given the newness and untested nature of aspects of the DDA 1995 and the DRC.

It was felt that the current distinction between specialist and mainstream employment support should be challenged where it does not maximise the enabling potential of the wider support systems for disabled people. It was also felt important that there is a clear need for evidence-based practice, programmes and policy. At present, evaluations of policy and programmes are largely focused on process rather than the effectiveness or outcomes of provision. Additionally, policy research evidence and dissemination is required based on typical career pathways disabled people have taken to enhance the knowledge base that employment support professionals use. Knowledge of and connectedness with labour markets was seen in some instances to be ad hoc rather than systematic in nature. Looked at more closely, we can say that a number of disability programmes, for example 'Work Preparation' have still to be comprehensively evaluated. Indeed, it is worth stating that many policies and programmes that explicitly set out to aid access to the labour market may have the opposite effect of reducing access, especially where punitive sanctions attach to disability benefit and employment access programmes. More worryingly, policy changes if evaluated (for example, New Deal for Disabled People, the DDA 1995) have to date been evaluated in process rather than substantive achievements and often treated as standalone programme entities which are difficult to connect to wider policy developments. This suggests that a clear attempt to address the value of current policy in this area needs to be made, while wider questions of governmental policy objectives need to be critically evaluated. This latter is important as questions of the valuation of disabled people without paid work in the 21st century is inseparable from any discussion of the value and likely success of employment policy for disabled people. A consensus emerged that it would always remain the case that some disabled people would never be able to or want to work and that valued futures without paid employment need to be addressed in policy terms.

The greatest labour market barriers were those facing disabled people with mental health problems and those with learning difficulties. This evidence further supports the call to widen and incentivise the 'place and train' model of employment support. There is need for more careful evaluation and reform of the relationship between national policy and regional/local experiences of disability programmes, especially an evaluation of the future relationship between the statutory and voluntary sector in employment provision. Good practice from the many voluntary sector providers of into-work support need to be better understood and lessons learned as to what works in disability and employment terms.

Reference

PMSU (Prime Ministers Stategy Unit) (2005) *Improving the life chances of disabled people*, London: PMSU.

Index

Social work and direct payments
Jon Glasby and Rosemary Littlechild

"This book will fill a gap in academic studies of direct payments. There is no other publication as comprehensive as this one." *Frances Hasler, National Centre for Independent Living*

This book summarises and builds on current knowledge and research about direct payments in the UK and considers developments in other European countries. It identifies good practice in the area and explores the implications of direct payments, both for service users and for social work staff.

Paperback £17.99 US$29.95 ISBN 1 86134 385 X
Hardback £50.00 US$69.95 ISBN 1 86134 386 8
234 x 156mm 184 pages July 2002

Disabled people and European human rights
A review of the implications of the 1998 Human Rights Act for disabled children and adults in the UK
Luke Clements and Janet Read

"This book is essential reading for parents, disabled young people and the organisations which work with them. By recognising that the exclusion of disabled children is a human rights issue - we can adopt strategies now to ensure that all disabled people are enabled to fully participate in society in the future." *Francine Bates, Contact a Family*

In the year 2000, the Human Rights Act 1998 came into force in the United Kingdom. This book reviews the implications of the Act for disabled people.

Paperback £17.99 US$28.95 ISBN 1 86134 425 2
234 x 156mm 144 pages February 2003

Thriving and surviving at work
Disabled people's employment strategies
Alan Roulstone, Lorraine Gradwell, Jeni Price and Lesley Child

This report breaks new ground in asking: how do those disabled people who are already in work get and keep paid work? Drawing on the experiences of disabled people themselves, it looks at the difficulties disabled people experience, the strategies they adopt and the policy context in which they work. The authors are all disabled people with a mix of practice and academic experience.

Paperback £13.95 US$23.95 ISBN 1 86134 522 4
297 x 210mm 56 pages July 2003
Published in association with the Joseph Rowntree Foundation

Frustrated ambition
The education and employment of disabled young people
Tania Burchardt

Improving educational attainment and raising employment rates among disadvantaged groups are key targets for the current government. This report shows that for one important group - disabled young people - these goals are far from being achieved. The report highlights the need for a new direction in careers advice and welfare to work programmes for disabled young people.

FREE pdf version available online at www.jrf.org.uk
Paperback £0.00 ISBN 1 86134 807 X
297 x 210mm November 2005
Published in association with the Joseph Rowntree Foundation

To order further copies of this publication or any other Policy Press titles please visit **www.policypress.org.uk** or contact:

In the UK and Europe:
Marston Book Services, PO Box 269,
Abingdon, Oxon, OX14 4YN, UK
Tel: +44 (0)1235 465500
Fax: +44 (0)1235 465556
Email: direct.orders@marston.co.uk

In the USA and Canada:
ISBS, 920 NE 58th Street, Suite 300,
Portland, OR 97213-3786, USA
Tel: +1 800 944 6190 (toll free)
Fax: +1 503 280 8832
Email: info@isbs.com

In Australia and New Zealand:
DA Information Services, 648 Whitehorse Road
Mitcham, Victoria 3132, Australia
Tel: +61 (3) 9210 7777
Fax: +61 (3) 9210 7788
E-mail: service@dadirect.com.au

Further information about all of our titles can be found on our website.